The City Works
Eric Parry Architects

Edited by Ian Latham and Chris Foges

R RIGHTANGLE
PUBLISHING

Published by Right Angle Publishing, London
Edited and designed by Ian Latham and Chris Foges

British Library Cataloguing in Publication Data.
A catalogue record for this book is available from
the British Library.

ISBN: 978-1-9997931-3-5

We are deeply grateful to the many contributors to
this book, some of whom have written new essays
and others who have reworked critiques of
buildings first penned when they were newly
completed. The book was initiated by Eric Parry,
developed in discussions with the editors, and
brought to fruition thanks to the dedication of
many members of the studio at Eric Parry
Architects, in particular José de Paiva who has been
tirelessly supportive throughout the project.

The City Works
Eric Parry Architects

Contributors

Simon Allford is a founding director of Allford Hall Monaghan Morris, and leads a studio of 200 architects working on the design and construction of projects around the world. His work aspires to the belief that 'outstanding architecture must last through time and accommodate different uses to those that called it into being, while offering an extraordinary and delightful backdrop to the theatre of everyday life'. Simon is a regular teacher, competitions and awards judge, writer and critic. He is currently a visiting professor at GSD Harvard, and a trustee of the London School of Architecture and Chickenshed Theatres Trust. A former chair of the Architecture Foundation, Simon is president of the RIBA for 2021-23.

Bob Allies founded Allies and Morrison with Graham Morrison in 1984, after his studies at the University of Edinburgh, and a Rome Scholarship in 1981. An architect, teacher and writer, he co-edited The Fabric of Place, which forms the foundation of the practice's urban masterplans that include Kings Cross, Olympic Games and Legacy, Greenwich Peninsula and Brent Cross Town. He has been a visiting professor at the universities of Reading, Edinburgh, Maryland and Bath, and taught at Cambridge, the Bartlett and North-East London Polytechnic. He was an Architectural Association council member, served on the Mayor of London's Design Advisory Group, is chair of the South East Design Review Panel and is on the council of the British School at Rome. He was awarded an OBE in 2016.

Biba Dow studied at the University of Cambridge and co-founded Dow Jones Architects with Alun Jones in 2000. She has led many projects including Grand Junction at St Mary Magdalene, Bevis Marks Synagogue and the crypt at Christ Church Spitalfields. Biba was shortlisted for Architect of the Year for the Women in Architecture Award 2018. She is a regular architectural assessor, writes about architecture and culture, and has lectured widely. She is a member of the Cathedral Fabric Committee at Coventry Cathedral, the Old Oak and Park Royal Place Review Panel and the Kensington & Chelsea Quality Review Panel. She has taught at a number of architecture schools, including a diploma unit at London Metropolitan University, where she is an external examiner, and as a visiting critic at Cambridge University and Kingston.

Chris Foges is a writer and editor working in architecture and the built environment. He is a contributing editor at the RIBA Journal and a regular contributor to publications including Architectural Record. He also works with architects and institutions to shape discussions on buildings and places in a variety of media. Chris was editor of Architecture Today magazine from 2005 to 2021, and previously edited magazines and websites for publishers in Europe and the USA. As a commissioning editor for Quarto Group he conceived and produced many books on graphic and product design. He studied english literature and architecture and has taught history and theory at London Metropolitan University and Kingston University.

Kenneth Frampton is Ware Professor Emeritus at Columbia GSAPP, where he has taught since 1972. He trained at the Architectural Association and has worked as an architect, a historian, a writer and teacher. In addition to Columbia, he has taught at the Royal College of Art, ETH Zurich, the Berlage Institute, EPFL Lausanne and the Accademia di Architettura in Mendrisio, and he has lectured and written extensively. His books include Modern Architecture and the Critical Present (1980), Studies in Tectonic Culture (1995), American Masterworks (1995), Le Corbusier (2001), Labour, Work & Architecture (2005), and A Genealogy of Modern Architecture (2015). Kenneth's teaching was the subject of the 2017 Educating Architects exhibition at the Canadian Centre for Architecture, where his archive is held. He was awarded the Golden Lion for Lifetime Achievement at the 2018 Venice Biennale.

Louisa Hutton studied at the University of Bristol and the Architectural Association, after which she worked for four years with Alison and Peter Smithson. Louisa founded Sauerbruch Hutton with Matthias Sauerbruch in London in 1989, which has been based in Berlin since 1993. The practice has always pursued a serious engagement with issues of sustainability, from the scale of the city to the individual's sensual perception of their environment. Louisa has taught at the Architectural Association and Harvard Graduate School of Design, and has lectured widely. She was a CABE commissioner, a member of the first steering committee for the Bundesstiftung Baukultur, and sat on the curatorial board of the Schelling Architecture Foundation. She is an honorary fellow of the American Institute of Architects, a Royal Academician since 2014, and in 2015 was awarded an OBE.

Edward Jones studied at the Architectural Association and has been a principal in private practice since 1973. In 1983 he won the competition for Mississauga City Hall in Canada and in 1989 co-founded Dixon Jones, whose projects include the Royal Opera House, the National Portrait Gallery and National Gallery in London, and Saïd Business School in Oxford. Edward has served on many competition juries, including the Laban Dance Centre and Hepworth Gallery, and on the Royal Gold Medal jury. He has taught at the RCA (1975-82), Harvard, Yale, Princeton, Cornell, Philadelphia, Rice, Toronto, Waterloo and Kent State University, Florence and UCD Dublin. Co-author of the Guide to the Architecture of London, his honorary awards include a doctorate at Portsmouth, a professorship at Cardiff, and a fellowship of the Royal Institute of the Architects of Ireland; he was awarded a CBE in 2011.

Rolfe Kentish was born in London in 1954 and received his MA and DipArch from Cambridge in 1980. He worked with David Roberts and Geoffrey Clarke, and Colin St John Wilson from 1982 to 1996 (as an associate from 1989), as an associate of MJ Long Architects from 1990-94, and then as partner in Long & Kentish. He has worked on many projects including the British Library, the British Library Centre for Conservation, the National Maritime Museum in Falmouth, an extension to Pallant House Gallery in Chichester, the Keeper's House at the Royal Academy in London, and the renovation of Porthmeor artists' studios in St Ives, Cornwall. As Cambridge-based Rolfe Kentish Architects, his current work includes restoration of the Anchor studio in Newlyn, visitor facilities at Trebah Garden and a villa extension near Izmir.

Ian Latham is a writer, editor and publisher. He studied architecture at Oxford Brookes and worked for Peter Moro, joining Architectural Design magazine in 1979 and Building Design in 1983. In 1989, with Mark Swenarton, he conceived and launched Architecture Today magazine. After three decades as AT's publishing editor, he now runs Rightangle Architectural Publishing, whose books include monographs on Dixon Jones and Allies & Morrison (both two vols), van Heyningen & Haward, Richard MacCormac and MJP, Feilden Clegg Bradley, Ted Cullinan and Peter Ahrends. He has twice served on the Royal Gold Medal jury, chaired the RIBA's dissertation awards panel for ten years and was made a RIBA honorary fellow in 2015.

Vivien Lovell founded art consultancy Modus Operandi in 1999, having directed the Public Art Commissions Agency from 1987, following roles at West Midlands Arts, Stoke-on-Trent National Garden Festival, Ikon Gallery and Tower Hamlets. Modus Operandi's art strategies and frameworks include BBC Broadcasting House, Liverpool Vision, Docklands Light Railway, St Martin-in-the-Fields, The Crown Estate and the Radcliffe Observatory Quarter, the new Bodleian and Westgate in Oxford. At PACA, Vivien led public art strategies for Cardiff Bay and Birmingham, and curated commissions for London Docklands Development Corporation, the British Embassy in Dublin and St John's College Oxford. She chaired the Public Art Forum, initiated an Alliance for Art Architecture & Design with RIBA, and wrote the Arts Council's Percent for Art: A Review in 2017. She was chair of the Fine Arts Faculty at The British School at Rome from 2013-20.

Patrick Lynch studied at Liverpool University and Cambridge University and took a PhD at London Met (formerly The Cass) in 2015. In 1997 he founded Lynch Architects, whose projects include The Zig Zag Building and Kings Gate in London's Victoria. Young Architect of the Year in 2005, Patrick has taught at the Architectural Association, London Met, the Bartlett, Cambridge and, as honorary professor, at Liverpool. He exhibited at the Venice Biennale in 2008 and 2012. His books include The Theatricality of the Baroque City (2011), Mimesis (2015), Civic Ground (2017) and On Intricacy (2020), about architect John Meunier. Patrick is a member of The Art Workers' Guild, The Worshipful Company of Architects, and Islington Council's design review panel, and he is editor and publisher of the Journal of Civic Architecture.

Daniel Rosbottom is co-director of DRDH, based in London and Antwerp, which he founded in 2000 with David Howarth. Alongside a number of large-scale city projects, including a tower in Antwerp's Nieuw Zuid urban extension, the practice is concerned with the design and role of public buildings in contemporary culture, with projects ranging from an acclaimed concert hall and library in Bodø, Norway (2015), to the current transformation of Ghent Opera. Daniel pursues an academic career in parallel to practice and since 2015 has been a professor at the Technical University Delft. Prior to that was head of the school of architecture and landscape at Kingston University (2008-15) and postgraduate director at The Cass (2004-08). Daniel writes on art and architecture, has been a judge on a number of international awards and competitions, and in 2016 joined the editorial board of Architectural Research Quarterly.

Deborah Saunt is co-founder of DSDHA, a practice known for its innovative buildings, high-profile urban strategies and research. Recent projects include refurbishment of London's Economist Plaza, the reimagining of Tottenham Court Road and a new park in the City of London. Deborah gained a doctorate with RMIT's Practice-Based PhD Program and held a Research Fellowship in the Built Environment from the Royal Commission for the Exhibition of 1851. Much of her work is concerned with democratising architecture and she regularly talks and writes on issues of diversity and innovation in the built environment. Deborah has taught widely and in 2015 helped co-found the London School of Architecture, of which she is now a trustee, with the intention of broadening access to the profession and building new collaborative forms of research and practice.

Jonathan Sergison is based in the Zurich studio of Sergison Bates, which he co-founded in 1996, and which is a recipient of the Schelling Prize for Architecture and the Tessenow Gold Medal. After graduating from the Architectural Association in 1989 he worked with David Chipperfield and Tony Fretton, since when he has combined writing, teaching and practice. Jonathan has taught at the University of North London, the Architectural Association, ETH Zurich, the Ecole Polytechnique Fédérale in Lausanne, Oslo School of Architecture & Design and Harvard University Graduate School of Design. Since 2008 he has been a professor at the Accademia di Mendrisio, Switzerland, and in 2019 became director of the Istituto di Studi Urbani e del Paesaggio (ISUP).

Cindy Walters was born in Australia, studied in South Africa, and moved to London in 1990 to work for Foster & Partners. In 1994 with Michál Cohen she set up Walters & Cohen, which works across education, leisure, cultural and commercial sectors. In 2012 Cindy and Michál were awarded the inaugural AJ Woman Architect of the Year Award. Cindy contributes to academic and professional institutions as an external examiner and guest lecturer. Her longstanding involvement with the RIBA awards group has included judging the Lubetkin Prize, Stirling Prize and the President's Research Awards. In 2019 Cindy became chair of the Architecture Foundation. She is a trustee for the Young Women's Trust, a Design Council associate, and a regular judge at the World Architecture Festival. Cindy is currently undertaking a doctorate at the Bartlett.

An Architecture of Urban Exploration:
Ian Latham

'A great poet... must have the ear of a wild Arab listening in the silent desert, the eye of a North American Indian tracing the footsteps of an enemy upon the leaves that strew the forest, the touch of a blind man feeling the face of a darling child.'

The kind of evocative, free-spirited sensitivities prescribed for creative writers by Samuel Taylor Coleridge at the start of the nineteenth century could apply across much modern artistic endeavour, and not least architecture.
A heightened appreciation for context, history and construction — for place, time and substance — is what we might expect in an architect, but it is that elusive spark of imagination that can truly raise the game.

Coleridge was intrigued by the creative mind, describing its 'esemplastic' or 'shaping' ability to synthesise images, words and emotions, in the case of writers, into a unifying whole. The artistic imagination, he suggested, held a 'mysterious power' to bring forth 'hidden ideas and meanings'. But while Coleridge may have intended to cultivate the impression that his poetry was freely spontaneous, his notebooks betray that it was meticulously crafted.

In a world that has become increasingly dislocated by internationalisation, as Kenneth Frampton and others have argued, architects might seek a sense of rootedness in their work. The dilemma this seemingly contradictory ambition poses for those, such as Eric Parry Architects, who operate in the milieu of global real estate, is obvious. Is it even possible to embody rootedness in a commercial office building — where the client is rarely the occupier, so denying the creative frisson of that relationship, and where market norms define the parameters of the brief? And if so, how can any rootedness be rendered meaningful? Should it be specific to the sense of place, of time, of a collective memory?

A defining characteristic of Eric Parry Architects' work is its capacity to embrace both imaginative speculation and carefully calibrated rootedness. It is telling in this respect that the trajectory of the practice's workload has not been confined to the cultural and elite educational spheres into which Parry might have comfortably settled, and the series of office buildings completed since the millennium represents a substantial and coherent body of work in its own right. This dalliance with the sharp end of capitalism has served the practice well, and its experience in matters of commercial realism and consensus consultation informs all of its work with a rich stream of pragmatism.

These urban office buildings were by no means born out of austerity, however — most have been beneficiaries of London's buoyant post-millennial property market — but they each represent the hard-won consequences of an over-riding architectural ambition subjected to planning, investment and financial pressures. In this the practice has fully embraced engagement with clients and developers, planners and artists as part of a creative process to help enrich and bring new impetus to a building type that had become moribund in the hands of other architects.

The allusive toponomy of the London streets where Eric Parry Architects has made its interventions give some indication of the rich layers of history, memory and myth written into the fabric of the city. Linking the City of London's five-street focus at Bank with Bishopsgate, Threadneedle Street (formerly Three Needle Street) could derive its name from the 'thrig' (three) needles depicted on the arms of the Worshipful Company of Needlemakers, or from the older Merchant Taylors, whose livery hall has been sited here since 1347. However, it may also be a corruption of Thryddanen, Anglo-Saxon for the third street from Cheapside.

Nearby, Fenchurch Street, like Finsbury Square, probably refers to its original marshy, 'fennie' location. Or maybe 'foenen' or 'fein', Saxon for the hay once traded here. Further west, the seventeenth-century tailor Roger Baker, who specialised in 'piccadill' lace collars, built Pickadilla Hall, which was short-lived due to a property boom, but its name has endured. Aristocrat, painter and patron of Handel, Lady Dorothy Savile (1699-1758) lent her family name to Savile Street (later Row), developed to the designs of William Kent in the 1830s by her husband, the third 'architect' earl of Burlington. There are layers of contextual material aplenty with which an attentive architect can get to grips, should they be so inclined.

Parry's determination to imbue his buildings with contemporary relevance by bringing together universal types with local references is exemplified in the use of sophisticated construction systems alongside crafted components. The approach resonates with the Deutscher Werkbund's 'handcrafts versus machine' debates of a century ago between Henry van der Velde and Hermann Muthesius which set artistic independence against standardisation, craft versus mass production. It also recalls the work of academic architect William Lethaby, whose sole commercial project, the Eagle Insurance Building in Birmingham (1900), placed arts and crafts theory in an industrial urban context, employing hand-carved stonework and reinforced concrete floors. While Lethaby's compelling writings anticipated a progressive architecture that could escape the shackles of the past, his own buildings reflect his fascination with fictive histories.

Examination of the Eagle Insurance Building's Colemore Road facade is instructive, not least in relation to the Piccadilly elevation of Eric Parry Architects' One Eagle Place, where the responsibility to the public realm is perhaps the most heightened among all his buildings. Lethaby plays compositional games, with a triple five-bay ground-floor facade restating the fenestration above, where trabeated pilasters form horizontal balconies, and the uppermost windows are set within a syncopated renaissance array, surmounted by a jazzy chequerboard frieze and sporting a sculpted eagle. The elevational narrative rises from earth to the heavens, fusing 'ancient' symbolism with 'modern' structure in the search for a universal architecture of common agreement. This reconciliation of modern construction methods, traditional architectural values and notions of what contemporary architecture should represent are the concerns with which Eric Parry also wrestles.

Above
William Lethaby's Eagle Insurance Building (1900) fuses historical and poetic references with contemporary construction methods. Eric Parry Architects' One Eagle Place at London's Piccadilly.

The City Works
Ten Buildings

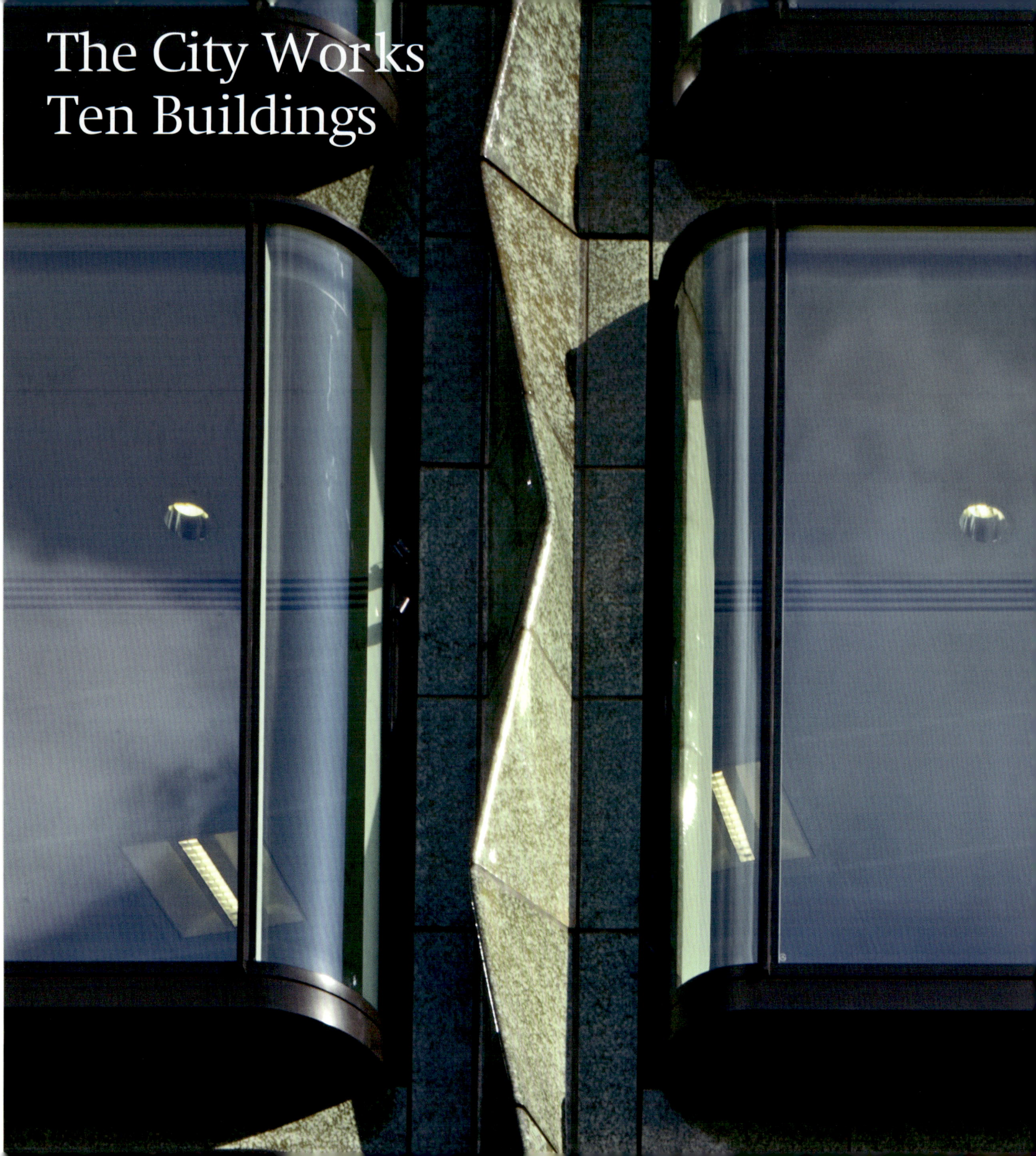

30 Finsbury Square

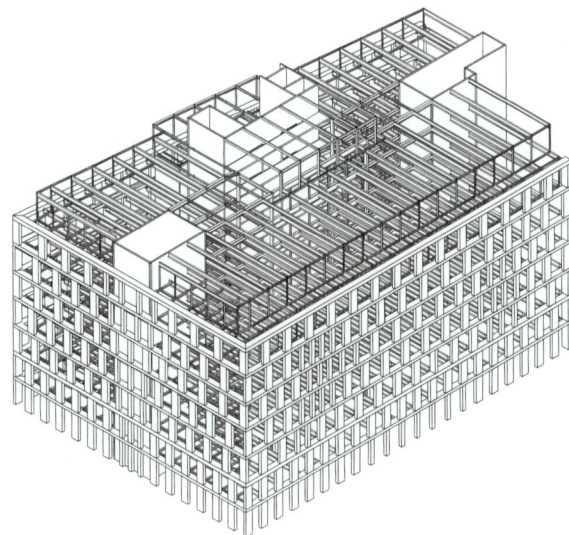

A Story in Stone:
Edward Jones on 30 Finsbury Square

I remember an occasion at a student thesis jury in Princeton in the mid-1980s when Alan Colquhoun dismissed an office building under review as '95 per cent real estate and five per cent architecture'. At times in the intervening years I have reflected on this comment on designing an office. Does this mean that after attending to the site plan and building volume, the building's appearance is the architect's principal and outstanding task? Does this further suggest that the majority of the remaining tasks are guided solely by commercial, environmental and industrial standards, whereby surveyors, engineers and letting agents direct the design within the straight and narrow expectations of the marketplace? Yet set against all this the client wants a building of great visual distinction, a building that will be prominent in the city, and a building that will be a commercial success. If all this is true, how then do the offices in Finsbury Square by Eric Parry Architects deal with these apparently contradictory pressures?

On the outside 30 Finsbury Square is an urbane but paradoxical building. The first impression is that, within its acceptance of conventional urban design guidelines, it appears unusual. On the one hand, the building wears the same suit of Portland stone as its neighbours and conforms obediently both to the building line and to Islington's 30-metre (six storeys and two attic floors) height limitation. On the other, the almost universal structural convention of placing load upon load has been put aside in favour of a policy of structural transfer. Added to this, the introduction of the picturesque in the ad hoc arrangement of the piers sets the building subtly in contrast to existing conventions.

Above
Rafael Moneo's Murcia town hall (1998), John Weeks' Northwick Park Hospital under construction (1970) and Eric Parry Architects' Foundress Court, Pemboke College, Cambridge (1998).

Left/right
The structural Portland stone columns on the north-west corner are variously orientated with Finsbury Square and Christopher Street.

Approaching closer, you notice that the piers are audaciously loadbearing masonry and that they also act as a brise soleil to the fully glazed facade behind. This is a remarkable achievement and a definite upping of Colquhoun's five per cent. There is an agreeable counterpoint between the regular rhythm of the stainless steel window mullions and the syncopation of the stone piers in the foreground. The silver stripes of the reflecting stainless steel create a constantly changing relationship with the matt textured finish of the stone piers. This pictorial device brings a sense of visual interest generally missing in the office elevation as a type — a significant contribution that takes architecture into double figures!

As to references, Parry characterises the west elevation facing the square as a giant sundial, speaking of sciagraphy — the branch of perspective that deals with projections of shadows. One is reminded of the self-supporting stone facades of Parry's work at Pembroke College, Cambridge, where shadows play a part both in the carving of the handsome stone elevations and in the literal use of the sundial ('the art of finding the hour of the day or night by observation of the shadow of the sun, moon or stars upon a dial'). Another reference is Rafael Moneo's Murcia town hall, and the lesser known facade of John Weeks' 1964 Northwick Park Hospital, where ideas of indeterminancy in the design of the elevations made a much earlier appearance.

Left
Principal elevation facing
Finsbury Square.

Right
Finsbury Square elevations
'before' and 'after'.

Below
Sequential urban plans of
Finsbury Square in 1799, 1879,
1929 and 1999 as residential
terraces make way for larger
commercial buildings; view
across the square before
redevelopment.

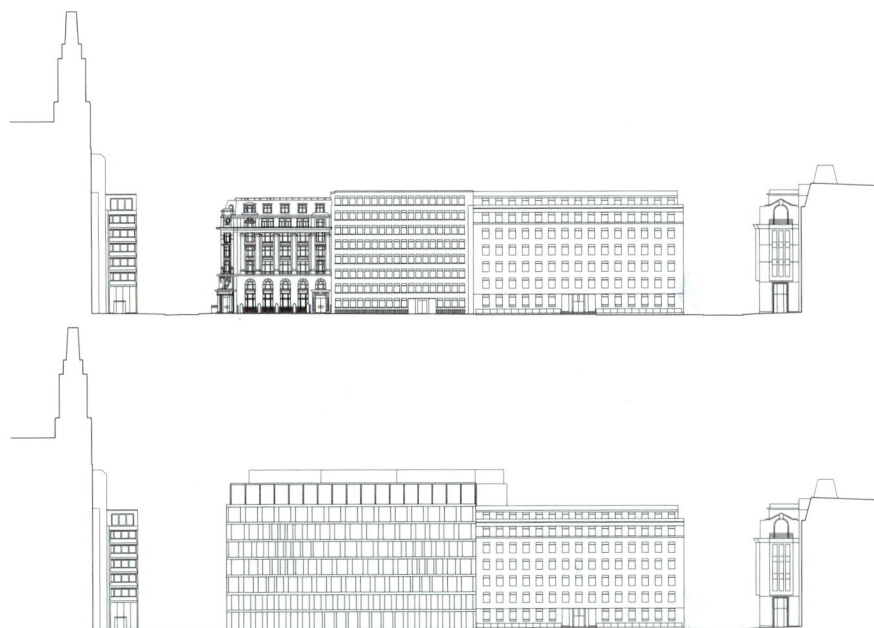

240m

20m

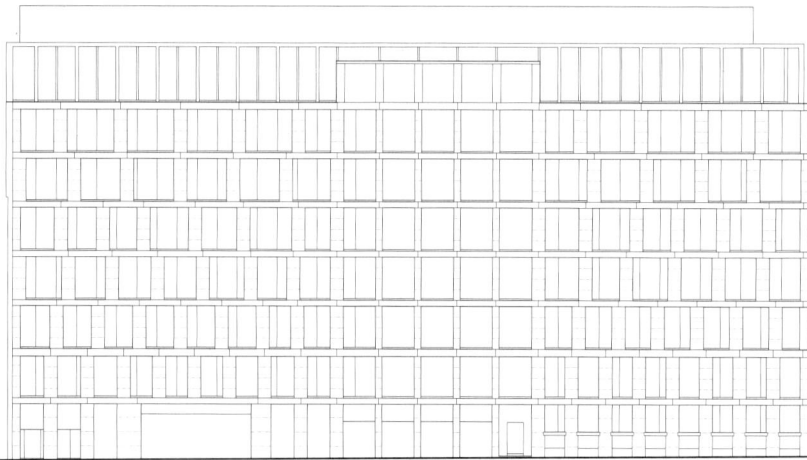

Unlike Moneo's town hall, however, Finsbury Square is horizontal in composition, with floor-to-floor heights that are equal throughout. This conveys an expression of evenness not unlike rock strata. Moneo on the other hand introduces a solid base, in contrast to the hierarchical and varied apertures above, and evades the dilemma of the entrance by tucking it around the corner. Parry is locked into a game of strata and understates the front door accordingly. Earlier versions of the facade either emphasised a tripartite division with exaggerated vertical slots crossing the floors or developed a more explicit piloti arrangement on the ground floor. In either case I believe the understatement of the entrance would have remained.

The building is more secure in distinguishing between a facade for the square and a facade for the interior. As Parry acknowledges, this is not a new idea. The reference here is to the work of SOM in the Gordon Bunshaft era, notably the 1965 Banque Lambert offices in Brussels, where the structural frame is clearly distinguished from the more transitory requirements of the interior. Parry also sets back the ground floor from the building line and creates a double-height space, bringing light and habitability to the basement, reinstating the 'area' of the traditional London house.

Following the fuel crisis of the 1970s and the emergence of concerns for cold bridges in enclosure design, a more neutral and banal expression became prevalent in office buildings; Richard Rogers' preoccupation with the expressive possibilities of services and circulation and Norman Foster's interest in sensuous profile, for example at Swiss Re, can alike be seen as a reaction to this reductio ad absurdum of the architect's expressive territory and the loss of structural visibility. 30 Finsbury Square proudly reclaims this territory for architecture.

Walking through the compressed (2.9-metre-high) entrance hall, the visitor approaches the dramatic nine-storey high atrium and crosses via a bridge to the core. There is a particular drama to this sequence, belied by Parry's rather matter-of-fact description of it as a 'sock'. The vertical structure here (ground to first floor) is gathered together into a vierendeel truss at first floor emphasising the horizontality of the space (on reflection this horizontal cut might have been used to signify the front door to the square).

On arrival from the lift lobby the visitor stands on a bridge in the atrium and looks across the void to the column-free space of the offices opposite. These are bounded by the regular screen of stainless steel window mullions, the irregular spacing of the masonry piers behind, and by the large dimensions of Finsbury Square beyond. The whole within its frame represents the office interior as a contemporary tableau, suggesting the enlarged photographs of Andreas Gursky. The generosity of the column-free space recalls more distantly the interiors of SOM's Union Carbide offices, as featured in Billy Wilder's 1960 film 'The Apartment'.

The general use of stainless steel — brushed, polished and striped — for the windows, balustrades, soffits, grilles and lifts is reminiscent of the corporate American office interior but it has been extended beyond the purely practical. Stainless steel has surprising benefits in its capacity to reflect daylight into the plan: firstly from the atrium and secondly (and rather unexpectedly) from the double reflection from the exterior face of the window frame onto the back face of the Portland stone columns. So here the columns are acting as a light source as well as a brise soleil. The result is an interior of considerable quality, tranquility and unexpected luminosity. In addition, the tenant fit-out (by architect Orms for Invesco) is generally successful and respectful of the architectural intentions. For example the atrium is bounded by general circulation, thereby avoiding the exposure of private occupation which so frequently subverts such spaces.

Overall then Number 30 Finsbury Square is successful in significantly raising the percentage for architecture above Colquhoun's rather pessimistic ratio. This it has achieved initially by a tour de force in the production and achievement of the facade and then by working through this 'big idea' so that it raises the quality of life in the workplace itself.

Above
East, north and west elevations facing Wilson Street, Christopher Street and Finsbury Square respectively.

Right
Four stages in the design development of the Finsbury Square elevation. The composition responds to both the structural loads and the relationship to the square.

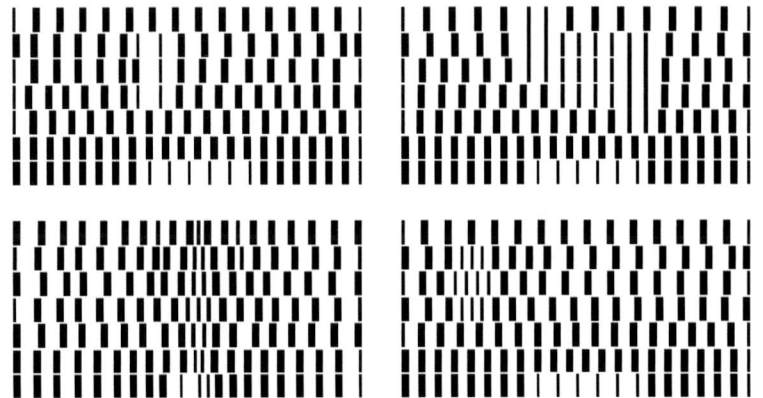

Eric Parry writes:

Ironically, had it not been for the vehement opposition of various conservation bodies to the demolition of the locally listed building occupying part of the site, the design stakes on this project would have been set much lower. Planning – so often the butt of inhibited and disgruntled architects – can also be a means of establishing ambitions that would otherwise be ignored in the rush to achieve the investor's bottom line and the earliest possible completion.

Prior to our rather unlikely engagement, there had been unsuccessful attempts to design a replica facade based on the 1929 building, a bizarre consequence of planning guidelines on facade retention in conservation areas.

In the words of David Williamson, national director for development and project management at Jones Lang LaSalle, 'the replica scheme would have worked commercially but did not reflect the ambitions of the owner, Scottish Widows, and the needs of the potential tenant for a contemporary flexible office building. We needed a new approach to convince the doubters, something special and of a high architectural order'.

Another positive aspect of the planning process is time. It would have been difficult to develop and interrogate many of elements of the design without this space between idea and implementation.

Looking back at the design stages, the 'first thought' sketch of May 1999 (above) highlights a number of key ideas: the tyranny of the office grid challenged by the aleatory rhythm of stone piers; the trabeated system of piers and lintels with secret guttering to accommodate weathering; the entrance as a low, wide mouth leading to the sheer wall of the atrium and lift core; the tripartite order of the facade as a response to the scale of the wall to the square; and the reflective soffit at the entrance.

It also shows the conflict between the idea of creating a 'open' ground floor and the proposed weight of the facade as it developed, which incorporates the structural idea. But in the initial conversations with Whitby Bird it became clear that it would be a constraint to maintain the continuity of the horizontal edge beam to avoid accumulated loads. Many facade studies followed as the structural logic and aesthetic plus proportional constants were explored.

The detailed design developed as an unusual hybrid of stone, precast and steel. The apparent simplicity of the set of construction drawings belies the difficult task of drawing together the precast sections that reflect the shifting position of the piers, and the rigour of the 1.5-metre fenestration rhythm behind.

Above right

Preliminary study exploring the massing and composition, prior to its resolution as a more consistent trabeated structure.

Right

Perspective view of the Finsbury Square frontage at a point in the design development close to the planning application.

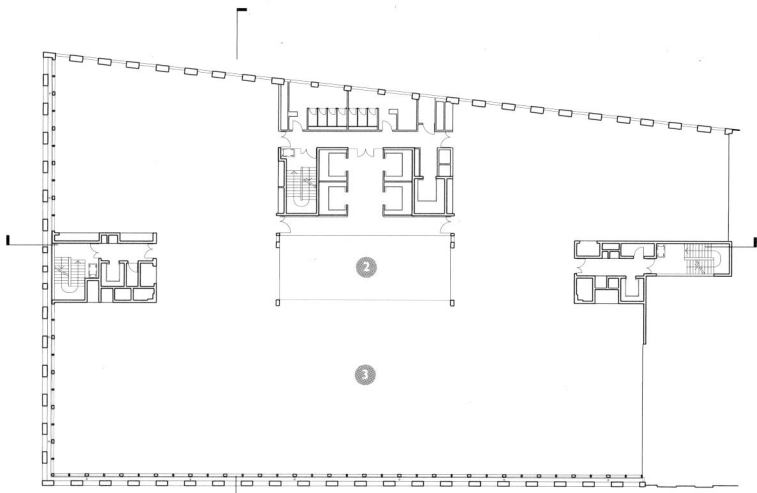

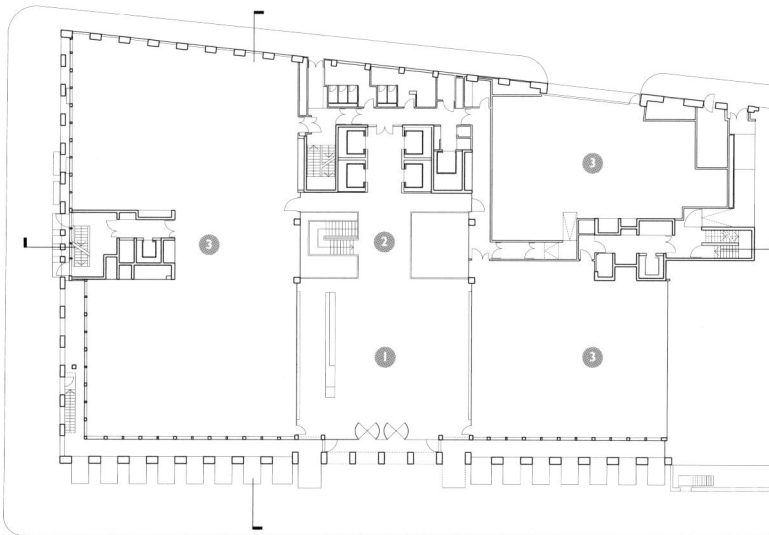

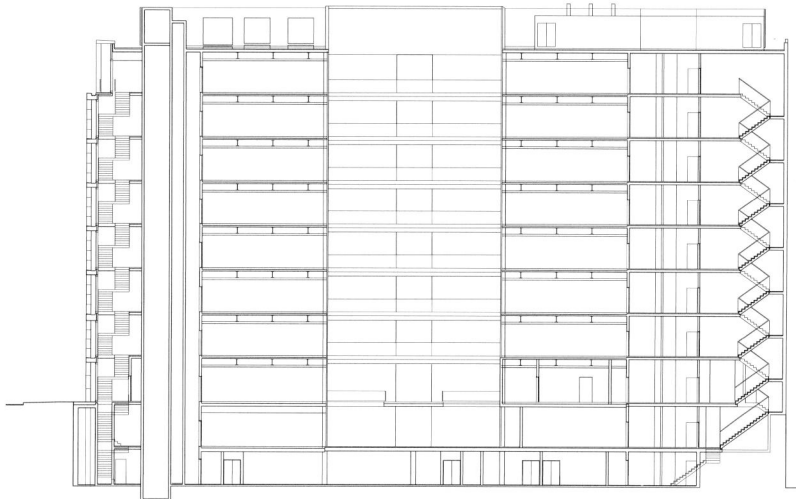

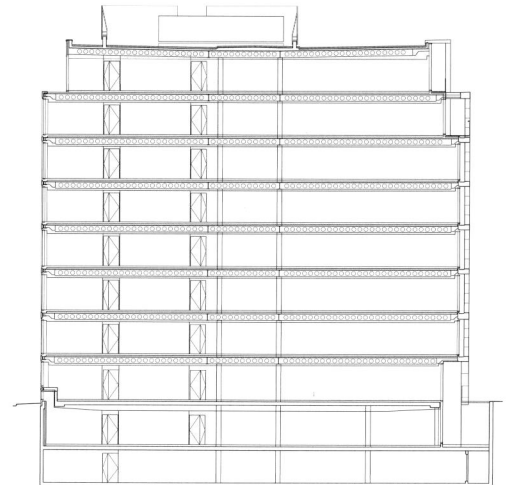

10m

Right
Junction of Christopher Street and Finsbury Square, where solid stone piers support precast concrete lintels, behind which a glazed wall encloses the office spaces.

Left
Ground and typical upper floor plans, longitudinal and cross sections. Key: 1 reception, 2 atrium, 3 office.

Right

Construction section and
cutaway axonometric of the
Finsbury Square frontage.
Key: 1 precast concrete beam,
2 pre-tensioned Portland stone
pier, 3 elastomeric bearing,
4 steel cell beam, 5 stub beam,
6 in-situ lightweight concrete
slab, 7 steel beam cast into
precast beam, 8 raised floor,
9 aluminium curtain walling,
10 stainless steel capping,
11 insulation with dpm and
vapour barrier, 12 hopper and
downpipe cast into precast
beam.

Left

Sequential construction photos;
interior view of typical office
space, prior to fit-out.

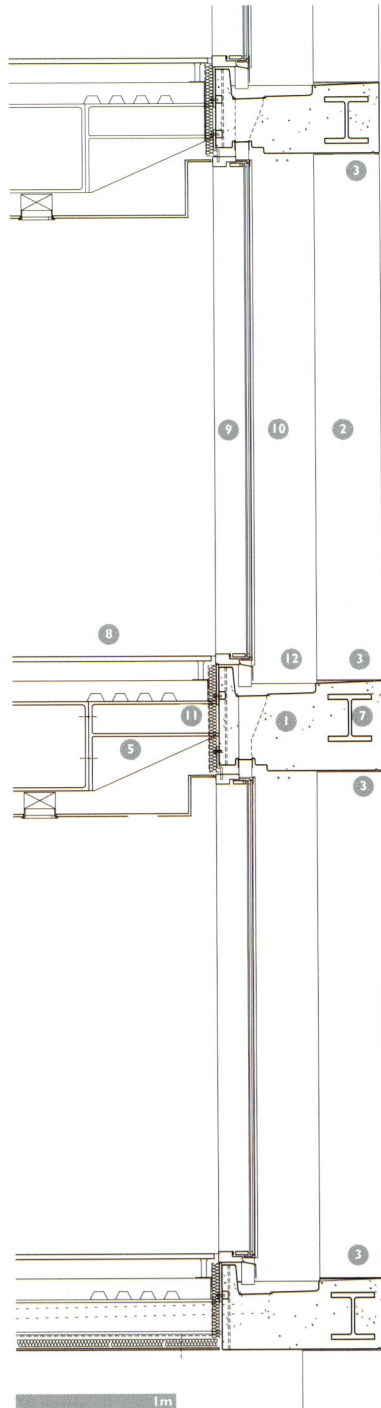

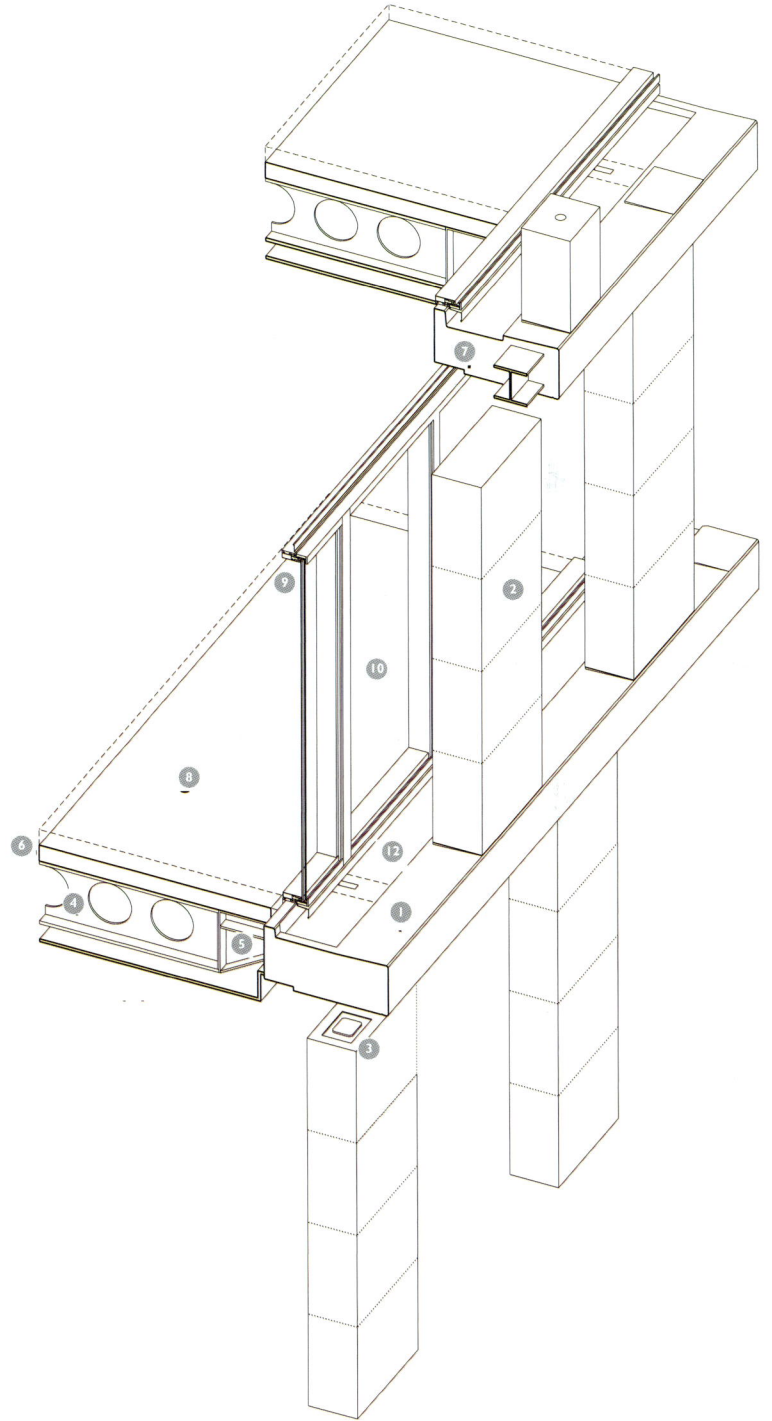

Above
The lift lobbies open to a gallery facing the office spaces across the central atrium.

Left/right
Atrium at lower ground level.

Left
The lower ground level is accessed by a glass staircase.

Right
A glass bridge crosses the atrium at ground level, helping to maximise daylight penetration to the below-ground atrium floor level.

Left
Stone quarry at Portland.

Right
Precast perimeter beams and stone quarry. The columns were developed following an extensive testing regime as little detailed design data was available for the use of stone as a structural material. A large number of cubes were crushed, both dry and fully saturated, to establish a characteristic compressive strength value. Tests were then carried out on one-third scale piers to confirm the relationship between cube strength and pier strength, and the effects of potential creep and different mortars on the load capacity. Finally a full-scale pier was placed in a test rig to test the maximum ultimate and working loads.

Below
Eric Parry Architects' Southwark Gateway public realm project included an inclined 'marker' made from stone, shown here under construction.

Left
Interstitial facade space; pavement lights along the main frontage bring daylight to the lower ground floor.

Right
The stone piers sit flush with the glazing on the Wilson Street elevation. Here the perimeter beam also consists of a steel section, but a precast facing beam was attached on site, rather than encasing the complete section as elsewhere.

5 Aldermanbury Square

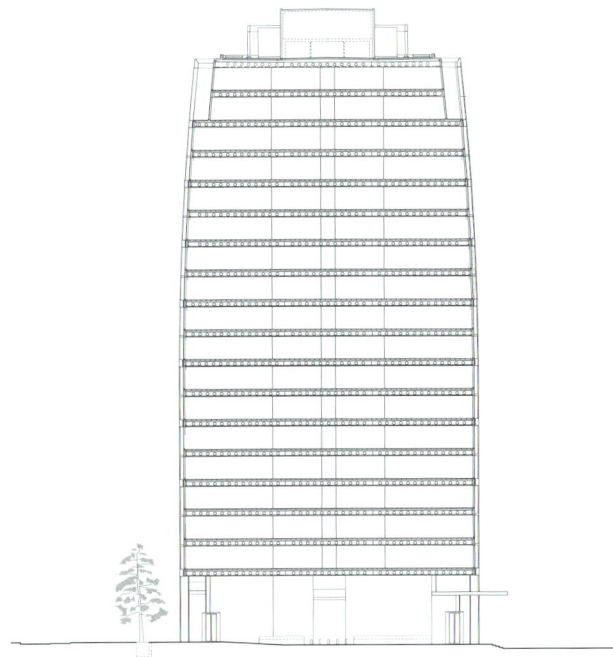

Crossings and Connections:
Bob Allies on 5 Aldermanbury Square

The plan of 5 Aldermanbury Square is, at first sight, a simple one. A large office floor, 34.5 metres deep, is served by a main core located centrally on the northern side with a satellite core positioned towards the south. On the north face the rectilinear geometry of the plan first adjusts to the angle of London Wall and then gives way to the looming presence of Terry Farrell's Alban Gate — the facade of which is no more than four metres away — by stepping back half way along its length, dividing the north elevation into two.

On the south facade a similar sub-division of the form is adopted, but to much more deliberate effect. Here the building is designed to be read as two tall slabs, linked at the centre by a recessed plane of glass which, as it descends towards the base of the building, curves inwards to allow the sun to penetrate the new public space that Eric Parry has created outside the building's entrance.

One immediate consequence of this arrangement is the way in which it changes the perception of the building from the south, where it forms a critical component of two historic views, one across the pinnacled roof of the Guildhall and one looking north up Wood Street past the residual freestanding church tower of St Alban and then the soaring stone chimneys and gables of McMorran & Whitby's Wood Street police station (1963). From these locations the articulation of the form gives the building an emphatic verticality that denies its bulk and allows it to sit happily in its context.

On these narrow, south-facing facades, Parry has allowed the cladding to develop an informality which acknowledges the absence of any intermediate columns, but which is also capable of accommodating another striking aspect of the building, the gentle curving back — or entasis — that he has introduced into the main east and west facades. For as the building rises above the more typical scale of the surrounding urban fabric, the facades begin to lean away from the street, diminishing the apparent scale of the building by exploiting the consequences of perspective. This is a device that operates not at the scale of the structural bay or glazing mullion — the constituent parts from which the facades are composed — but at the scale of the building as a whole.

Of course, a great deal of contemporary architecture operates exclusively at this scale. A building's shape and configuration can be generated from a single formal move which is deemed sufficient to define the entire architectural proposition. In consequence, the components from which the building is actually made take second place, relegated to performing a merely technical role.

And it is true that in the design of tall buildings where the structure, of necessity, stands apart from its surroundings, there is a need for the architectural proposition to satisfy at this much larger scale, the scale of the city as a whole. Now that we are again facing the task of building tall, the relationship between the form of a tower and its wider urban context is something which must be confronted again.

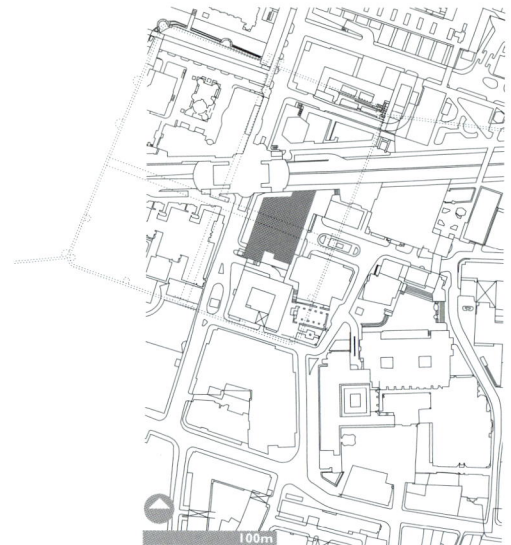

Right
View from the north-east across London Wall.

Left
Location plan; designed by Richard Seifert, Royex House (1962) was demolished in 2004 to make way for the new building.

What are the expressive modes appropriate to the shaping of a tower? What formal responses might be made to the transformation of a tower from its base to its head? And how might this transformation transcend the repetition of its constituent parts — either in terms of plan or construction — without succumbing to the weary pursuit of increasingly idiosyncratic shapes?

In Parry's work, the significance attributed to making has always encouraged respect for the process of construction and, more significantly, a concern to represent that process directly, if not literally, in the building form. So it is perhaps not surprising that at 5 Aldermanbury Square the entasis has not been created through the adoption of complex computer production techniques but through the simple stacking of straight steel box sections, the only complexity in the process arising from the wedging of the joints. In fact the east and west facades are models of tectonic clarity.

The steel columns which are located outside the curtain wall in order to create a clear internal floor plate are clad in billets of stainless steel, as are the beams which span between them. The billets, like the majority of the columns they enclose, rise over two storeys — another technique adopted by Parry to reduce the apparent scale of the building. The structure is set out on a six-metre grid, but additional billets are also introduced on the three metre module, transforming the proportion of the frame and — because these elements stand proud of the facade — creating an element of shading. Further shading is provided by stainless steel 'eyebrows' which project out from the facade, and mask the presence of the spandrels behind. From the street, the facade possesses considerable depth, a quality which also enhances the experience of the office space itself where the layering of elements contributes to the play of light in the interior.

One curious by-product of this rigorous identification of cladding with frame is that when the stainless steel is deployed instead to wrap the cantilevered canopy that projects over the Aldermanbury Square entrance, the benefits of consistency in the use of a limited palette of materials seems outweighed by the disadvantages of the more complex assembly that this involves. Everywhere else the stainless steel is so direct, so matter of fact, that here it feels as if it has too much to do.

Left/below
A glazed interstitial 'belly' on the
south side curves inwards
towards ground level to
enhance daylighting to the
undercroft. public space.

Aldermanbury Square itself is a wonderful piece of urban recovery, a new public space created by a combination of intelligent building placement, careful ordering of a ground floor plan and the introduction of an elegant landscape, designed again by Parry but through a separate commission from the City of London. Because the main core of the new building is located at the northern end of the site, Parry has been able to establish a generous route under the building to link the new Aldermanbury Square to Wood Street, and to include within it a small urban garden with fountain and seats, the beneficiary in terms of sunlight of the set-back of the south facade. It is an important public gain, and an interesting space, although its slight indeterminacy and somewhat difficult relationship to the back of the police station left me wondering if a more modest arcade could not have succeeded equally as well. Put simply, to sit amongst the silver birches that Parry has planted in Aldermanbury Square always seems a more attractive option.

For Parry, however, the ground floor spaces beneath the building — public and private — have become the focus for a sequence of poetic explorations which extend from the large-scale woven hanging that he designed with Merit Claussen, through the office reception where he contributed the furniture, into the undercroft where he designed the circular seats and the water piece that provides the southern enclosure to the space. Hovering above all of these is a polished black granite ceiling, mirroring literally and metaphorically the textured granite of the floor.

This is art. Not public art as it is conventionally deployed today, but rather the controlled manipulation by a single hand of material, colour, texture, light and even sound to add intensity and richness to one's understanding and experience of the building and its site.

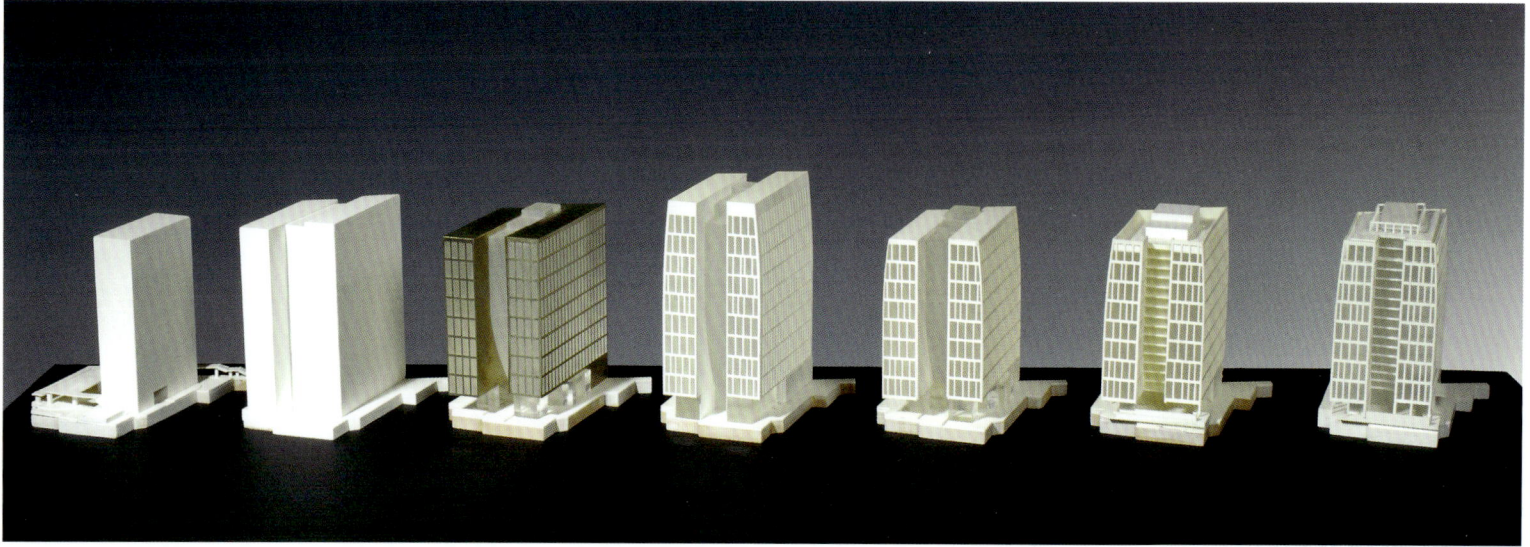

Eric Parry writes

Number 5 Aldermanbury Square is an architectural story of connections and crossings: it lies at the intersection of the axial roads of a Roman fort and draws together Wood Street and Aldermanbury Square in a new public space under its curtilage.

London Wall seen through archival images (for instance a sequence in Michelangelo Antonioni's 1966 film 'Blow Up') conjures a nostalgia for the abstract clarity of Le Corbusier's urban vision, but the pedestrian experience was banal. On Wood Street the base of the building was a ramp rising to the planned Barbican highwalk.

Addle Street, a taxi rat-run, connected the street to the square which itself was a sad post-war invention with some miserable architecture to match. Replacing Richard Seifert's 18-storey, 16- by 60-metre plan Royex House (1962) was not a difficult case to make, particularly as it was an ugly backdrop to the view of Guildhall Yard from Gresham Street. The brief was to maximise the net floor area of the existing building which was challenging given the limitation on height deriving from the site's prominence behind St Paul's and the congestion of adjacent buildings.

Looking to reinforce positive aspects of the existing urban scene, the generous eight metre reception ceiling height at 88 Wood Street suggested the datum for the new public space under the building. To create this space it was necessary to relocate the public ramp which has been designed to improved standards and is placed to the north, parallel with Wood Street and woven into the northern skirt of the building.

To maximise the new public realm at ground level and take advantage of wonderful views to the south from the upper floors, the principal lift core was pressed as far to the north as possible.

The theme of crossing is reflected in the east-west axis of the reception and public spaces, and in the building's form – two wings separated by a belly allowing the penetration of south light to the undercroft. Against this is set the triple-height entry into the lift lobby framed by a giant board-marked concrete wall. It has been a real bonus to design the metal textiles, rugs and furniture of the reception and public space.

The plans are as simple and flexible as possible. The synthesis of the facade design and the 'clean' plan began with the decision to place the vertical structure outside the line of the curtain wall.

Facades that recede from an uninterrupted external plane have been developed in a number of our projects, particularly Foundress Court, Cambridge (1997) and 30 Finsbury Square (2002).

The stainless steel panels that cloak the structure have a shot peened finish which, unlike a brushed finish, has no pronounced direction, creating a surface very responsive to light. The pattern of joints responds to structural elements of the bay design and involves very long sections to create the double order. The bending skywards, 'levitation' of the shadow billets and the inverted reflections from the polished soffit all contribute to a 'floating' world.

Above

Massing study models, with a comparative model of Royex House (left), which was demolished to make way for the new building. The bipartite form was introduced as an early concept, while the canted elevations were introduced in later iterations.

Right

West, south and east elevations; ground, second and 16th floor plans. Key: 1 entrance, 2 reception, 3 lift lobby, 4 car lifts, 5 loading bay, 6 retail, 7 water feature, 8 silver birch garden with seating, 9 London plane trees, 10 new pedestrian ramps and stairs to London Wall, 11 office space.

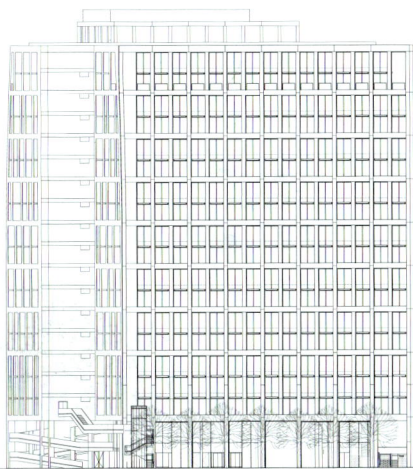

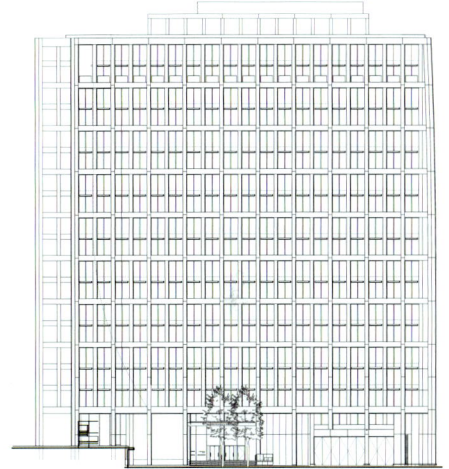

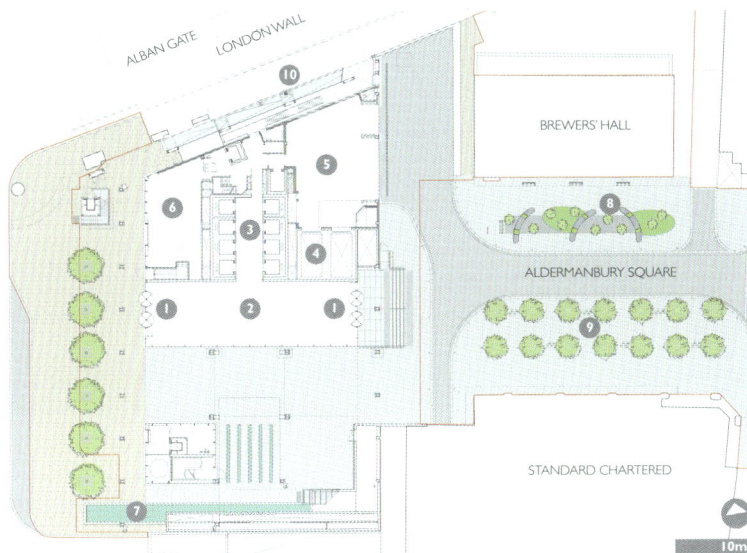

ALBAN GATE   LONDON WALL

BREWERS' HALL

ALDERMANBURY SQUARE

STANDARD CHARTERED

10m

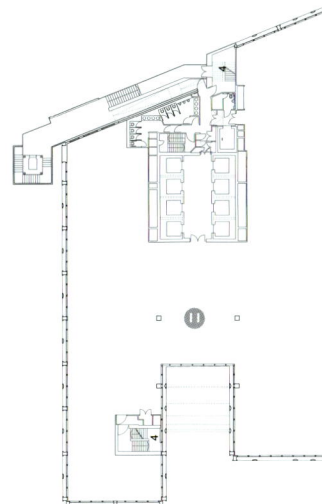

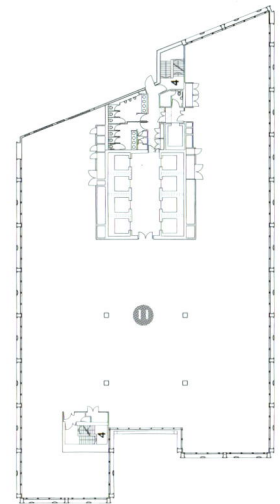

Left
View east across the landscaped space that forms a new public route linking Aldermanbury Square with Wood Street.

Right
The landscaped public realm on the south side is partially framed by the flank of Wood Street police station.

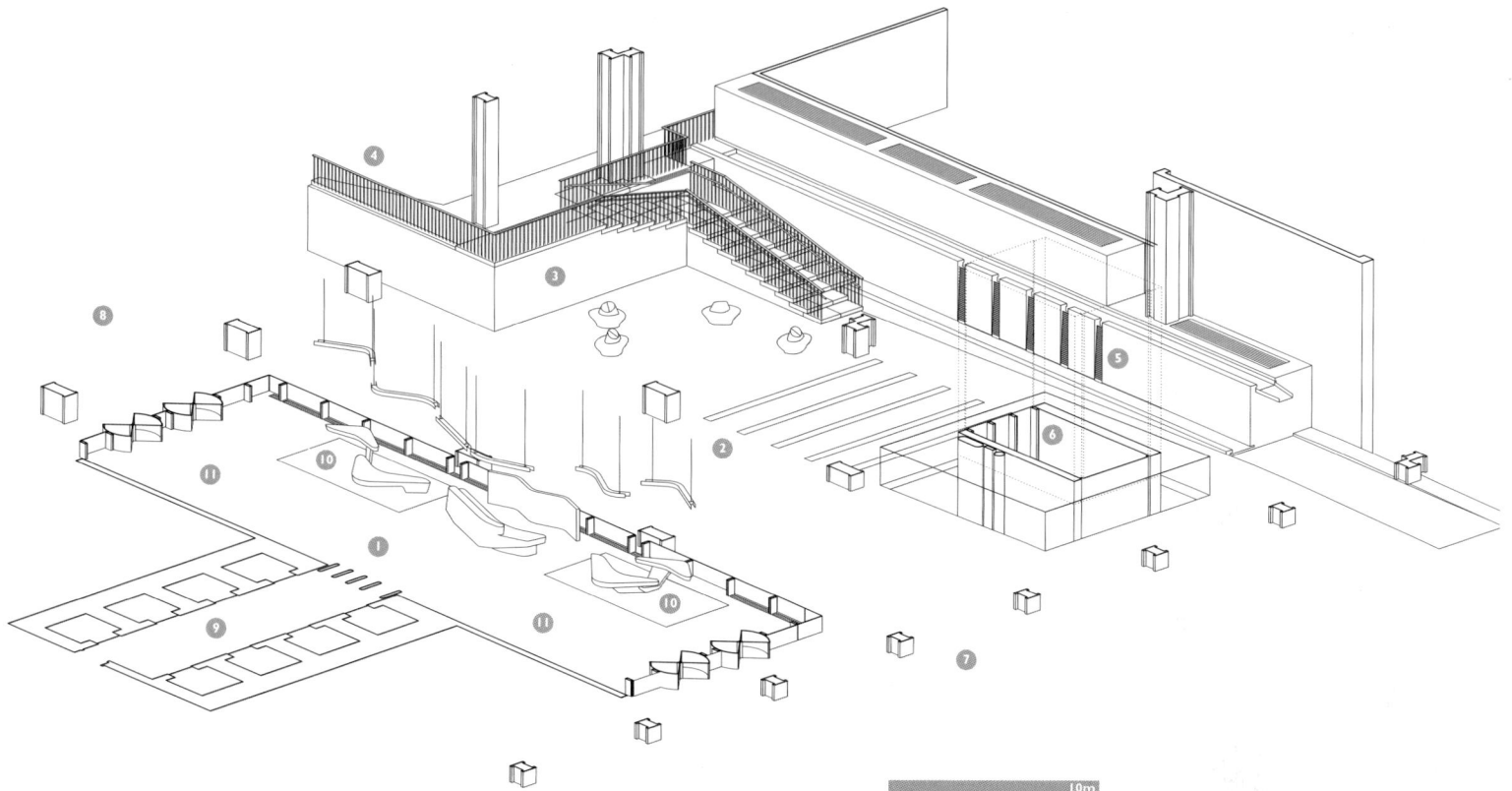

Above

The linear reception space, accessed from both Wood Street and Aldermanbury Square, aligns a new external space that extends across the site, forming a public route and landscaped with benches and a water feature. Key: 1 reception, 2 public space, 3 lookout benches, 4 public passage to Love Lane, 5 insitu concrete water wall (rills, rivulet and bronze gargoyle), 6 entrance to retail/restaurant below pavement, 7 Wood Street, 8 Aldermanbury Square, 9 lift core, 10 seat/worktop, 11 textile wall hanging.

Right

Board-marked concrete panels form a backdrop to the water feature.

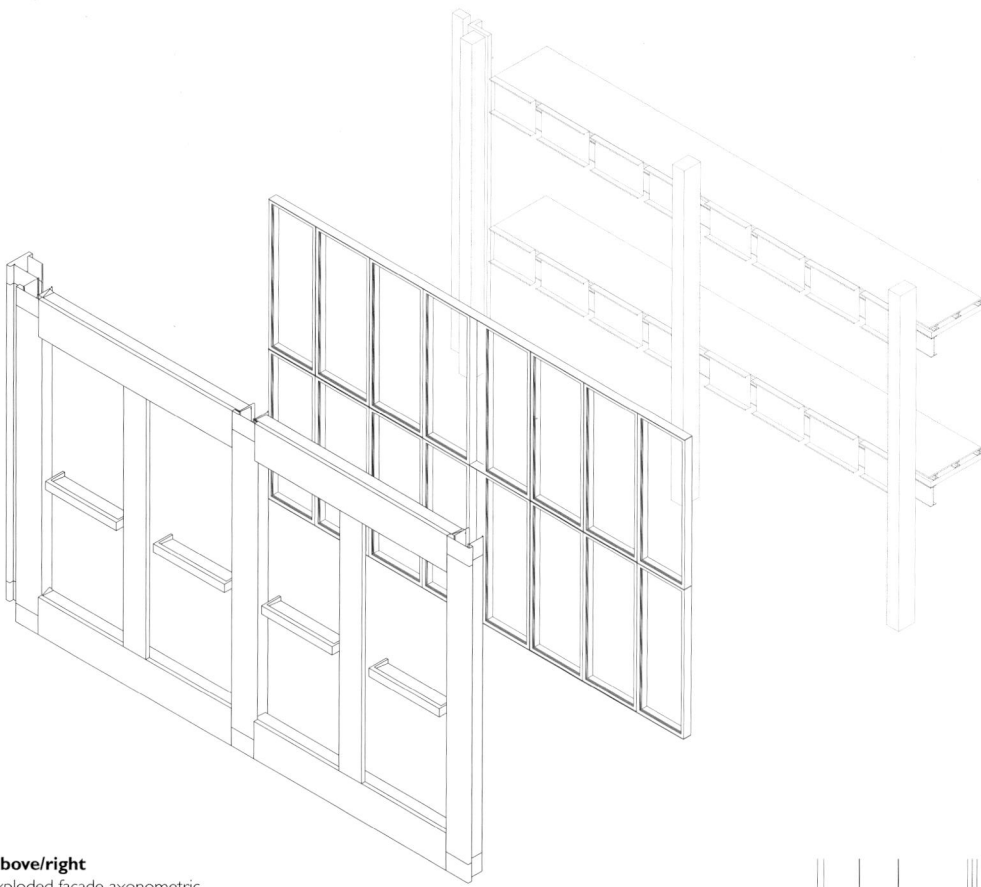

Above/right

Exploded facade axonometric, elevation, section and plan at seventh and eighth floor levels. Key: 1 shot-peened stainless steel, 2 shot-peened stainless steel vertical solar baffle, 3 structural column clad in shot peened stainless steel, 4 spandrel panel/shadow box, 5 stainless steel brise soleil, 6 double-glazed unitised cladding unit, 7 stainless steel cover caps, 8 raised floor, 9 structural slab, 10 structural beam with service apertures, 11 ceiling and lighting void, 12 insulated spandrel panel, 13 powder-coated aluminium mullions to internal faces, 14 blind box, 15 guides in mullion for future blinds, 16 fire/smoke stop.

Opposite

The 'giant' order of the facade is composed of stacked stainless steel elements punctuated by joints and gaps. The shot-peened stainless steel panels, alternately attached to concrete-filled Cor-ten structural columns, form a screen in front of a unitised aluminium cladding system which is in turn supported on the steel and concrete structure.

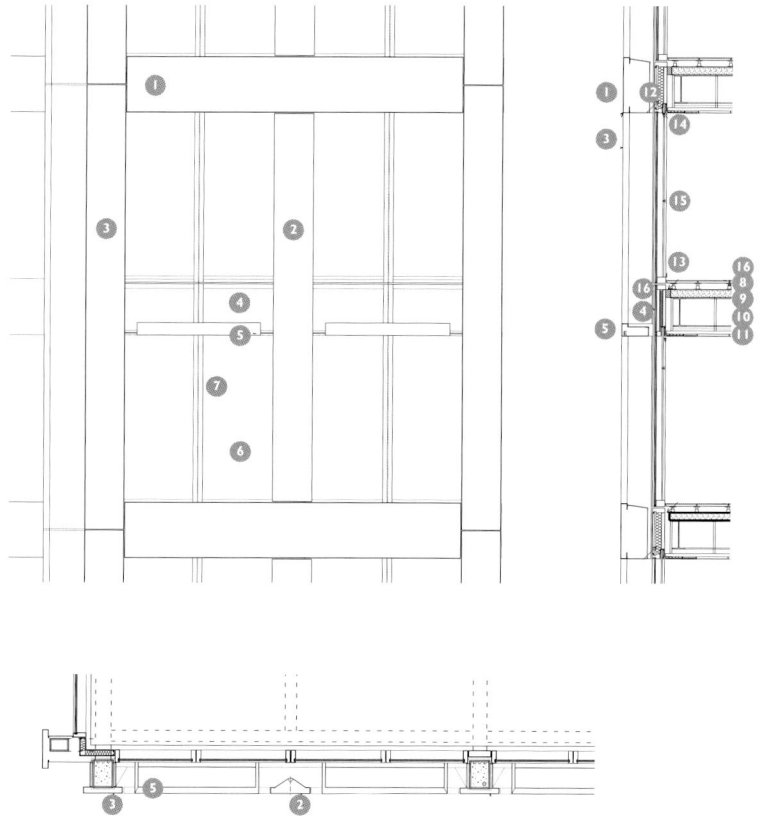

2m

Left
The building's south flank addresses the church tower of St Alban and Wood Street police station.

Right
To the north Aldermanbury Square abuts Alban Gate, the postmodern building designed by Terry Farrell that straddles the busy thoroughfare of London Wall.

60 Threadneedle Street

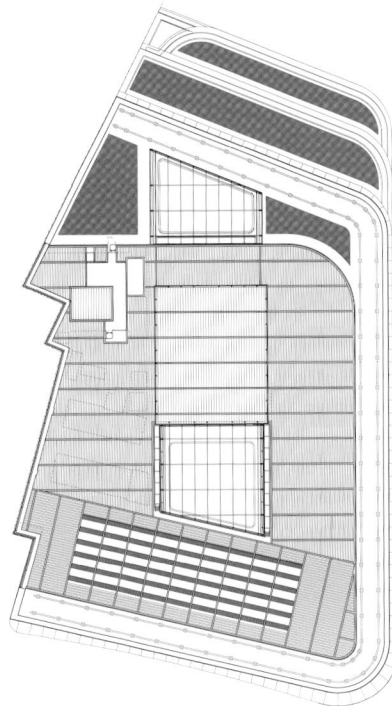

A Purposeful Paradigm:
Patrick Lynch on 60 Threadneedle Street

Eric Parry's office building on Threadneedle Street sits halfway between James Stirling's No 1 Poultry and Richard Rogers' Lloyd's building, in more than a simple geographical sense. If the former posthumous work exudes an almost science fiction attitude towards the past — like one of Joseph Gandy's ruination watercolours — then Lloyd's too can be seen today as an example of nostalgia for the future. Rogers' atrium is reminiscent of Georgian industrial architecture as well as 1980s dystopian movies such as 'Blade Runner' and 'Brazil'. No 1 Poultry is infused with a similar collagist sensibility, and Parry has been known in the past to adopt a similarly eclectic approach. His neighbours Soane and Cockerell and Tite were inspired by antiquity and the Renaissance, and the City of London is a kind of museum of grand architecture, both of the foolish and ambitious attempts to engage money with civility.

The City has a latent urbanity, whereby medieval streets and arcane rituals force neoclassical facades into displays of decorum that never quite come off. It is as if the Anglican fudge of 'English Catholicism' compromises both architecture and commerce and what results are marooned examples of Grand Architecture on tight plots, mean and exaggerated. On Threadneedle Street, in retrospect, it is obvious that something else was called for than yet more stone. Yet the temptation to join in the choir of Soane, Cockerell et al must have been difficult to resist, and one could be forgiven for expecting Parry to have adapted his success at Finsbury Square to this similarly masonry setting.

He resisted, and the result is an intriguing and singular act of imagination that appears like a shadow or a lacuna in the streetscape, one that reflects as much as it absorbs. He confidently holds his own amongst his fellow Royal Academicians.

A new street amplifies the medieval setting, and 'glass vitrines' offer up the hope at least of a commercial public realm. Opposite the entrance an existing square is given scale and definition by the new building, and a forgotten space now seems obviously lovely. Breaking away from the former Stock Exchange tower defines Parry's building as a block and the planners must be applauded for encouraging this. It enables Parry to put his energy into focusing and directing the movement of the sun and of pedestrians, in a context where both are usually subservient to cars or the bogus classicism of overblown porticos. Instead, his building can play a delightful game of repressed recession and surprise on the one hand — the glass skin — and sexy, slightly louche enticement on the other. Cast into shadow but illuminated within from above, the lobby seems to extend the public realm deep into the plan and section.

Upon arrival the lobby ceiling compresses your view until the startling full-height south atrium offers release. Glass is cast in elliptical curves that appear solid and reflective. From inside the wells appear like bodies of light, densifying the space. On the floors above they appear also as dense pools of light and reflections, and the edges of the floors dissolve so that your peripheral vision is drawn out to the landscape of rooftops beyond. Standing on the upper floors is a fresh and exhilarating experience, more akin to being in the natural world than the deadening interiors of most offices. I cannot think of any other commercial building where the world beyond the interior is brought into focus by the experience of being in one.

Right
The principal office entrance is placed on Threadneedle Street, where an inflection at ground level forms a transitional space between the columnated streetline and the reception space within.

Parry is justly proud of the structural clarity of the 15-metre spans achieved, and this canny agility has enabled money to be spent on the special paint finish of the aluminium facade. While the building received planning consent before changes to Part L2 of the Building Regulations, the design team worked hard to achieve an 'excellent' BREEAM rating. The facade shades the interiors while also responding to the scale and rhythm of its neighbours. Both inner and outer worlds are brought together by a facade composed as a multiplication of the ubiquitous 1.5-metre tiling grid that is to modern commercial buildings what the Venetian piede was to Sansovino or the Mantovan braccio was to Alberti. Proportion, order, scale and tectonics were the lingua franca of educated architects until recently, and Parry manages to make architecture that seems at once appropriate and also catalytic. He understands the technical and economic challenges facing the architect today yet somehow his rigorous approach to problem solving is not dominant and neither is his rhetoric. Instead, his building recalls the most optimistic aspects of modernism and the more sensual aspects of classical architecture.

Allowing the midnight blue structural frame to oscillate between solar shade and portico liberates the facade from a literal obsession with structural purity. It is both responsive to questions of scale and decorum whilst being a 'state of the art' response to practical questions in a way that both Lloyd's and Poultry never were. Parry's architecture sits at the threshold between instrumental and representational notions of ecology, fusing a contemporary attitude towards energy usage with the best aspects of what Karsten Harries calls for in Infinity and Perspective (2001): 'an altogether new post-postmodernist geocentrism'.

What do I mean by this? If architecture is to develop beyond the mutually antagonistic discourse of theory on the one hand and commercial opportunism on the other, then this building offers us another paradigm. Harries suggests that post-modernists valued 'sublimity over beauty' and that on the other hand the 'price of pursuing objectivity appears to be the progressive loss of whatever gives significance to existence'. Parry neither refuses nor entirely accepts the plight of modernity and the lessons of post-modernism, finding a third way between the nihilism of both.

The key is the blue coloured facade that gives the building body and depth, and makes the sunlight appear at once orchestrated and free. The curves modulate light, and also shadows which read as coloured reflections rather than as an absence. Seen from afar the curves densify the mass of the block, defining the scale of the public square as a volume, and operate as mouldings that modulate the face of the house. Seen obliquely they add vitality and seem to ripple, like muscles under a thin dress. At this point in his career you could expect Parry to become at once overly emphatic and cautious, yet his work is becoming both more direct and more nuanced. His imagination blossoms out of sturdy limbs.

Right
The Threadneedle Street facade plays against the Bank of England to the west.

Left
Extended 'shadow shelves' serve to introduce curvature to the facade while emphasising horizontality and providing solar shading to the office spaces within.

Location plan; ground and third floor plans

Left
South and east elevations facing Threadneedle Street and the new Threadneedle Walk.

Left below
Model viewed from street level and above.

Below, right
Location plan; ground and third floor plans. Key: 1 Reception, 2 retail, 3 loading bay, 4 south atrium, 5 north atrium, 6 office.

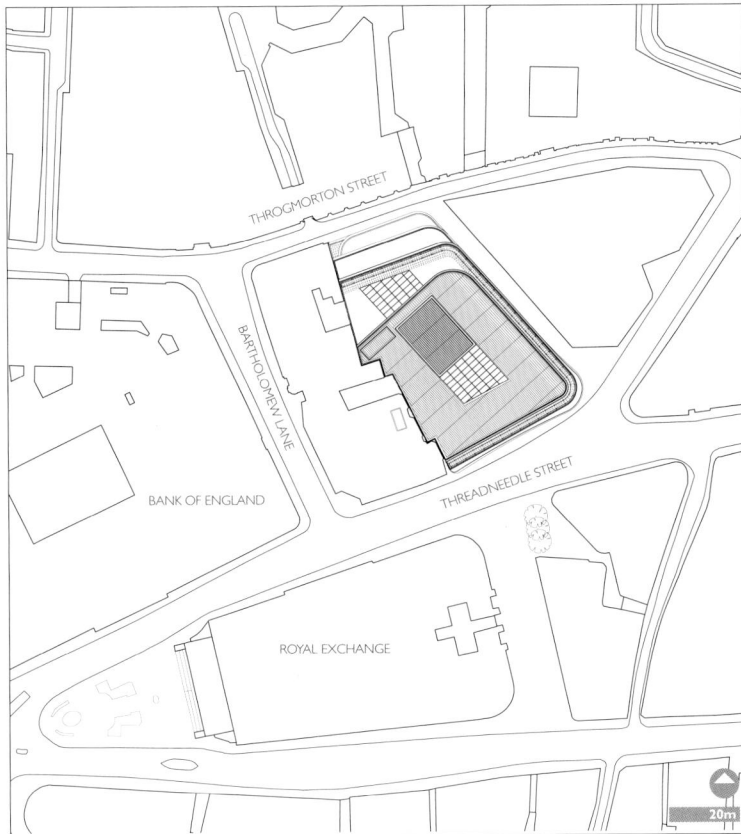

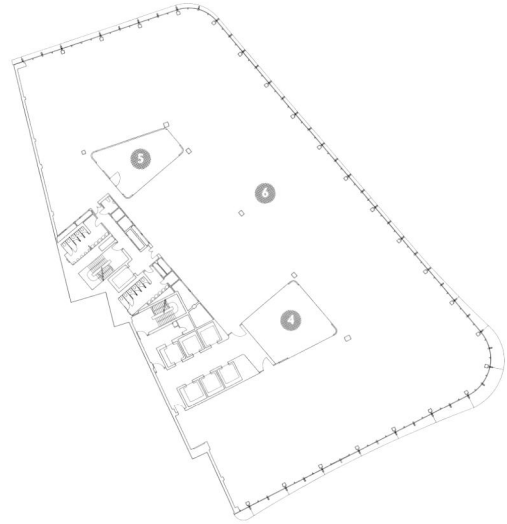

THROGMORTON STREET

BARTHOLOMEW LANE

BANK OF ENGLAND

THREADNEEDLE STREET

ROYAL EXCHANGE

20m

10m

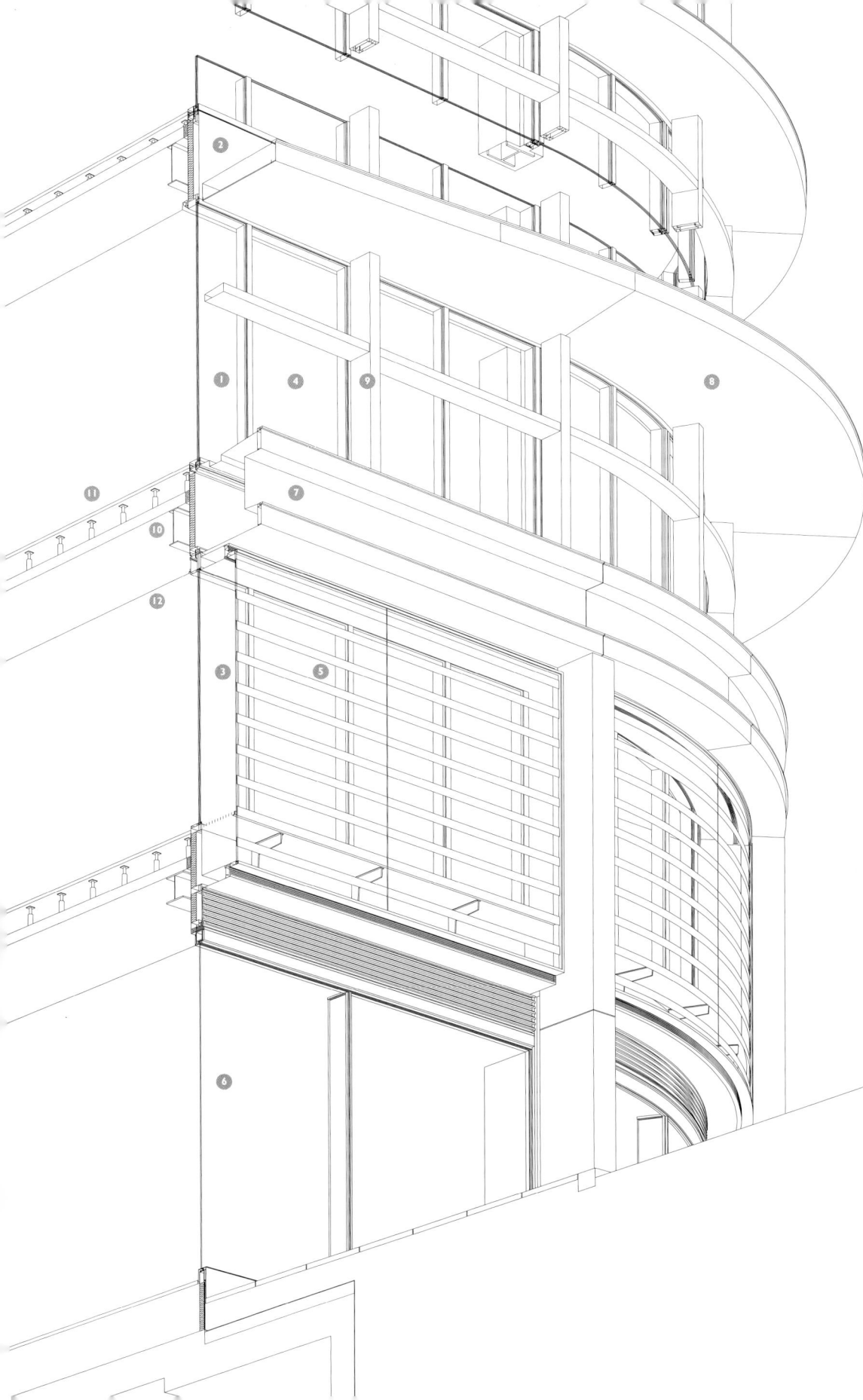

Left
Upview cutaway axonometric of the corner condition showing the 'shadow shelves' and external louvres that articulate the facade and reduce solar glare and gain. Key: 1 unitised six-metre-wide storey-height cladding with full-height double-glazed units and insulated flat spandrel panels, 2 pvdf liquid-applied external finish, 3 unitised three-metre-wide storey-height double-glazed cladding system to first floor with full-height inner double-glazed units, vented maintenance cavity and outer laminated dichroic glass screen, 4 36mm double-glazed units, 5 22mm clear low-iron triple-laminated curved and flat units, 6 16mm clear low-iron laminated glazing with structural fins to four-metre-high reception, 7 metal cornice with integral gutter, 8 cantilevered sun shelves with rubber buffer strip to leading edge, 9 metal light shelf and mullions, 10 perimeter edge beam with intumescent coating, 11 raised access floor on composite steel structural deck, 12 suspended metal plank ceiling with plasterboard margin and folded metal blind box.

Opposite
The articulated facade eschews the stonework that characterises its neoclassical neighbours in favour of more contemporary materials and character.

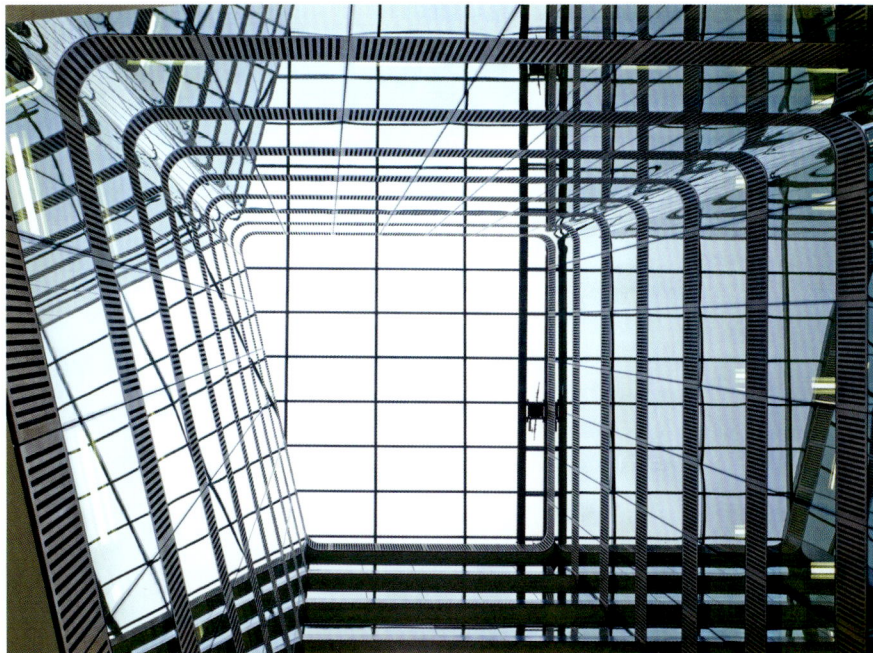

Above/left
Two atria punctuate the interior, introducing natural light to the deep-plan office floors. The smaller atrium extends only down to the third floor so as to maximise the area of the two dealing floors below.

Left/right
The main atrium extends
upwards from the reception
space, echoing the curved
exterior but with more
intimate detailing.

73

Left
The reception lobby occupies the full length of the Threadneedle Street frontage.

Right
The newly-formed Threadneedle Walk is aligned by glazed 'vitrines' to the retail spaces, echoing the shop windows of the medieval city.

Left
The upper floors are set back to the north, forming external terraces to the office spaces.

Right
The staircase that leads from the reception area down to the lower ground floor is sculpted so as to form part of the atrium that rises above.

23 Savile Row

Reading Places:
Daniel Rosbottom on 23 Savile Row

Eric Parry's spacious meeting room is screened from the rest of his bright Clerkenwell studio by a wall of books. Perusing them, the breadth of his interests quickly becomes apparent, encompassing among other things history and archaeology, a panoply of artists and an intriguing, eclectic range of architectural references. This is to be expected from a distinguished teacher. What is perhaps more surprising is that our discussion, which took place beneath a Richard Serra etching, across a large table filled with models and drawings, did not concern one of his various public commissions. Instead it related to a programme that, for an architect of his persuasion, might seem less enticing — the speculative office block.

Such prejudices appear justified when one remembers the earliest building for which Eric Parry Architects became known — a pair of studios for the painter Tom Phillips and the sculptor Antony Gormley. But in fact the practice was simultaneously working on another defining project, an office pavilion at Stockley Park near Heathrow. Strands of work have extended from each of these beginnings. However they should not be understood as parallel trajectories, with lucrative commerce economically underpinning cultural prestige — the usual cross-subsidy. Instead they have intertwined to achieve a refreshing level of equivalence, together becoming the DNA of a practice that has, with a singular degree of success, confronted the breadth of the heterogeneous urban condition that is London and which understands the need to consider both the figure and the ground of the city with equal concentration.

Twenty years on, this holistic view was eloquently demonstrated in Parry's project for a substantial office and retail building at 23 Savile Row in London's Mayfair. Here art, craft and commerce are drawn into quietly dramatic dialogue. The building also marked the conclusion of a more tightly defined period in EPA's oeuvre, completing a suite of projects born out of a seismic shift in the influence of corporate power and wealth within London during the last decade. The physical consequences of that transformation rippled across the urban fabric from its epicentre in the City before shuddering dramatically to a halt in the face of the economic downturn. The blossoming cranes have quickly withered but the effect on London's grain and scale will be lasting and Parry's contribution is a rather exceptional high point in what might generally be considered an unfortunate legacy.

The primary reasons for the quality and consistency of his work are encapsulated in Parry's remark that his first London office commission, Finsbury Square, arrived not because of a perceived expertise in the programmatic constraints of commercial office development, but rather in recognition of an attitude to the city. As with its predecessors, the Mayfair building is innately concerned with the particularities of its urban situation. Critically however, this relationship is not a subservient or passive one, nor is it the result of a predetermined attitude, indiscriminately applied. Instead each of the buildings seeks to become an active agent in reinforcing or transforming innate, but often latent, qualities found within its context.

Right
Generous floor heights are achieved in some of the retail spaces by exploiting the 1.5 metre drop in ground level across the Savile Row frontage. These are also signified by the use of black granite in contrast to the Portland stone above.

At Savile Row, EPA has confronted the issue of a prominent site and a scale of development that is considerably larger than its immediate neighbours. The project replaces Fortress House, latterly the home of English Heritage. This was built in 1950, itself the result of a fortuitous combination of bomb damage and demolition which had opened up the northern end of Savile Row to Conduit Street. While it was a building with definite qualities, its didactic plan and limited floor-to-floor heights made it difficult to re-appropriate and its introverted demeanour, concentrated around an axial entrance court, left it unresponsive to the wider context of the surrounding streets.

Parry's initial moves were akin to those of Alison and Peter Smithson within the similarly sensitive context of the Economist Plaza in St James — breaking down the site into an ensemble of pieces and creating an element of public space. However, the plan was subsequently 'hardened up' and the result is a building that at an urban scale straightforwardly reinforces the line of the pavement and the grid of the street, both predominant characteristics of the historic Burlington Estate, of which Savile Row is a part. The new building retains an axial relationship to the Row, with two wings of accommodation stepping forward to the street line, separated by a slightly set-back, canopied entrance. The foyer leads through to an atrium, with a densely planned core to the rear of the site. Street presence is reinforced by a ground floor retail unit on the prominent corner that opens to Conduit Street. Behind it, along the minor edge of New Burlington Place, are secondary and service access points.

Looking from Conduit Street, the building has a significant presence, with the 'vitrine' of the new shop introducing the refined world of bespoke tailoring that lies beyond. In its response to the surroundings, the building seeks to improve on the rather ponderous relationships that the similarly-scaled Fortress House had imposed. Seen obliquely, the two wings accentuate a rhythm that already echoes along the length of Savile Row. Sectionally, a tripartite strategy offers empathy with the scale of adjacent properties and the street as a whole, with the base and four storeys above establishing an eaves height. Set back from this, two further storeys, originally intended as residential but now converted to office use, form a visually lighter roof-top pavilion.

Commentators on his City buildings have noted the quality of light and optimised efficiency of Parry's office interiors, and this project extends that track record. But what particularly defines EPA's attitude to the office building as type is the role that the facade plays. Although Savile Row is as different from its predecessors as they are from each other, one can see a genealogical thread running through them. At its root, this familial quality stems from an innate belief in the 'idea' of the facade, both as an integral component in the ordering and optimisation of those interiors, but simultaneously as a separate, mediating element between the life of the building and the public world beyond.

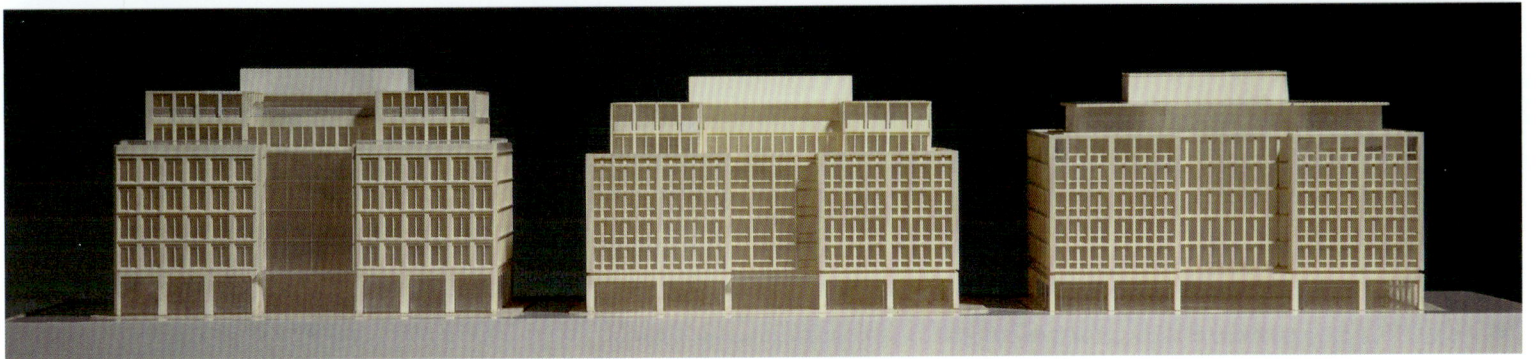

Left

Facade studies by Eric Parry explore the notion of 'weaving' in the composition of stonework piers and lintels.

The theoretician Colin Rowe regretfully concluded that 'face was never a preoccupation for modern architecture.' In giving his buildings a very definite physiognomy, Parry clearly places the work of his practice apart from the didactic urban machinery of high-tech. For while a fascination with the conditions of modernism is embedded in his work, the buildings collectively reject the orthodoxy that the free plan inevitably destroys the primacy of the facade as the representative moment of a building. Thus they bring the pre-modern, the modern and the post-modern into a satisfying continuity. Within these buildings, the ubiquitous multiplier of the 1.5 metre grid is respected, but it is not allowed to dissolve the exterior into the numbing repetition of a curtain wall. Nor is the problem of the face ignored through the application of veils or screens leading to a kind of de-scaled objectification. Instead, such pragmatic concerns become merely another system of order within a complex matrix of thinking that takes in issues of proportion, scale and tectonic, solid and void, window and wall.

Previous projects have demonstrated this through a layering of components that are allowed to slip past each other, interlacing tectonic clarity with experiential shifts in scale and depth, light and shadow. This is most immediately evident at Finsbury Square where the extraordinary screen of loadbearing, self-supporting masonry plays against tauter rhythms of bright stainless steel framing behind, with light bouncing in the space between. Close inspection reveals similar intricacies in the gridded, stainless steel facades of Aldermanbury Square or in the midnight blue frames of Threadneedle Street — although in that case it is shadow and structure that are almost interchangeable.

The development of the Savile Row facade began in a similar way, as a process of 'weaving' stone. However, this was quickly put to one side in the face of a sensitive planning conversation. Instead the project developed as a more traditional dialogue of Portland stone string-courses and pilasters, spaced at three-metre centres within a six-metre structural grid.

Parry has made a number of eloquent and expressive stone facades, notably at Pembroke College, Cambridge. Prior to this one, though, each worked with the idea of carving back from a planar surface. Perhaps it was the deep, sensuously curving, Mendelsohn-like projections of Threadneedle Street that emboldened him to express the horizontal strings in this case. Whatever the cause, the result is a strongly classical resolution but one which embodies an implicit modernity, recalling the Chicago School or the work of 'Greek' Thomson in Glasgow. Such resemblances are in part to do with the democracy of repeating floor-to-floor heights but are largely a result of the slenderness of each element of the composition.

Parry is rigorous but he is not a moralist and he is happy to announce that this lightness is the result of the stone being only partially self-supporting — tied back at intervals to the precast panels holding the window assemblies and hence to the steel frame. A slipping of layers within the facade is still just discernable within the 550mm wall depth. This is artfully registered through the slight shift in the grain of the larger pieces of stone used within the revealed openings and is made literal by the shadows of movement joints at the back of each pilaster.

These subtleties express something of the inevitable discontinuity of contemporary construction. The architect has worked hard to emulate traditional structures, however, using three metre unbroken Portland stone lintels and 3mm joints between each stone. Collectively these complementary expressions provide a satisfying tectonic clarity.

More ambiguously, a freestanding, ribbed aluminum extrusion stands centrally within each window bay. At first glance this appears to act as a prop to the long stone lintels. In fact its purpose is entirely visual, masking any intermediate partitions that might be erected inside and heightening the modulation of light and shadow. Such creative ambiguities and playful tensions exist within each of Parry's projects and these are what allow the apparently laconic forms and relationships to oscillate within one's consciousness, moving beyond mere well-tempered background.

The final element of the composition draws the building as a whole into such a dialogue. In direct response to the sense of restraint exhibited throughout, the shallow space above the entrance canopy has become a kind of votive niche at an urban scale — a space for a sculpture. 'Here' is a work by American artist Joel Shapiro. Specially commissioned, it was developed in dialogue with the architects and the building. The dynamic composition of five linear, raw bronze pieces is apparently weightless and yet obviously massive; both figurative and abstract. Suspended from the stone on either side, it creates a dialogue with the facades that feels both free-spirited and absolutely precise, a leading dancer to the building's corps de ballet. This does not feel like a 'percent for art' appendage but rather an intrinsic and essential element in the composition. Indeed, the minimalist, Dan Graham-like qualities of the reflective glazing that fills the recess behind it would feel a distinctly curious conceit without its presence. Seen as a whole, the warm, tonal colour of the bronze heightens the monochromatic qualities of the stone. Close to, the rhythmic marks of the sawmill, captured within the sand-cast surface, echo the larger urban rhythms of the facade. The loss of a public space at ground level, speculated on within the early schemes, is more than compensated for in this very different form of public event. It is a gift to the city whose arrival, as Parry suggests, might once have prompted a three-day festival of celebration.

If the Savile Row building concludes his sequence of latter-day palazzi, dedicated to the art of commerce and embellished, like their forebears, by the finest artists, then Parry's final office development, for the moment at least, promises a rather different urban expression — one that might be succinctly characterised as poché. Very close by, on New Bond Street, a mixed use development of office, shopping and housing expertly weaves its way through back courts and through both new and existing buildings. If Savile Row is a big man in an impeccably tailored, bespoke suit, then the striking infill piece emerging on New Bond Street is an agile youth in a hand-stitched snakeskin jacket. That project underscores the point touched on at the outset: while there may be architects in London who have built more, and more noticeably, there are few whose work is more encompassing. From the renewal of St Martin-in-the-Fields to 23 Savile Row, Parry has approached the complexity of the city and the diversity of its building stock with perception, precision and personality.

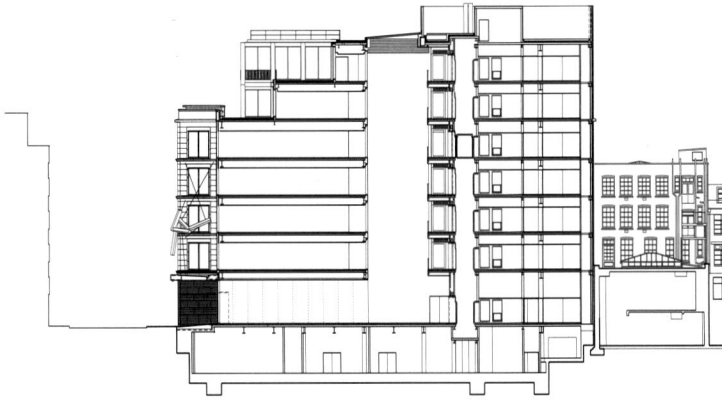

Right
Ground floor and typical upper floor plans with cross sections. Key: 1 Reception, 2 retail, 3 loading bay, 4 atrium, 5 office.

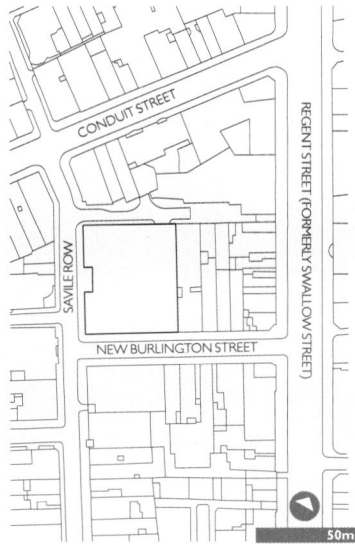

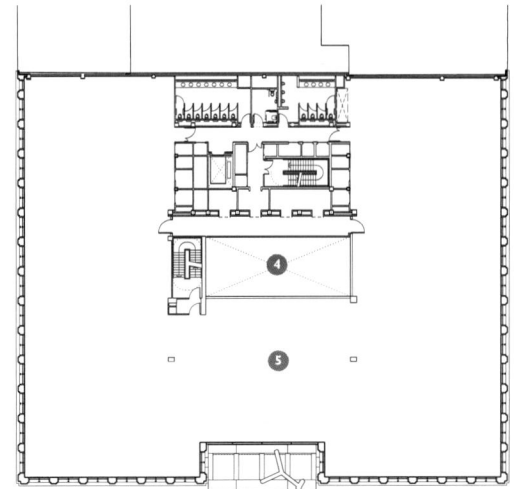

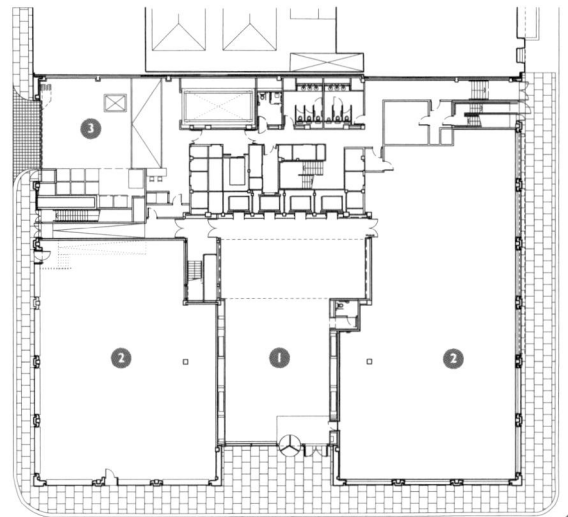

CONDUIT STREET

SAVILE ROW

REGENT STREET (FORMERLY SWALLOW STREET)

NEW BURLINGTON STREET

50m

10m

Left
The central atrium, flanked by a
lift and service core to the rear
of the site, rises above the
extended entrance foyer.

Right
The floor plates are
symmetrically arranged around
the central atrium and
overlooking the indented bay
on Savile Row with its
suspended sculpture 'Here' by
artist Joel Shapiro.

Left/right
The two uppermost storeys, which feature more extensive glazing than elsewhere in the project, are set back from the Savile Row frontage so they remain largely unseen from street level, and allow the elevation to correspond with its neighbours in terms of height and proportion.

Left

The suspended sculpture 'Here' was specially commmissioned from New York artist Joel Shapiro. The work is cast in bronze and left untreated.

Right

The layered window bays combine Portland stone, aluminium-framed glazing and a central natural anodised aluminium non-structural pier.

Left
Facade detail on New
Burlington Place.

50 New Bond Street

Civic Advocacy:
Jonathan Sergison on 50 New Bond Street

In recent years, no practice in the UK has considered the workspace as an area of programmatic investigation more profoundly than Eric Parry Architects. Often such projects are treated as technical exercises or become over-deferential to the client's fiscal interests. While Parry's work doesn't disregard such concerns, it has a different departure point. Each project begins as an urban work, makes accurate readings of a city and is clear about how it can be reasonably adjusted.

In the late 1980s, Parry's office refurbishment in Greek Street, Soho, made a series of insertions and adjustments to the existing building. Later, the practice completed a workspace project adjacent to St Martin-in-the-Fields, a work of masterly urban repair with a bold attitude to the question of heritage. These earlier projects rehearse and enforce an architectural position which is both generous, in that it offers a better sense of public realm, and exacting, as it considers the appropriate forms of intervention within sensitive preservation conditions.

Talking recently about his experience of designing and constructing workspace, Parry refers to a project he undertook as a student of Dalibor Vesely, Peter Carl and Mohsen Mostafavi at the Architectural Association. This particular studio adopted a forceful intellectual position informed by an understanding of history. It had a highly personal and somewhat poetic attitude, richly layered in ideas and resulting in an intense, almost existential vision of architecture. At its core, this work is steeped in a humanistic tradition. Notions of meaning in the city as an inherited fabric continue to inform Parry's work as much as the need to offer a sense of urban decorum and civic generosity.

As places of work, Parry's office buildings could be viewed in the same way in which one considers housing. Office space contributes to a normative programme of the city and represents a large component of the urban built fabric. Unlike housing, however, it has a more public role, and the manner in which an office building meets the city requires careful negotiation.

At 30 Finsbury Square, Parry proposed a solution that sensitively and boldly added to a somewhat fragmented square. At 5 Aldermanbury Square, the building acted as a tower in the city and became a formally bold example of this building type. It could be understood as a revision of a Miesian idea of an office building as tower, in the sense that it considers more than its own interest in purity, proportion and itself. Parry's approach takes all of these considerations as a starting point, but it adjusts to things that exist. The found situation is allowed to affect the formal and constructional ideas of each new project. Conversely, the project at 23 Savile Row is a more sober example of a relaxed relationship to the normative. An essentially classical building with a sense of symmetry, it works, however, more boldly with tectonic interest and a highly personal sense of proportion.

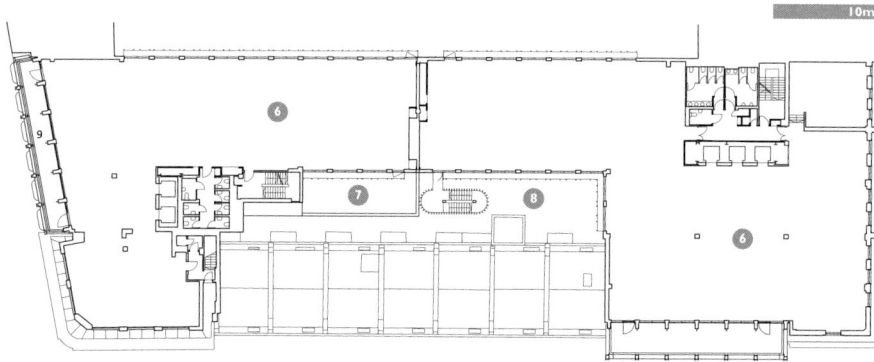

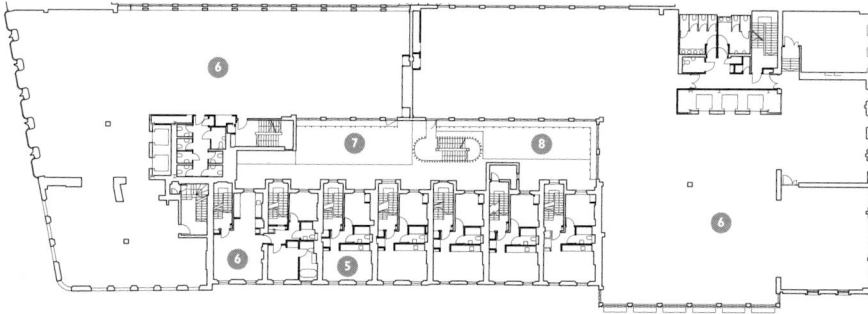

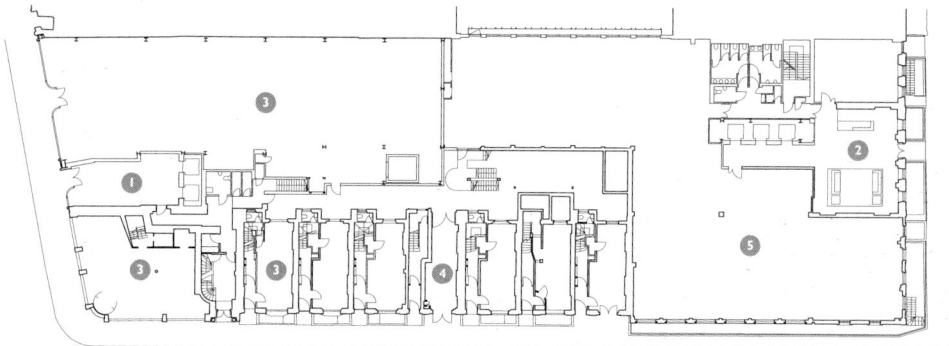

10m

Left
Long section and ground, first and fourth floor plans. Key: 1 New Bond Street reception, 2 St George Street reception, 3 retail, 4 service entry, 5 apartment, 6 office, 7 lightwell, 8 courtyard,

Right
Plans showing the historical development of the urban block in 1819, 1951 and 2011; elevations along New Bond Street, Maddox Street and St George Street. The mixed-use development comprises retail and office use within the new buildings on 50 New Bond Street and 14 St George Street, plus residential and retail in the refurbished terrace along Maddox Street.

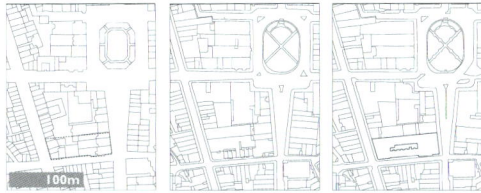

I have reviewed briefly these built projects for two reasons. First, I believe that this body of work is a great lesson and a catalogue of solutions to this type of building programme in the city and, second, I would argue that the sum of the observations I have made (and many more that I have not) is explored further at 50 New Bond Street. However, this project is a much more complex undertaking than its predecessors — an act of urban repair as well as adjustment and extension.

The project on New Bond Street is the third occasion that Parry has been invited to design a building for Scottish Widows. Repeat business is indicative of client satisfaction, but what is noteworthy in this collaboration is the extent to which the architect has been allowed to develop ideas and construction proposals that many developers would hardly find acceptable.

The facades to all the new-build public components of this project are deep. The new facade to 50 New Bond Street maintains a careful relationship to the surrounding nineteenth century buildings. It is, however, working much harder, as it contains structure, thermal barrier, external cladding and internal linings. The oriel windows offer a generous relationship with the street.

Parry's early sketches also explore another interest in this project: the faience, or ceramic elements create a vertical relief to the facade and reflect light into internal spaces in a subtle and unexpected manner. I am reminded of HP Berlage's Holland House in the City of London (1916) and the equivalent ordering of the elevation through a vertical element. Parry certainly understands the manner in which such an element is experienced obliquely in the street.

An early study of this component in the building — the ceramic pieces — suggests a somewhat playful interest. The projecting element shifts along its vertical length. It is an exercise in geometric manipulation, and clearly not structural, but it is not purely decorative because it contributes to the use of the building and does not simply embellish it. The handling of the joints, which are sometimes open and sometimes pointed in a dark pigmented lime mortar, makes it clear that in this instance the facade is not a further investigation of a tectonic expression. This is revealed in the sum of these details and most explicitly in the way that the ceramic facade sits over a substantial opening at ground level. In time, this will be filled in by a shop front with its own approach to display, and Parry has allowed the greatest freedom for this to happen.

103

The new facade to Maddox Street explores an entirely different set of concerns. If the ceramic New Bond Street facade has a gentle relationship to the Arts and Crafts tradition, this part of the building is indebted to the modern movement. It adopts a form of industrial pragmatism and the freedom to employ repetition in the making of things. Here, also, the force behind Parry's work is based on urban observation. The manipulation of the section is skilfully handled to bring light into the basement and ground floor spaces. At first floor, the building cantilevers over the pavement, its soffit adorned with a mosaic by Antoni Malinowski.

Up until this point I have dealt with the facades that open out onto the public realm. It should be pointed out that the possibility of creating any new component of building was made possible through the demolition of a piano factory built on the site in the 1930s. Eric Parry has been ingenious in the way that a quantum of additional office space has been added to this site without significantly affecting the urban presence of the buildings in this block. This has been done not only through the construction of the new buildings described above, but also through the addition of a new floor to the Hanoverian buildings on St George Street. A volume has been added here for compositional reasons, in terms of the relationship to the new facade on Maddox Street, but this has been done in a way that is impossible to read when you see the completed building from the street. Internally, however, this work becomes very evident.

Along Maddox Street, seven early Victorian buildings have been converted into apartments above ground floor. This fulfils a local planning requirement to provide a residential component that is at least 50 per cent of the area of new office space. The requirement has been followed seriously and its purpose respected. It will positively contribute to the success of the building, because the mix of programme will bring a greater sense of life overall.

Another aspect of this project that should be noted is its environmental strategy. This building has an Excellent BREEAM rating, reflecting the serious attitude adopted. Decisions about the possibility of retaining and extending the life of buildings have been taken carefully. When it was felt appropriate to demolish a building, the replacement has been responsibly considered. The depth of the plan is in all cases reasonable and the level of natural daylighting is excellent. Natural ventilation is available as an option as all new office spaces have opening windows, and a brown/green roof allows natural habitats to be established. This is an environmentally responsible set of decisions rather than a box-ticking exercise, and the building does not overtly display the intention at work.

50 New Bond Street is a complex, rich and urbanistically subtle project. It makes for an interesting complement to what is an impressive body of work demonstrating how to make buildings for office use in London. I now eagerly await the next instalment.

Left/right
The new facade on Maddox Street comprises glass blocks and aluminium sections. The soffit incorporates a mosaic by artist Antoni Malinowski. The bay offers views towards the eighteenth-century church of St George's on Hanover Square.

Right

Maddox Street perspective section. Key: 1 300×300×100mm ribbed glass blocks in panels with silver anodised aluminium frame, 2 unitised aluminium glazing unit with window and glass block spandrel panel, 3 unitised aluminium column unit with primary steel RHS and 40mm high-performance insulation, 4 primary steel structure, 5 column cladding formed from 300×70mm extruded aluminium channel and two 180×15mm extruded aluminium RHS, 6 insulated window head and reveal, 7 insulated window cill with 70mm projection of folded 3mm aluminium sheet, 8 double-glazed argon-filled unit with low-e and solar coating, 9 dummy mullion from 50×15mm extruded aluminium profile, 10 brise-soleil from 3mm folded aluminium sheet, 11 external aluminium profiles with satin dark brown metallic hyper-durable organic powder coat to resist UV degradation, internal profiles finished with matt white polyester powder coat, 12 opaque spandrel panel with 100mm mineral wool insulation, 13 fire and smoke seal, 14 stack joint, 15 130mm-deep in situ steel hollow-rib deck and reinforced concrete composite floor slab, 16 100mm-deep raised floor, 17 suspended ceiling with 570mm void containing steel beams and services, 18 recess for roller blinds, 19 plasterboard lining to columns, 20 Venetian glass (tesserae) mosaic installation by artist Antoni Malinowski, 21 aluminium support frame to mosaic soffit, 22 70mm high-performance rigid insulation, 23 140mm blockwork cavity wall, 24 stainless steel cavity wall lintel, 25 painted render with string line features, 26 satin white polyester powder-coated aluminium frame to ground and lower ground floor windows, 27 ventilation grille.

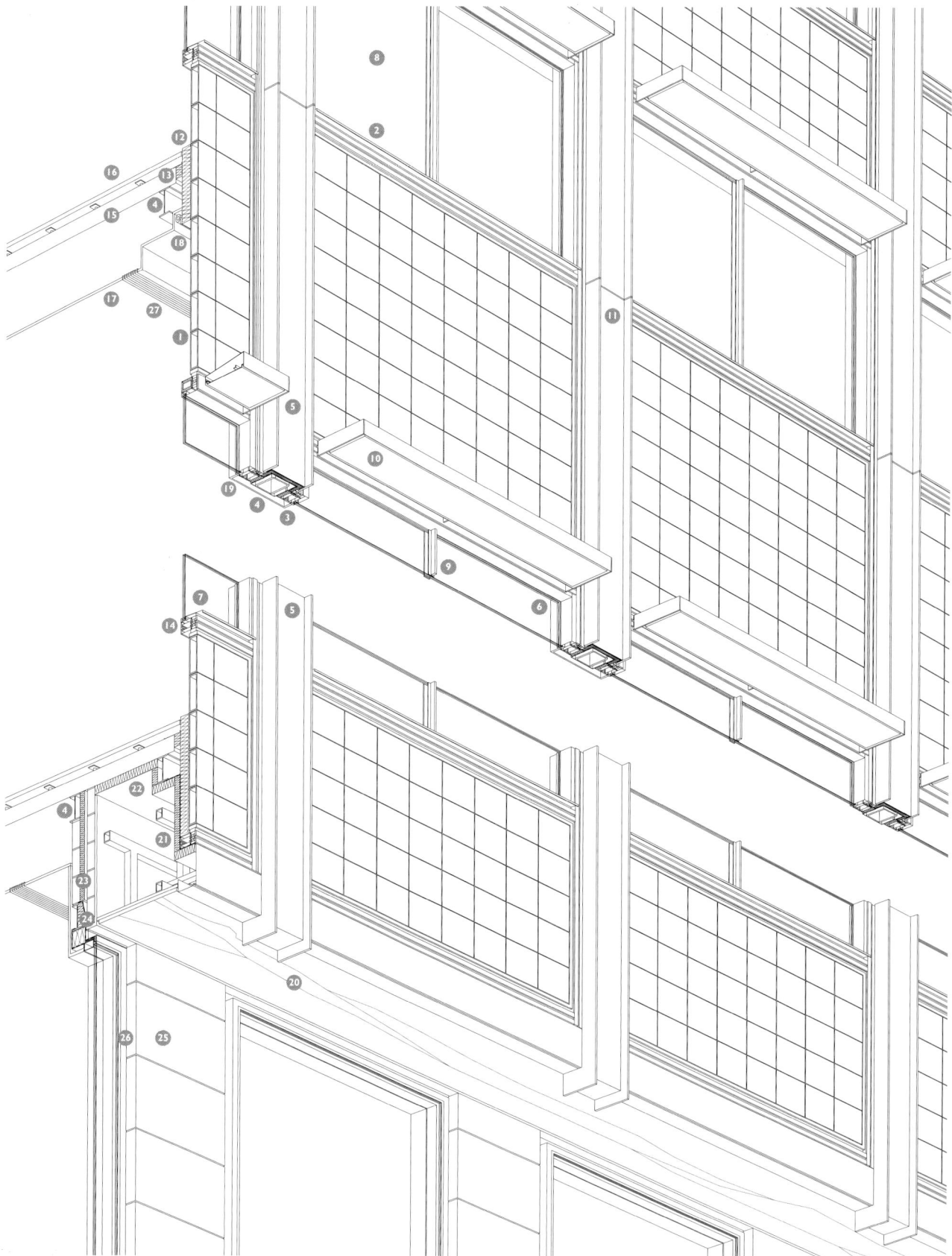

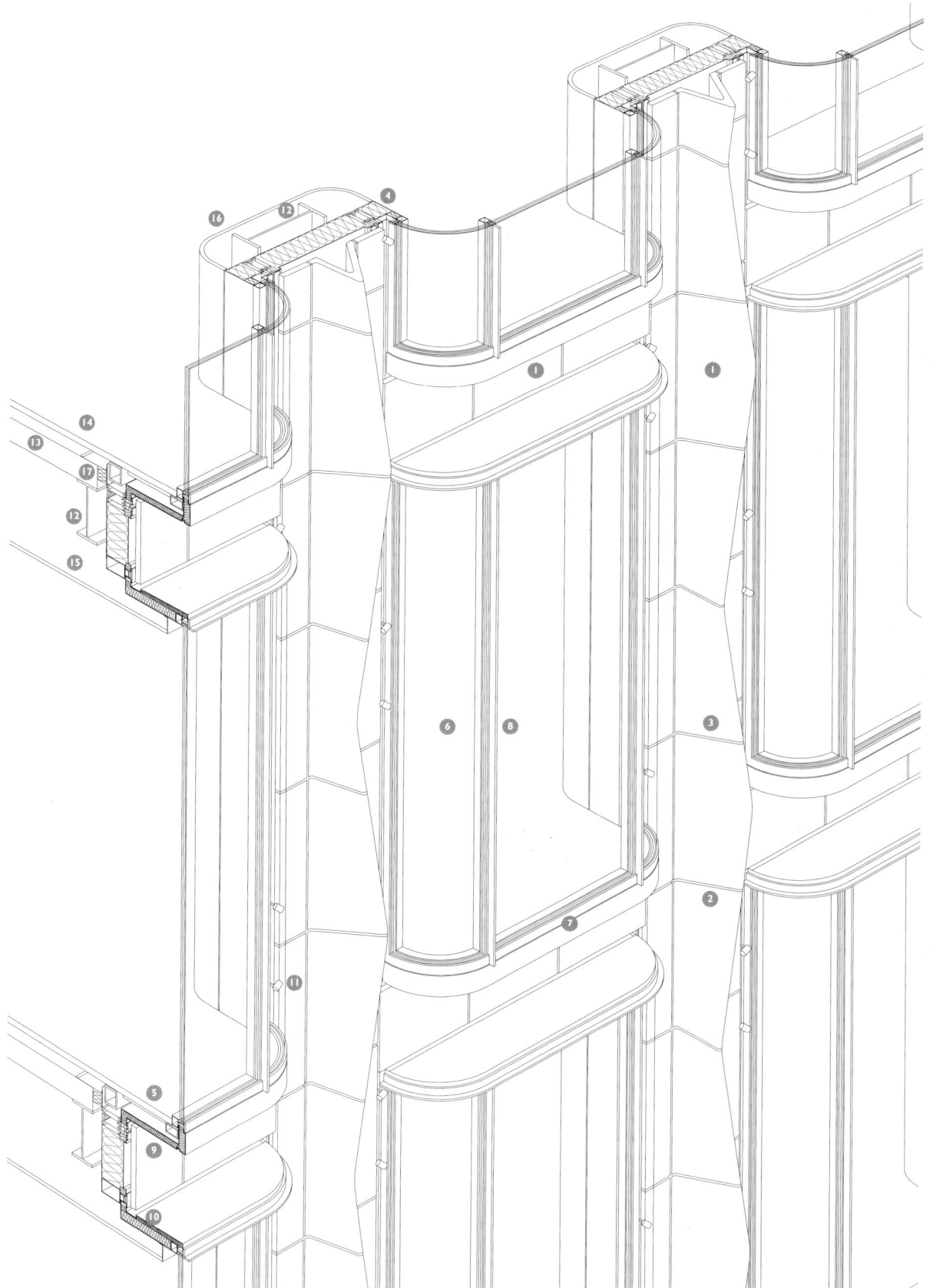

Right
New Bond Street facade. Key:
1 40mm-thick faience (glazed terracotta) cladding on stainless-steel brackets fixed to unitised cladding via stainless-steel channels, 2 column units stacked on support brackets at each floor with restraint brackets at each subsequent joint, 3 joints bedded on and pointed with dark grey lime mortar (except key movement joints), 4 aluminium unitised cladding system with 160mm mineral wool insulation and galvanised steel framework to transfer loads from faience cladding to primary structure, 5 bay windows integrated with unitised cladding system (opaque areas are insulated), 6 flat and curved argon-filled double-glazed units with low-e and solar control coatings, 7 aluminium window profiles and panels with satin dark brown metallic organic powder coat (internal profiles finished with matt white polyester powder coat), 8 50x15mm extruded aluminium fin fixed to mullion with aluminium spigots, 9 soffit panels to bay windows finished with a high-gloss black polyester powder coat, 10 aluminium gutter along rear edge of bay window roof, 11 LED lighting installation by artist Martin Richman,
12 primary steel structure,
13 130mm-deep in-situ steel hollow-rib deck and reinforced concrete composite floor slab,
14 100mm-deep raised floor service void, 15 suspended ceiling with 570mm-deep void containing steel beams and services, 16 curved fibrous plaster lining to column, 17 fire and smoke seal between slab edge and back of cladding.

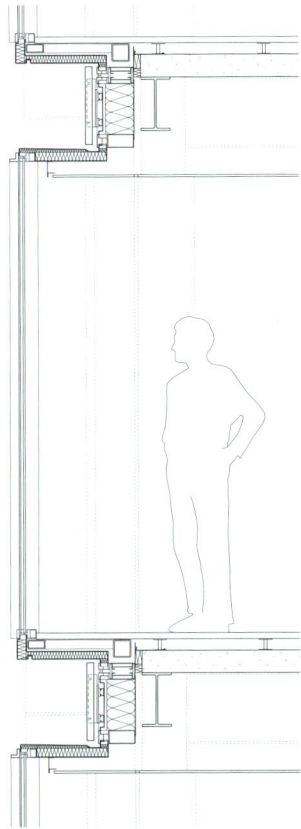

1 m

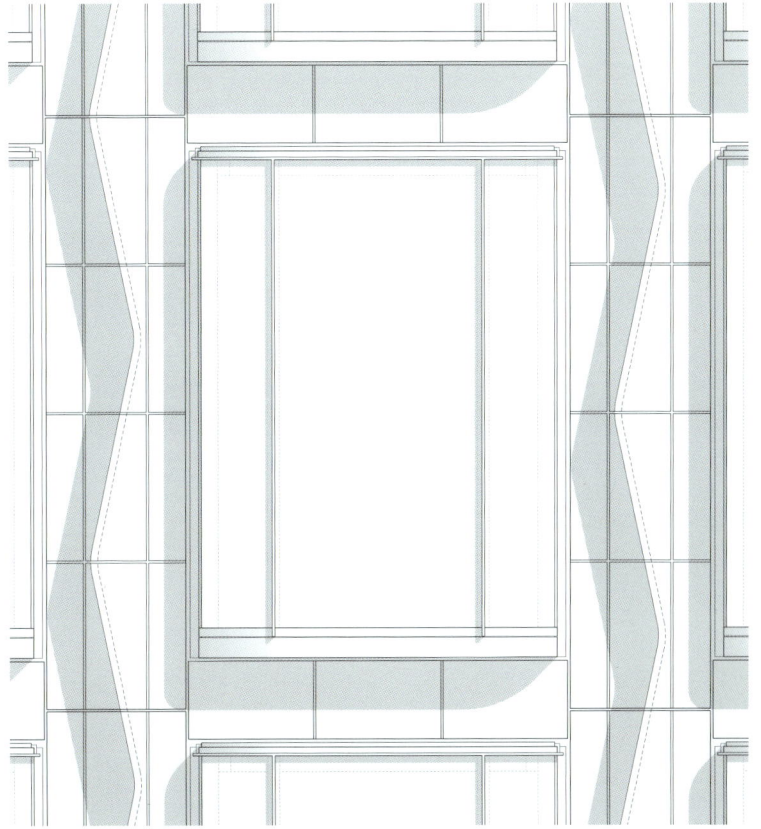

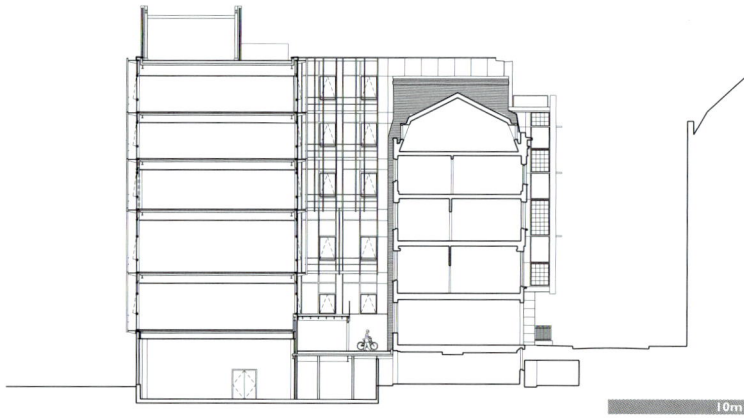

Left

North-south cross section through residential buildings on Maddox Street and office space across the interstitial court; 14 St George Street office interior.

One Eagle Place

Continuity and Change:
Simon Allford on One Eagle Place

London, the 'Unique City' whose continuity so engaged Steen Eiler Rasmussen, is a unique city in which to make architecture — one where architects and informed clients are combining new into old to challenge ideas of programme, place and development. Having established its reputation by inserting new architecture into historically charged parts of the city, Eric Parry Architects have now delightfully refined this model of development-as-palimpsest with One Eagle Place, an office and residential project in St James's.

This project is in part Parry's response to Blomfield and Nash's interest in the use of the facade to define the West End as an urban stage set. As I was working with the same client, The Crown Estate, to build a city sandwich between Regent Street and Parry's own 23 Savile Row building, I followed progress from the near distance, and have enjoyed witnessing the emergence of Parry's considered but bold risk-taking as he confronts comfortable ideas of taste.

Parry articulates the relationship of the site's urban and architectural history to the cultural, financial, technological and political context in which he operates, then utilises this to define the architectures of his response. Following surgical removal of failing and exhausted fragments, the retained is combined with the new to accommodate a rich mix of uses in an urbane, coherent yet commercially astute block. This repair and remaking is made more complex by the fact that the site is bisected by a building and theatre whose long leases preclude the possibility of negotiated adaptation.

Eagle Place references an interest exhibited in Parry's 'palazzo' at 30 Finsbury Square, still for many a touchstone for its intelligence and wit. There, he detached structure from the cage-like constraint of the planning module expressed in the thermal envelope, and thus facilitated an independent exploration of architectural aesthetics — one where the loadbearing structural stone facade references the rationalism of both Gruppo Sette and the engineer. At Eagle Place the two new facades offer a richer take on Finsbury's bald idea of 'back'. Again the facade is structural, but this time used not to support a frame but to enable a material to be explored in depth; to generate an alternative idea of the aesthetics of the punctured wall.

The first of these, a ceramic facade fronting Piccadilly, is sandwiched between elderly stone neighbours, while the second, faced with stone, forms a new corner where Eagle Place meets Jermyn Street. Parry likens the project's challenge to extracting and replacing teeth, though I note that one tooth — the Baron building, formerly a menswear shop owned by the family of comedy actor Sacha Baron Cohen — has been dismantled and re-erected five feet higher up (these are buildings designed in imperial dimensions) on a new base that is carefully related to, but inevitably somewhat different to that which was vandalised in the 1960s. The shock of the new ensures that the Piccadilly facade, with its polychromatic Richard Deacon frieze and red reveals, has already achieved a certain notoriety.

Above/right
The Piccadilly facade, seen from the Shaftesbury Memorial Fountain, popularly known as 'Eros'. The ceramic-clad facade incorporates a 25-metre-long cornice, designed by artist Richard Deacon, that consists of 39 sculptured components.

The programme behind provides three 'new' buildings — one office, two residential. While the office sits behind new and reconstructed facades, the two residential buildings are behind historic facades, one retained and the other carved out of a listed building. This is definitely a single project, however, concerned with the remaking of the city block, and challenges orthodoxy by prioritising the programme of the city over the programme of use — which is entirely logical: the use will change. The city will change, too, but the former much more rapidly than the latter.

The commercial programme is skilfully woven in plan and section. A sequence of interlocking parts that work together, sharing servicing, lifts and stairs to create an urban whole, reminding us that London's urban blocks — even when in single ownership — are a collection of parts, of uses, of leases, of buildings. Large-scale development is challenged not just by commerce and conservation but by the urban morphology that can be traced through the language of facades expressing party walls. Parry's skill is in undertaking large-scale redevelopment while celebrating the complexity. Modern servicing and infra-structure weave between new volumes which, through engagement with the 'found', have acquired more specific and thus memorable characteristics.

Above
Contextual study by Eric Parry for the Piccadilly street facade.

Left
Two buildings on Piccadilly were demolished to make way for the new development.

In the office, beyond the crafted volumes of the entrance hall (which like its neighbour, Lutyens' banking hall, has longevity) Parry understands that a lesser level of architectural control, reflecting the inevitability of fit-out and change, is appropriate. In the apartments, however, he has designed everything beautifully, simply and economically, from the carving out of habitable space in unique found volumes down to the throws on the beds. The refurbished and reinvented interiors of these apartments are a microcosm of the project: in the architecture of remaking and the urban palimpsest, Merzbau becomes Gesamtkunstwerk.

Relationships between new and old, inside and out and building and city are never quite as might be anticipated. The new Piccadilly facade is traditionally constructed of jug-white glazed ceramic and lime mortar, specifically so that it can be sculpted to capture reflections from the famous neon of Piccadilly Circus. Versions of this material have long been used to bounce light, but in secondary elevations, lightwells and courts, and always for amenity not effect. Here ceramic is used on one of London's greatest, widest streets.

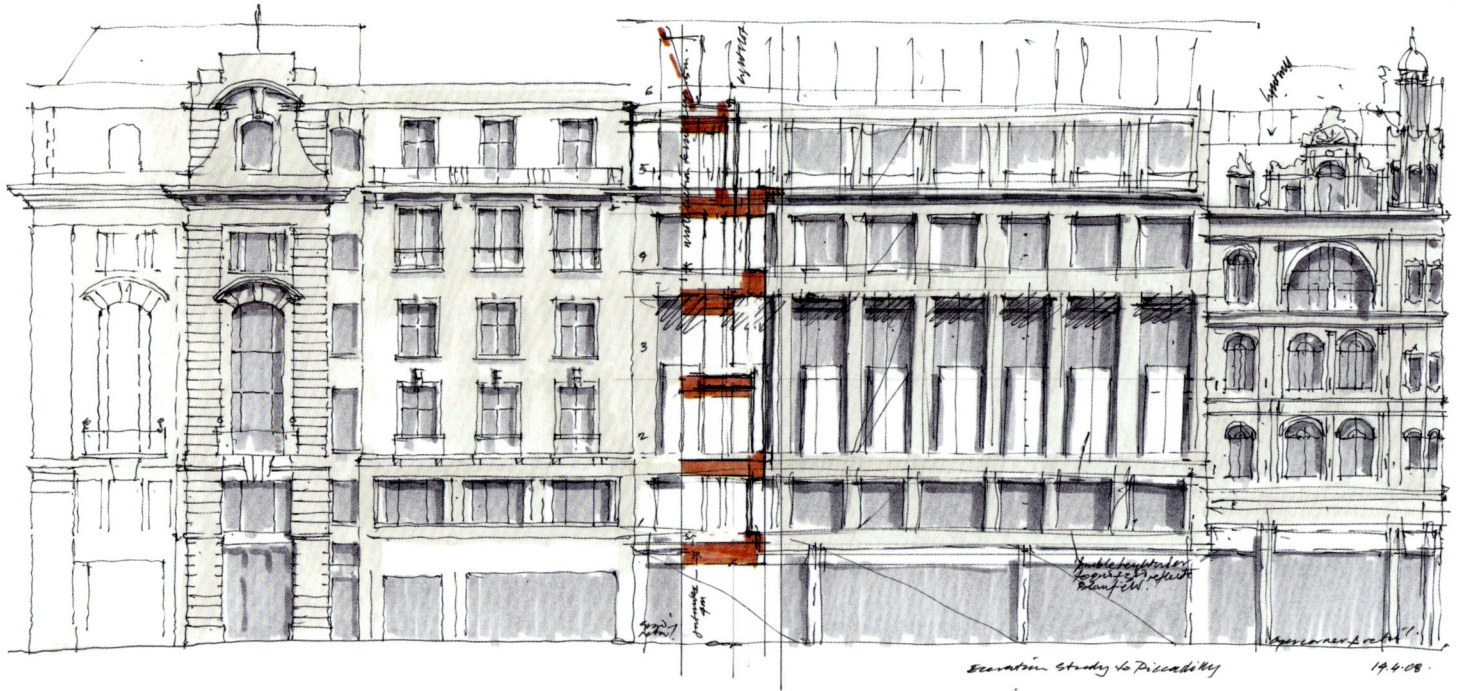

Elevation study to Piccadilly   19.4.08.

Again, in contrast to the norm, Portland stone is then used on the 'lesser' Jermyn Street and Eagle Place, in a rich mix of bed types articulated by string courses and worked transoms (a nod to a history of tailoring and the figure of the dandy) and topped by Stephen Cox's sculptural relief. There are of course other logics at play here: following conservation battles, the neon of Piccadilly Circus is celebrated as an important urban and historical asset while commercial logic dictates the use of Portland stone on Eagle Place to give this reinvented address the stature that the office requires.

Both new facades are studies in scale and proportion, in light, shadow and depth, and in bay widths, rhythms and modulation — a play of the neutral and the vibrant. Which is neutral and which vibrant is perhaps less certain than first glimpses might suggest. The Piccadilly facade is actually a modest and subtle play of black and white. The stipple effect stencil around the windows is, on inspection, not red but a 'blush'. This elevation is a play of modulated interlocking bays that decrease in size, complexity and evidence as they rise to the open loggia and then to the sky beyond. Its vivacity is largely concentrated in a polychromatic frieze by Richard Deacon, whose 39 steps draw a sculptured line across at cornice height. While this line harnesses the technology of the same architectural craft that constructs the facade, the mark of its maker ensures that artifice is transformed into art.

Through its detail, depth, oriel and terrace, this new Piccadilly facade allows the inhabitation and enjoyment of the threshold between room and city. It also questions our understanding of the likely longevity of building and facade. Parry's engagement with the detail of its making suggests to me that he believes that the 'facadists' Nash and Blomfield were in fact right to construct an urban stage set that is still the locale's defining quality.

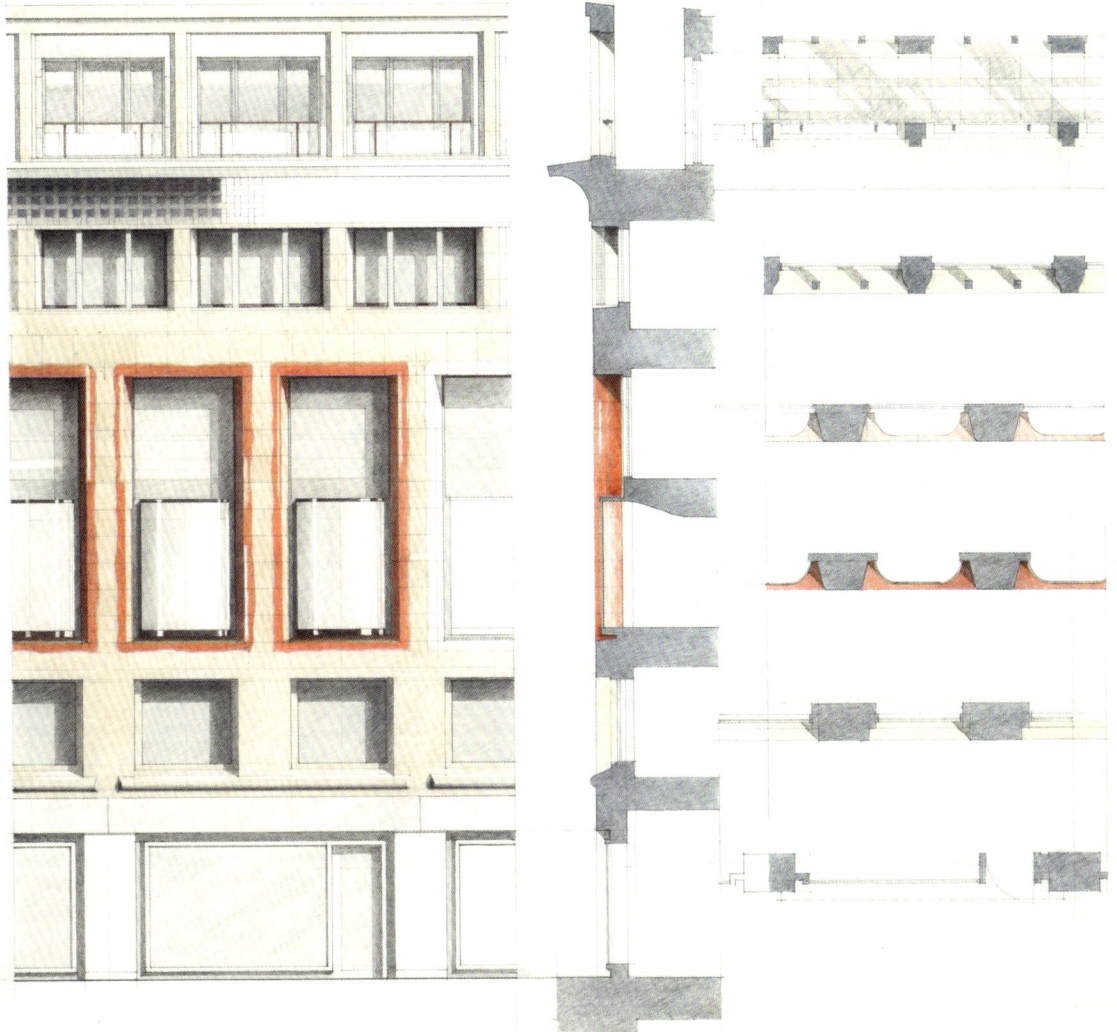

This challenges my 'flat cap rule' that suggests no-one ever sees above the shop front, so a demolished facade is instantly forgotten by even the most assiduous observer of architectural detail. (Ask yourself what you recall of the supposedly much-loved facades that preceded Parry's). Alan Powers' 2012 Royal Academy exhibition, 'Eros to the Ritz: 100 Years of Street Architecture', offered the same challenge, encouraging me to scurry from Burlington House onto Piccadilly to discover for the first time the facades of the street that I believed I knew.

One Eagle Place is a variegated container of uses, architectures, histories and technologies, and challenges our thinking on design strategies, on the relevance of use and on the urban importance of the aesthetics of the constructed facade. It questions aesthetic and artistic predilections and speculates on ideas of time and context. It is a project in which the architects are testing themselves, their audience (both lay and professional) and our shared ideas of history, present and future.

At the unveiling of his frieze, Richard Deacon diverted eyes from his art by doffing his cap and thus elegantly drew attention to the fact that it was adorned with but two words: 'No Fear'. I can think of no more appropriate an epithet for this most particular, creative and challenging project.

Left
Street view with entrance to
the offices on Eagle Place; office
lift lobby.

Right
Portland stone facade to Eagle
Place

Piccadilly facade with bay
details. The red window reveals
were made using a ceramic
transfer method, first
developed in the eighteenth
century but not used in a
building application since.

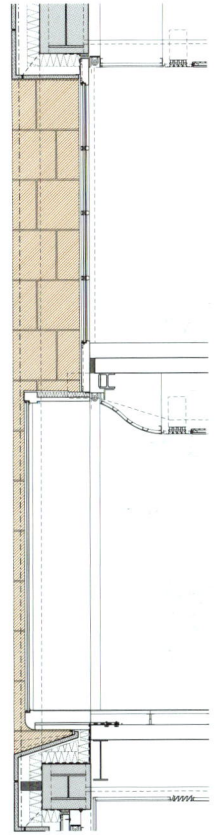

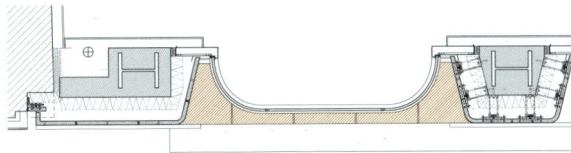

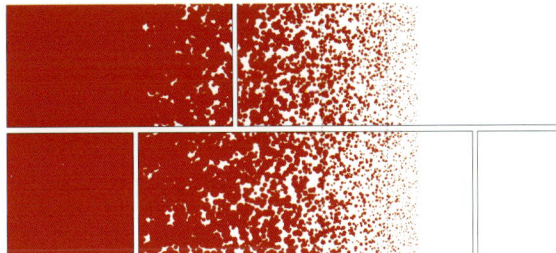

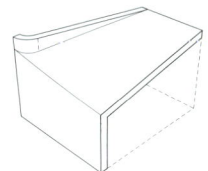

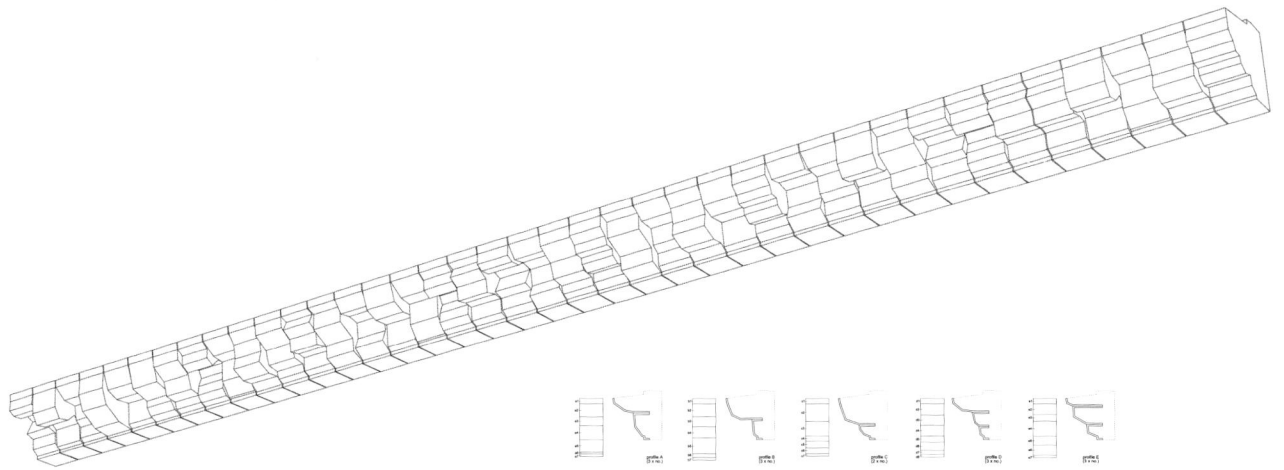

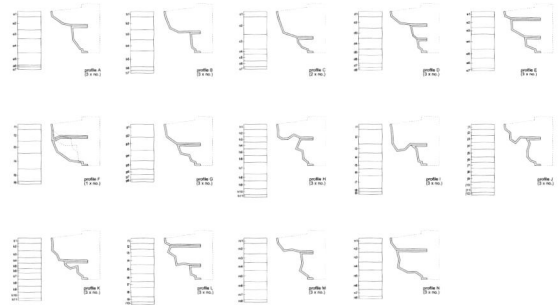

Left
View to Piccadilly Circus from the second-floor offices.

Above
Detail drawings for the components of the Richard Deacon cornice.

Right
Section through the Piccadilly facade and corresponding plans at key heights.

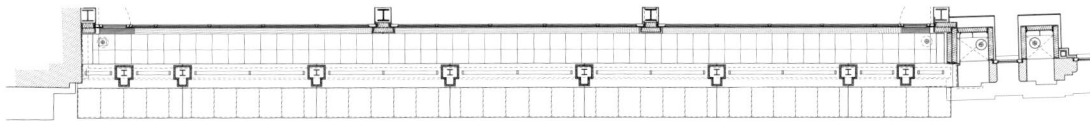

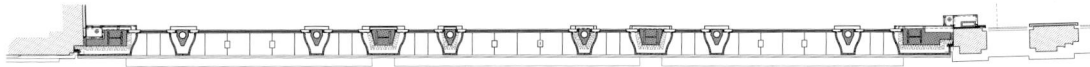

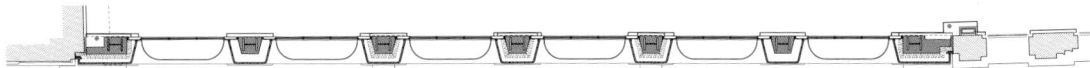

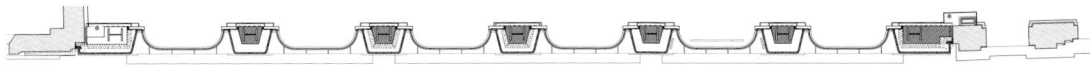

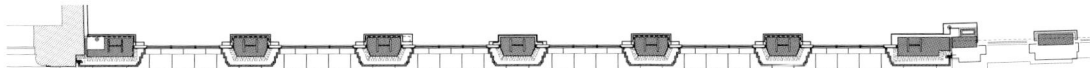

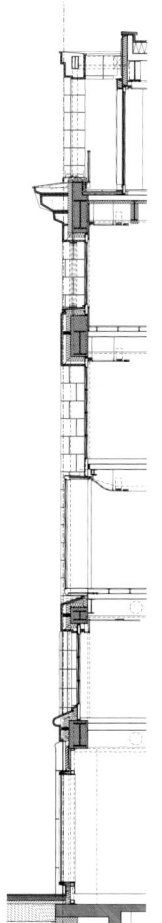

5m

8 St James's Square

Remaking the City:
Cindy Walters on 8 St James's Square

Eric Parry calls himself an 'urban repair man'. Prior to the office building at 7 and 8 St James's Square, his practice completed a number of significant projects within the tight confines of the Cities of London and Westminster: 30 Finsbury Square, 60 Threadneedle Street, 23 Savile Row, 50 New Bond Street, One Eagle Place and 5 Aldermanbury Square. In this series of convivial urban office buildings, elevations are crafted and sculpted with a care akin to that usually invested in civic or cultural buildings. Each building has achieved better and better environmental credentials, or what Parry refers to as 'the other stuff'. The deft and well-considered addition to St James's Square is further evidence of the refined sensibility that informs the work of the practice.

The site is located between Apple Tree Yard to the north and St James's Square to the south, with the longest frontage on Duke of York Street to the west. Christopher Wren's St James's Church, Piccadilly, can be seen at one end of Duke of York Street, and the open greenery of the square at the other. The Survey of London shows that the site was previously occupied by deep plots that facilitated very dense urban development.

St James's Square itself was laid out by Henry Jermyn, 1st Earl of St Albans, and was always intended to be a good address: by the mid-nineteenth century it contained a bank, an insurance society, two government offices, the London Library and three clubs.

In 2005 Eric Parry Architects (EPA) won a design competition to develop the site, including reconfiguration of the listed 7 St James's Square — rebuilt by Edwin Lutyens in 1911 and formerly home to the Royal Fine Art Commission — and the demolition of its neighbour, a rather pedestrian building whose replacement is smaller and less bulky. The first fund sold up at the height of the last speculative cycle and the site was passed from one owner and architect to another until, at the end of 2009, Kish Twelve, managed by Green Property, acquired the site and returned to Parry's office for a revised scheme, which was delivered under a two-stage design-and-build contract with the architect novated to the contractor.

The revised project comprises a single residence at 7 St James's Square and a nine-storey office building at number 8, with three distinct elements to the new Duke of York Street elevation, which was formerly characterised by service entrances. A dark brick building occupies the lower corner facing the square, an intermediate building with a loggia forms the middle part of the new elevation to Duke of York Street, and a third building turns the corner from Duke of York Street into Apple Tree Yard. A common theme is the robust materiality and the relationship between the new building and the back edge of the pavement.

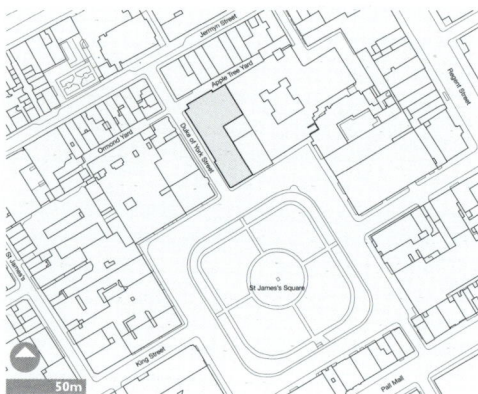

Much love and care has gone into the building corner at Duke of York Street and Apple Tree Yard, where a projecting granite bay overhangs the street. A granite sculpture built into the wall, by Parry's fellow Royal Academician Stephen Cox, was inspired by Michelangelo's pronouncement that 'a figure lies within the stone waiting to be discovered'.

Parry and Cox have carried on a conversation about the relationship between art and buildings — and the use of granite in particular — for many years. The Impala Black granite that Cox has used for his corner piece is similar to the stone selected by Parry for the building's tectonic base; some of the granite is riven, some is honed, some is polished, and the colour ranges poetically from light grey to shiny black.

There is a generosity of spirit in Parry's acknowledgement of the work done by other architects working nearby: the projecting granite window is a corbelled reference to the work Edwin Lutyens did on the masterplan for New Delhi while based at 7 St James's Square, and its rippling glass echoes that found in Wren's church, framed at the end of Duke of York Street.

The next large block in the composition forms the longest frontage on Duke of York Street. The ground-floor windows increase in height towards St James's Square as the 'Renaissance' base to the building responds to the significant fall in the ground from north to south. Above is a loggia and a stucco-rendered elevation with punched windows. Triple-glazed curtain walling to the top two floors leans back by two degrees to reflect the sky.

10m

Left
View south along Duke of York Street towards St James's Square showing the transition from stone to brick facade.

Right
A granite 'base' with a recessed loggia runs along much of the Duke of York Street facade, taking up the slope of the street. the upper storeys are finished with a lighter stucco render and limestone.

The lower corner of the site is occupied by a dark brick building that references its neo-Georgian neighbours and other houses on St James's Square. Where the other two replacement buildings have a grey granite base and pale limestone details to the upper floors, the entrance building is the reverse, with white horizontal bands breaking up the dark brick.

The corbelled stone soffit that appears on the projecting window bay on Apple Tree Yard is echoed by the ceiling of the reception area. Beautiful porcelain ceramics by the London-based potter Carina Ciscato are displayed in bronze-framed display cabinets, and bespoke light fittings, designed by Parry, illuminate the white corbelled ceilings.

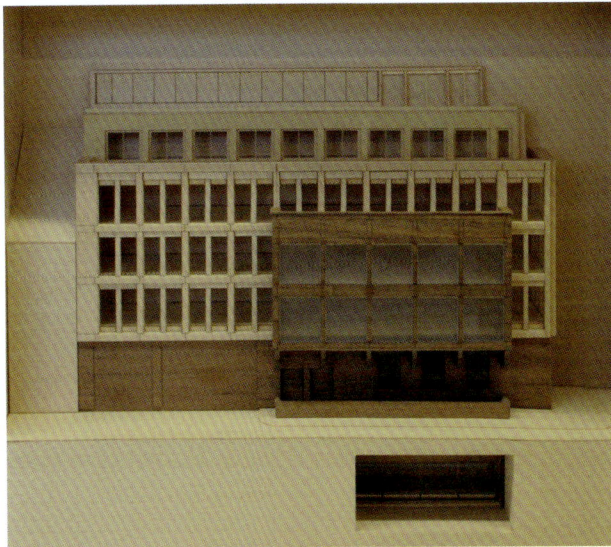

The new office building's plan is arranged so that a longitudinal core aligns the party wall to 7 St James's Square, preventing overlooking of its new enclosed courtyard. The resulting narrow floor plates are easily lit from one side. The plan is effortless and confident, reflecting Parry's significant experience of balancing the requirements of developers, agents and occupants.

This project underlines the importance of Parry's work within architectural discourse. Having held long-term lectureships at Harvard and Cambridge, and the presidency of the Architectural Association, he has always moved effortlessly between practice and academia. His work in London reflects his fascination with the history and qualities of the European city, developed over the course of numerous conversations with his friend and mentor, the late Dalibor Vesely, about what it means to situate architecture in its cultural and urban context.

Architects dislike the idea that clients feel they need to have 'made one earlier', but in the hands of the right architects, repeat commissions for the same building type can allow each building to be better than the last. Through the delivery of so many diverse London office buildings, Eric Parry has continually added to his urban repair toolkit. His buildings have an ongoing dialogue with the city and are built to last.

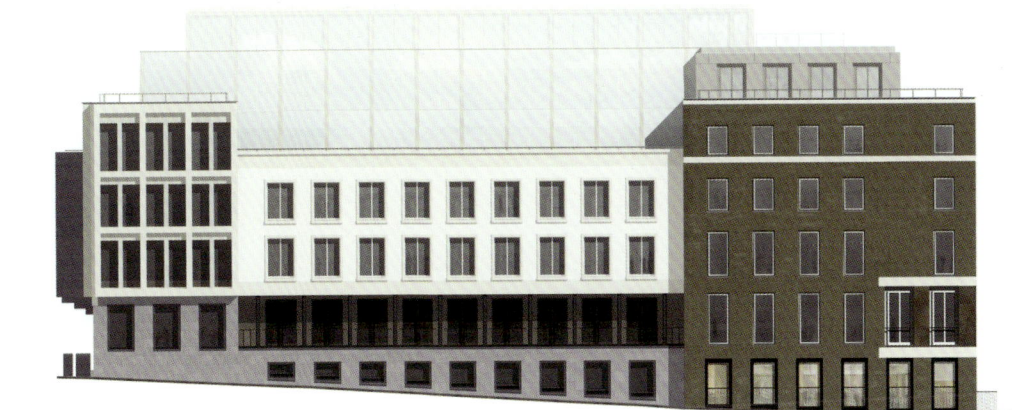

10m

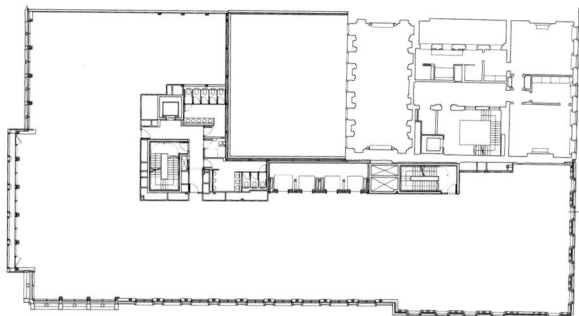

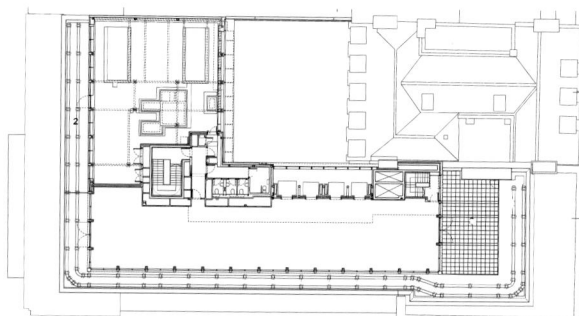

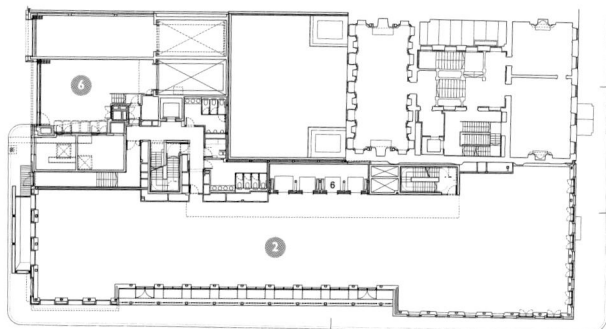

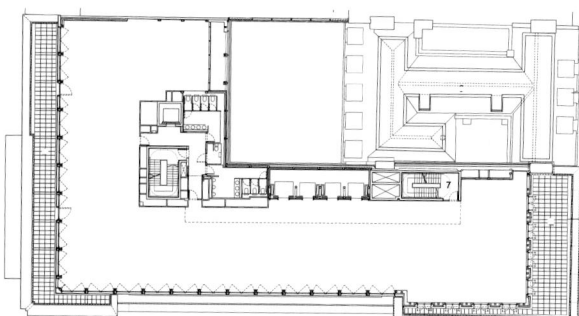

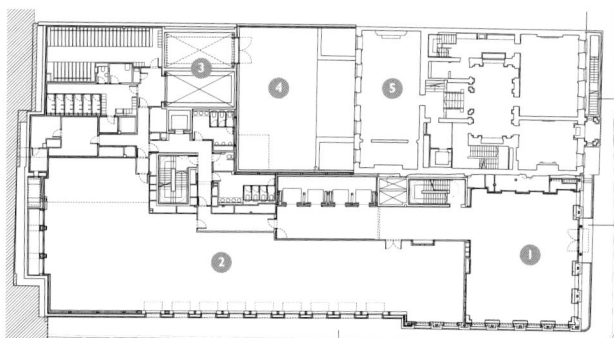

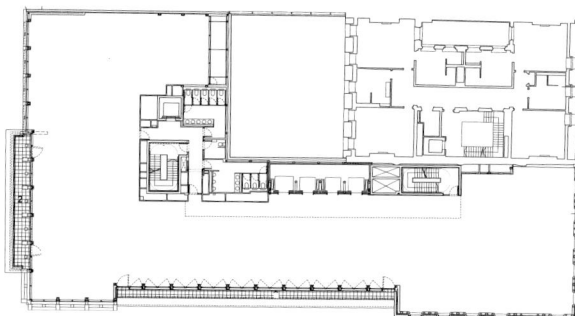

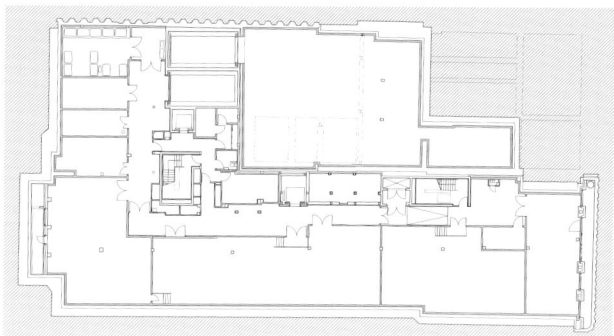

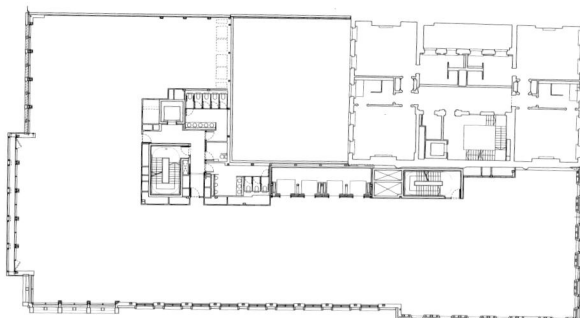

10m

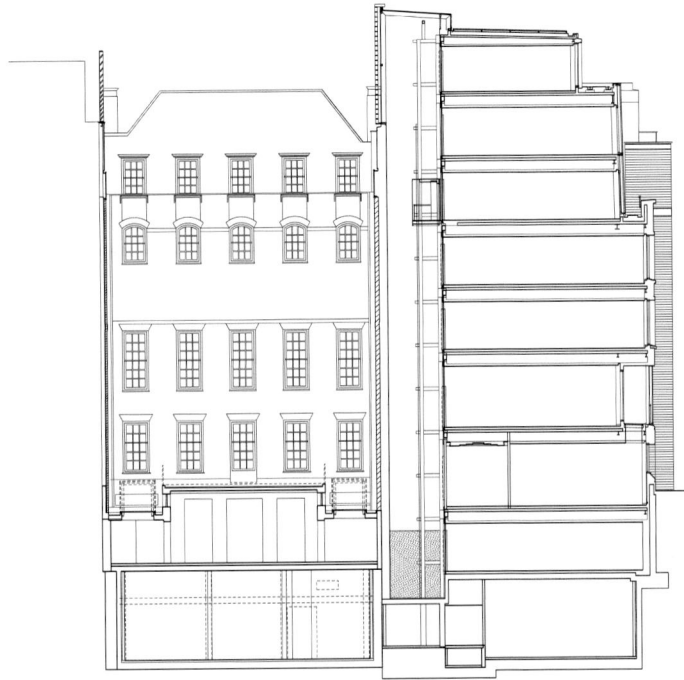

Far left
Basement (bottom), ground, first and second floor plans. Key: 1 Reception, 2 office, 3 car lifts, 4 courtyard, 5 existing building, 6 loading bay.

Left
Third (bottom), fourth, fifth and sixth floor plans.

Right
East-west cross section and south-north longitudinal section.

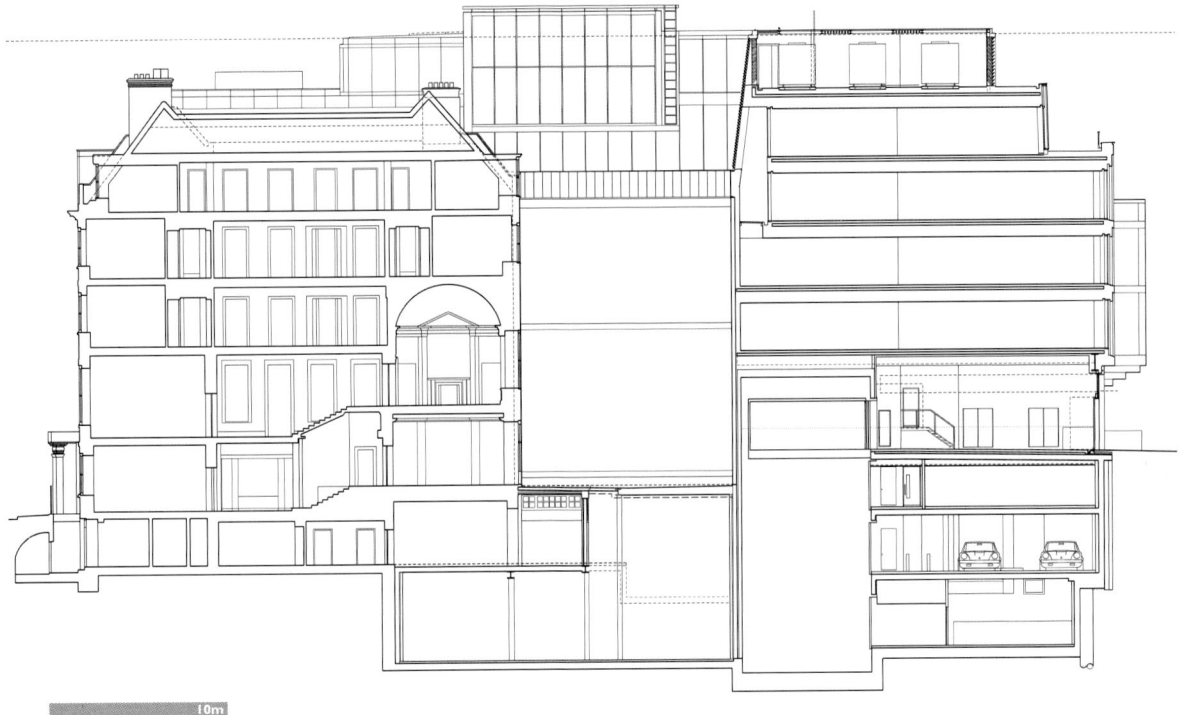

10m

Left
The dark brick corner building,
faces St James's Square and
flanks onto Duke of York Street.

Right
Entrance detail facing St James's
Square

Above/right

The reception to the office building at 8 St James's Square incorporates a coffered ceiling that resonates with the stone soffit that projects over Apple Tree Yard. The window surrounds feature recessed sliding panels that can be drawn to enhance privacy. A custom-made bronze display cabinet serves to articulate the space.

Left/right
Handmade bricks in a range of colours and textures were produced by Coleford Brick & Tile for the project.

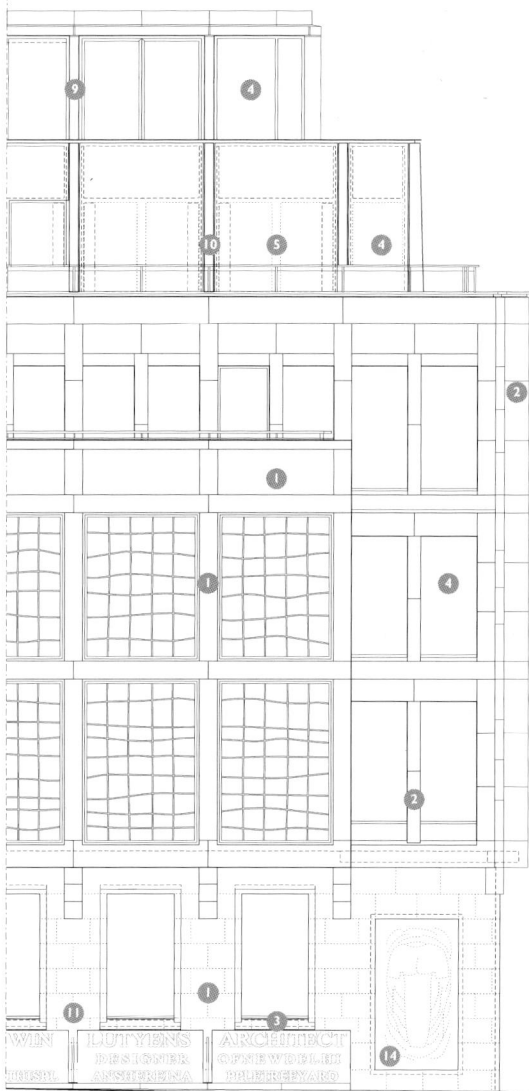

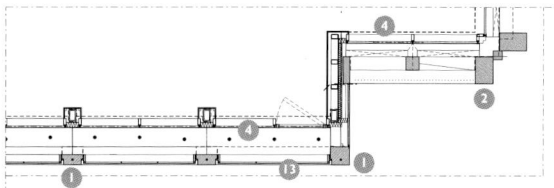

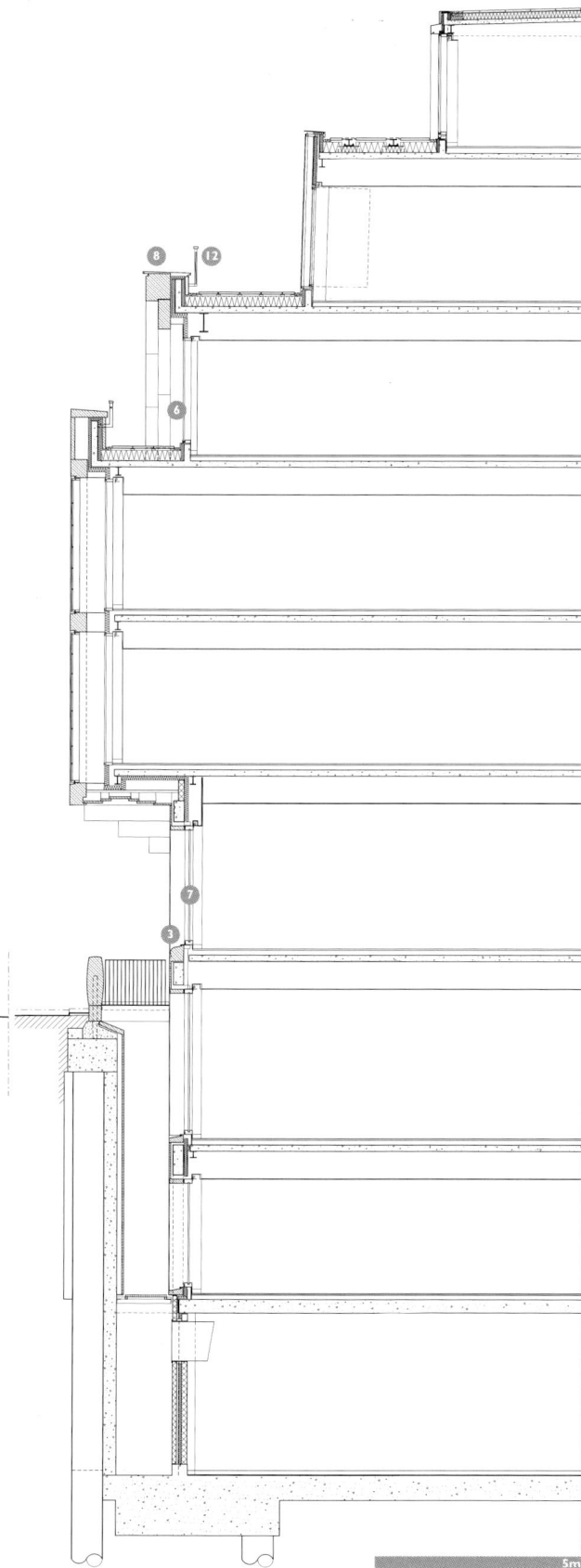

Left

Apple Tree Yard elevation, section and plan detail. Key: 1 Picked granite, 2 honed limestone, 3 polished granite cill, 4 glazing, 5 fritted glazing, 6 grey powder-coated aluminium windows, 7 dark-grey powder-coated aluminium windows, 8 mid-grey powder-coated aluminium coping, 9 powder-coated finish to aluminium cladding, 10 anodised finish to aluminium cladding, 11 black-painted steel railings, 12 black-painted steel railings with glass infill, 13 hand-drawn glass within bronze frames, 14 sculpture by Stephen Cox.

Right

Projecting bay facing Apple Tree Yard. Artist Stephen Cox has contributed a sculpture entitled 'Relief Figure Emerging (2015)', carved from granite in India, as well as an adjacent inscription that marks an earlier use of the site as the location of Edwin Lutyens' studio, from where he planned New Delhi.

Four Pancras Square

Urban Calibration:
Kenneth Frampton on Four Pancras Square

Ever since 30 Finsbury Square was completed in 2002, Eric Parry's reputation has been linked to the facility with which he designs medium-rise office buildings, a type which one may well regard as an endangered species given the current spate of freestanding mega-high-rises which, irrespective of their programmatic content, are popping up ad-infinitum in every capital city around the world; a dystopic 'value-free' cancer capable of destroying the socio-civic fabric of every historic city. This, fortunately, has so far not been Parry's destiny as an architect, which raises the imponderable question as to how does a reasonable, ethical developer — a rare species — find an appropriate architect and vice versa. In this instance we are referring to one David Partridge of Argent, the lead developer behind Parry's Four Pancras Square at London's King's Cross.

Eric Parry Architects' 11-storey office building, which completes the enclosure of Pancras Square, is an exceptional one-off; a quality that arises in the first instance from its compact civic form — which stems as much from its carefully calibrated height as from its site-imposed trapezoidal plan — but equally from the subtle topography of the square itself, warped to accommodate below-ground servicing (all factors determined largely by the King's Cross development masterplan, originally devised by Allies & Morrison and Porphyrios Associates).

At the same time it is patently an abstract, rhythmic composition of great refinement which not only depends on its modelling and proportion but also on a particular alternation between advancing and receding planes, the displacement of which gives an all-but musical structure to the building in section. Thus where the ground-floor foyer is recessed, the floor above (the traditional piano nobile) is advanced behind a monumental long-span steel vierendeel truss that establishes the tectonic language of the building, not only for the front-facing square but also for the other three sides, enabling the use of widely-spaced steel stanchions upon which the building rests.

The building is articulated in section into two groups of four floors each, of which the first group is recessed and the second advanced within an eight-floor sequence above the foyer level, while the building is crowned by an attic that is recessed by an open, steel-framed loggia continuing around its perimeter in lieu of a cornice. An equally syncopated rigour obtains in the detailing wherein prefabricated, welded spandrels of weathered steel make up the structural facade, rhythmically articulated by pairs of mullions in five-bay units. These spandrels are hoisted into position in a manner reminiscent of the construction of the facade of Mies van der Rohe's twin apartment towers at Lake Shore Drive, Chicago, completed in 1951.

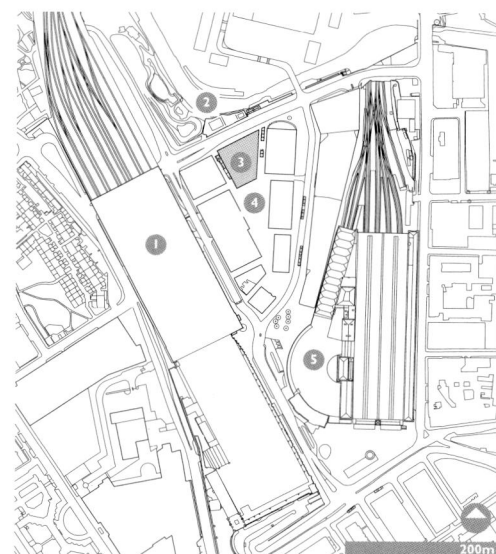

Above
1 St Pancras International station, 2 Regent's Canal, 3 Four Pancras Square, 4 Pancras Square, 5 King's Cross station.

Right
The principal, narrowest elevation faces south to Pancras Square.

Left, right
The external weathered steel frame evokes the industrial heritage of the area, with its gasholders, warehouses and rail infrastructure buildings.

At Four Pancras Square, however, the entire perimeter is loadbearing, so that the facade rises in coordination with the internal columns and the central structural core. This woven, loadbearing wall may be seen as an evocation of Mies's 'beinahe nichts' (almost nothing); a representational tectonic in welded steel, comparable to the flutes of a classical column.

At the same time, the weathered steel, the structural perimeter wall, the cast glazed terracotta brise soleil and the white soffit panels and glazed terracotta facias over the inset balconies on the second to fifth floors, jointly testify to the aim of achieving a low-maintenance, enduring structure.

A rental office building, as opposed to a bespoke corporate headquarters (though in this case a pre-let has made the building quasi-bespoke), is always a challenge for an architect, since apart from its capacity to produce income it tends to lack cultural significance. It may also afford well-serviced, well-lit, commercial space at grade, which Parry has succeeded in doing at Pancras Square. Otherwise the only gratuitous provision is a landscaped green roof, which apart from its ecological potential (as wildlife habitat and to counter the heat-island effect) provides for a certain amount of 'park-space' for the use of the occupants at the top of the building. It is noteworthy that the western flank accommodates a ramp giving access to bicycle racks, showers and lockers. This is a sustainable touch par excellence (as well as servicing a fire escape).

Appropriate to its situation, close to the threshold of Thomas Cubitt's King's Cross station, this is a twenty-first century tour-de-force playing a discreet homage to the heroic engineering achievements of the second half of the nineteenth century.

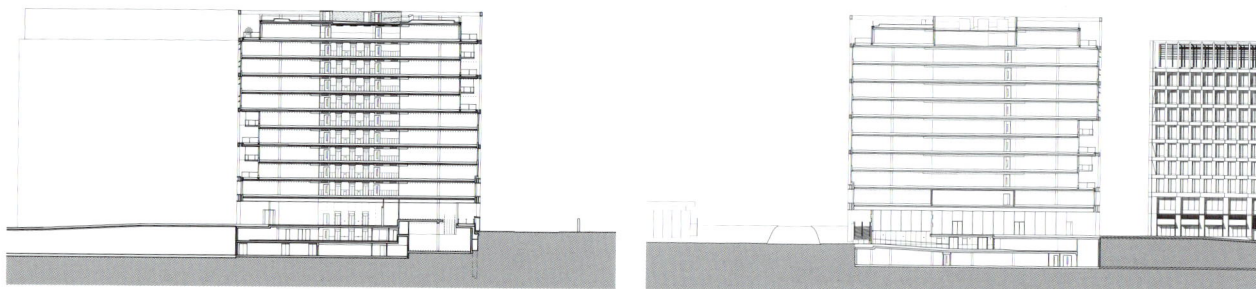

Above
The widest, northerly elevation viewed from the Regent's Canal.

Left
South-north section through atrium; north-south section through cafe area.

20m

South elevation and section: 1 weathered steel structural pillar; 2 weathered steel panel, 3 extruded glazed terracotta brise-soleil panel, 4 full-height glazing, 5 structural glazed parapet with vitreous enamel handrail, 6 aluminium ceiling cladding, 7 honed precast terrazzo paving, 8 inverted roof, 9 landscape by Todd Longstaffe-Gowan, 10 weathered steel vierendeel truss.

5m

Left, below
Office reception with cafe area,
entrance and lift lobby, typical
office floor shell before fit-out.

Right
Cycle racks and escape stair.

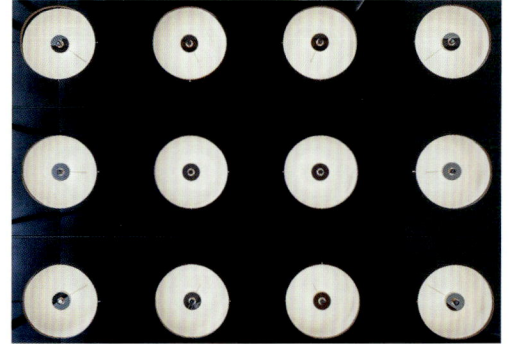

Right
The planted roof terrace was designed with landscape architect Todd Longstaffe-Gowan.

Below
The southerly aspect affords views .across Pancras Square to the Gothic-revival tower of the Pancras Hotel.

Right
Pancras Square at dusk.

Below
The weathered steel structural
frame in the factory and in situ.

Cambridge
Assessment

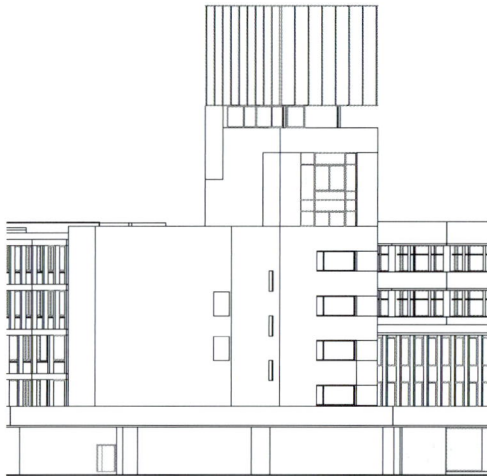

Grade Boundaries:
Rolfe Kentish on Cambridge Assessment

Arriving in Cambridge by train there was, for many years, a large sign, illuminated at night, announcing 'Cambridge University Press'. Now a new symbolic gateway has arrived in the shape of The Triangle, the 35,000-square-metre headquarters of exam board Cambridge Assessment, designed by Eric Parry Architects.

Cambridge station was completed in 1845, together with an adjacent goods yard and mill. No doubt to appease the university, which had already stipulated that the station was located a mile from the city centre, the mill buildings were topped out with references to San Miniato al Monte and the Palazzo Vecchio in Florence, while the station building echoes the loggia of the Ospedale degli Innocenti.

In 2010, the redevelopment of land around the station began, with office space for more than 2,500 workers, homes for 600 residents and 1,100 students, and 400 hotel rooms; further buildings are planned. Not all reviewers have been sympathetic. "An embarrassment to the city: what went wrong with the £725m gateway to Cambridge?", asked Oliver Wainwright in The Guardian in 2017. EPA's Triangle should help to counter this view.

Cambridge Assessment has roots which go back 160 years. A not-for-profit department of Cambridge University, it incorporates several exam boards and provides English language and admissions testing, serving over eight million learners in 170 countries, and employing over 2,500 staff.

Cambridge Assessment was previously spread over 11 sites around the city, but the new Triangle building will be able to accommodate up to 3,000 staff by 2025. The 2.5-hectare site was made available by the demolition of the 1981 Edinburgh Building, a warehouse belonging to Cambridge University Press. It is well located, just 15 minutes' walk from the station, next to a cycle path, the busway (serving North West Cambridge, the city centre and Biomedical Campus), and with road access from the broad residential Shaftesbury Road.

From the train The Triangle's curved and angular forms, the belvedere tower, warm buff brick, precast stonework and brise-soleil resonate with the urban approaches to Milano Centrale or Florence's Santa Maria Novella stations. The curved elevation and subdividing street of Giovanni Muzio's 1920s Ca' Brutta, and the layered facade and black-stuccoed entrance hall ceiling of Giuseppe Terragni's Casa del Fascio also come to mind. There's even a classicising remnant of rustication in the ground-floor brick piers, marked by inlaid glazed bricks at the entrance and recessed elsewhere, not unlike HP Berlage's Holland House in London.

Alvar Aalto was among the 'other tradition' modernists to employ brick and ribbon window cladding on a concrete column-and-slab structure with intermediate precast spandrels. The theme was developed by Leslie Martin at Oxford's Law Library and Colin St John Wilson at the British Library. At the Triangle, Parry uses precast stone spandrels, rather than powder-coated or anodised aluminium, and glazed clay brick for the mullions and transom of the entrance screen.

Above
Located south of the city centre, The Triangle occupies a site bordered by rail and road routes. 1 The Triangle, 2 Cambridge University Press, 3 Shaftesbury Road.

Right
The west-facing terrace is overlooked by a tower that acts as a beacon.

The building sits firmly in the tradition of large-scale Western civic and institutional typologies that extends from Dudok's Hilversum town hall and Wright's Johnson Wax to Hertzberger's Centraal Beheer and Foster's Bloomberg. The ground floor contains an auditorium, archive and multiple meeting rooms for visiting examiners and exam writers. Car and bike parking is accessed from the north and east via a perimeter road; the first floor spans over and forms a true piano nobile. From the large double-height entrance hall, stairs lead to the first floor.

The shallow open-plan office fingers, 19 metres from side to side, have excellent natural lighting and views. Glare is significantly reduced by external solar shading. The concrete soffits, walls and columns are left fair-faced. Multi-service finger beams extend from lower central spines to provide air, light, security and communications. There are four main service cores and four subsidiary escape stairs. The tower has large meeting rooms from the second to the sixth floors and a belvedere on the seventh.

The overall form of the building, with its three podium-level and two ground-floor courtyards, is seemingly carved from a single triangular mass, yet at the same time it is articulated as a set of extrusions, terminated with 'gables' or stop-ends.

Left
East-facing court and tower; entrance foyer and mezzanine in the link building.

Opposite
Principal west entrance foyer.

There are six main facade types, which differ according to orientation and location. The predominant type is to the east, west and prow of the perimeter, and the north and south facades to the link courtyard. Columns, on a nine-metre structural grid, and floors are expressed by precast concrete pier casings and lintels, with continuous ribbons of brickwork between sill and lintel. The ground-floor columns are encased in rusticated nine-inch brickwork. Powder-coated aluminium windows alternate with solid opening panels, and incorporate an anodised aluminium brise soleil. The facade depth — relatively generous for the type — gives a zone for relief modelling of 450-550mm for the brick elevations and 900mm in the courtyards, allowing for a maintenance walkway.

The second facade type, facing onto the three podium courtyards, consists of a freestanding trabeated precast concrete brise soleil set 600mm in front of aluminium windows and rendered spandrel panels. The shape and spacing of the piers varies to maximise solar shading, as at Parry's 30 Finsbury Square. The upper parts of the three-sided courtyards — which suggest academic cloisters — can be glimpsed from beyond the site. The gable facade type — used at the end of the northerly 'fingers' and by the main entrance — comprises deep-set individual windows separated by precast piers. Another variant occurs between buildings of different height, in which precast framing is used instead of brick to articulate the dégagement. The entrance elevation to the link building has closely-spaced glazed-brick piers in front of a glazed facade, while its rear courtyard elevation has simpler vertical aluminium fins in front of aluminium windows.

The Triangle features a major two-part art commission, one at the entrance and the other at the top of the tower. 'In Other Words', by artists Vong Phaophanit and Claire Oboussier with EPA, features layers of script in different languages enamelled onto the glass. The tower artwork, subtly lit at night, is in warm parchment colours, and the 33-metre-long entrance artwork, in shades of indigo, is integrated with the glazed bricks.

By responding to the long-term ambitions of Cambridge Assessment, Eric Parry Architects has given specific form and identity to a building that otherwise might have been anonymous, undifferentiated grade-A office space — examples of which abound around the railway station. Added to this, bringing together disparate departments from eleven sites around Cambridge is a significant challenge, not least in terms of human resources, but one that this welcoming building will go a long way to facilitate.

Right
'In Other Words', an artwork by Vong Phaophanit and Claire Oboussier with the architect, becomes more apparent when lit at dusk.

Left
Office floor interiors.

Fen Court

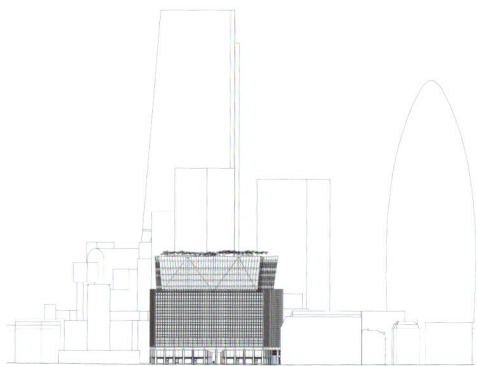

City Crown:
Louisa Hutton on Fen Court

The sheer chutzpah with which Eric Parry Architects has placed a vast shimmering crown on the top of its latest building in the City of London both surprises and intrigues. The blatant contrast that exists between the well-mannered, glazed terracotta-clad 11-storey building that sits so effortlessly in its context and the uninhibited swagger of the glassy structure above is not exactly what one might have expected from a practice that has established a reputation as the author of serious, finely conceived, highly contextual, beautifully crafted office buildings in the City.

However, it is not only the seductive nature of the building's polychromatic crown that makes a highly unusual and positive addition to the cityscape — there are three further characteristics concerning its place in the city that equally convince: the sculpting and surface treatment of its body, the generosity given to the public realm at street level, and a sizeable public garden at roof level.

There is an assuredness with which Parry has created the lower building's gently zig-zagged form. Approaching in either direction along Fenchurch Street the mass of Fen Court presents itself as four cranked planes that catch the light and one's eye with pleasing alternate rhythm. On account of the double inflection, the pavement area has been increased which is both a significant plus for pedestrians and expands the street's volume of air, now positively sculpted and held by the pair of shallow 'V's of the quadripartite facade.

A similar moment is found to the east on Billiter Street, where a single inverted 'V' again breaks the body into two. The Fenchurch Avenue facade has a subtler but nonetheless perceivable inflection, while the facade facing Fen Court is the only one whose articulation is a single outward crank that follows the line of the site. Through these inflections the building gains an idiosyncratic morphological language and a certain tautness. The systematic, rhythmic folding of the nine-sided body gives the whole an apparent lightness that belies its actual physical mass.

As is the case with many buildings in dense urban situations, Fen Court is nearly always approached anamorphically. So any three-dimensional treatment of the facades is first condensed and then released as one walks past. A fine-ribbed verticality is given by the pronounced array of engaged columns that rise uninterrupted from the second floor to form their own raw, spiky parapet at the eleventh. In between these, and somewhat set back, short, thick, shadow-creating horizontal brise-soleils are woven in like stitches.

This textile-like character invites a tactile response, and though it is well out of reach, one's eyes are encouraged to roam. Drifting diagonally upwards and across the well-crafted solidity and texture of the facade they eventually land on the slippery face of the crown, whose glassy inclined planes offer no such physical certainties.

Right
Fen Court comprises 10 Fenchurch Avenue, One Fen Court and 120 Fenchurch Street. The 39,670-square-metre building is on a 75- by 55-metre plot. It has a two-storey base and a new public passageway lined with retail, a main body with nine storeys of offices, and a glazed 'crown' providing four floors of offices and a restaurant.

Inspiration for the building's massing came from Hamburg's deep-plan Chilehaus (Fritz Höger, 1924) whose form includes acute angles, punched courtyards and a celebration of sky in its use of copper roofs.

Left
Model views and roof plan.

Left, below
City context; urban grain plans showing the district around Fenchurch Street in 1677, 1896, 1945 and 2017, with Fen Court highlighted.

Sometimes disappearing into the sky and at others appearing as a brash neon-striped facetted vase, this five-storied polychromatic crown could hardly be more subversive. While the 11-storey tectonic base building is appropriately and politely sited, the crown with its bright, changing, glassy surfaces introduces a totally new game.

EPA's project underwent many iterations. A change of client resulted not only in the loss of a proposed atrium but also in the desire for a considerable increase in area. Many rounds of negotiations between architect, client and planners produced a quite brilliant bargain: more square metres — as long as they were in an independent volume that was set back from the main body — in exchange for a publicly-accessible roof terrace.

The inventiveness with which EPA has resolved this challenge is admirable. While the plan of the crown was derived from the form of the base building, its outward splay coupled with additional faceting introduces both formal independence and the offer of varying degrees of reflection. However, it was the bold decision to clothe this sharp-cornered volume in a candy-striped dress of dichroic glass — whose appearance changes according to light conditions and one's angle of view — that brings its unmistakeable character and identity.

Below
Ground (bottom left), mezzanine
(below), fourth (bottom right)
and 10th (below right) floor plans.
Key: 1 Fenchurch Avenue reception,
2 southern reception, 3 retail,
4 banking hall, 5 security, 6 loading
docks, 7 office, 8 management suite,
9 security office, 10 switch room,
11 generator room, 12 lobby,
13 building maintenance unit,
14 terrace.

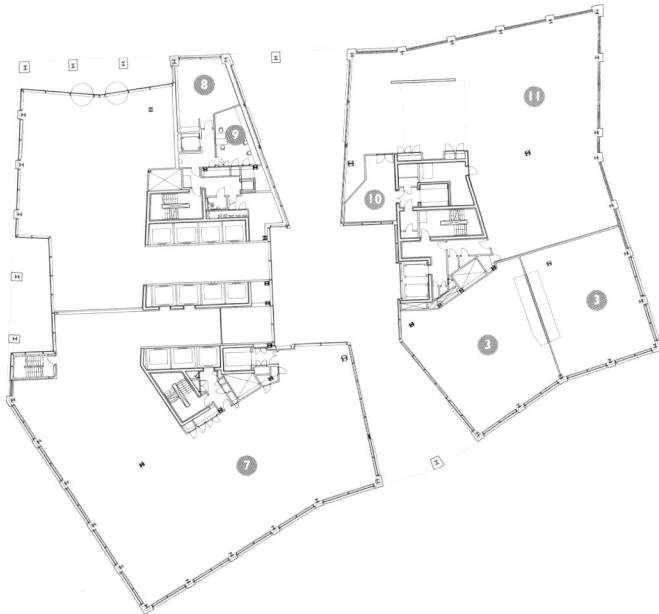

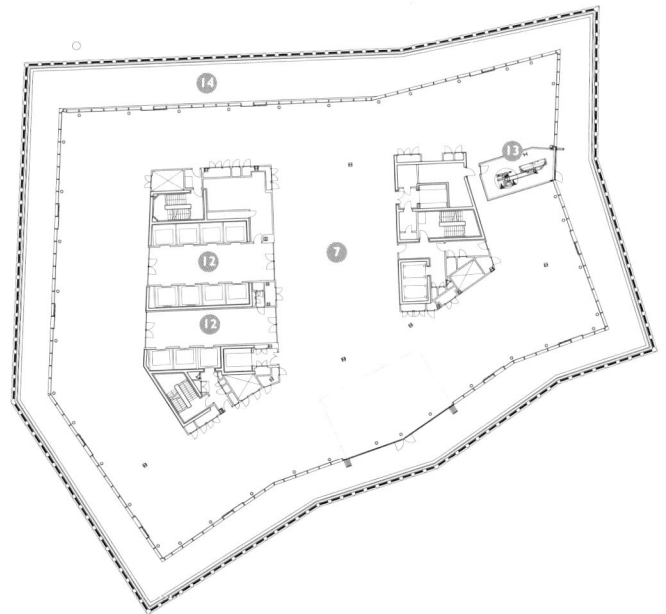

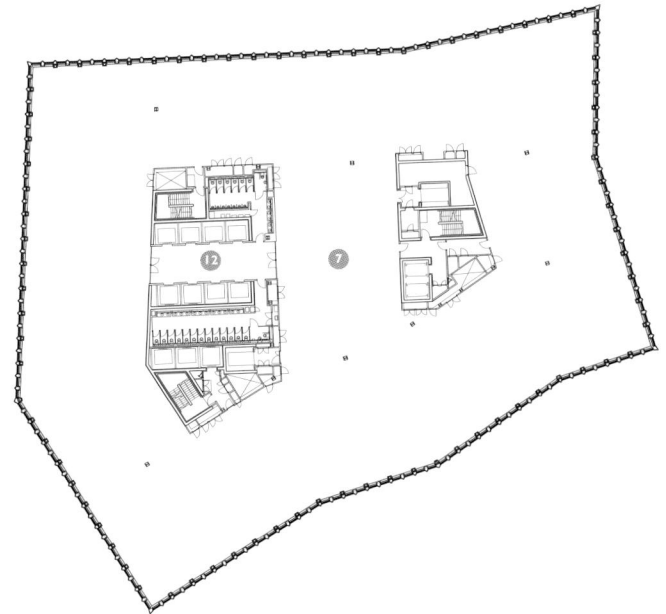

FENCHURCH AVENUE

BILLITER STREET

FENCHURCH STREET

20m

185

There is a particularly enjoyable theatricality to the 'banking hall' — the quotidian grind of our work-lives is suspended, as the shifting silhouettes of passers-by become the protagonists in a public performance. The surprise of the pedestrian's experience in the 'banking hall' more than meets its match in the delight of the roof garden, which is easily reached via dedicated lifts. Finding oneself among the neighbouring towers — perhaps closer to the corpulence of the Walkie Talkie than one would rather be — and looking out over the skyline of London is both thrilling and fascinating. Seeing the immediate rooftops of neighbouring structures disfigured by ugly arrangements of plant, one regrets all those missed opportunities.

Planned by landscape architect Latz & Partner, the terrace offers a 360-degree walk around the perimeter, an impressive variety of sensual spaces, timber seating, abundant planting and haptic surfaces. The latter range from the modelled York stone paving, highly textured concrete walls, steel pergolas whose triangulated geometry echoes that of the crown, a long pool of water, various hedges and roses and 80 wisteria trees that offer a huge shady canopy. A public restaurant situated on the floor below is accessible by stair or lift. Apparently seven of the next 14 towers to be completed in the City will have public viewing galleries; would that even half of them might be as sophisticated and pleasurable as the roof garden at Fen Court.

This is a project with, as Parry puts it, civic soul. It displays an extraordinarily generous attitude towards both the physical and visual public realm that is all the more remarkable in consideration of the fact that the building was not conceived for a specific end user but as a speculative project.

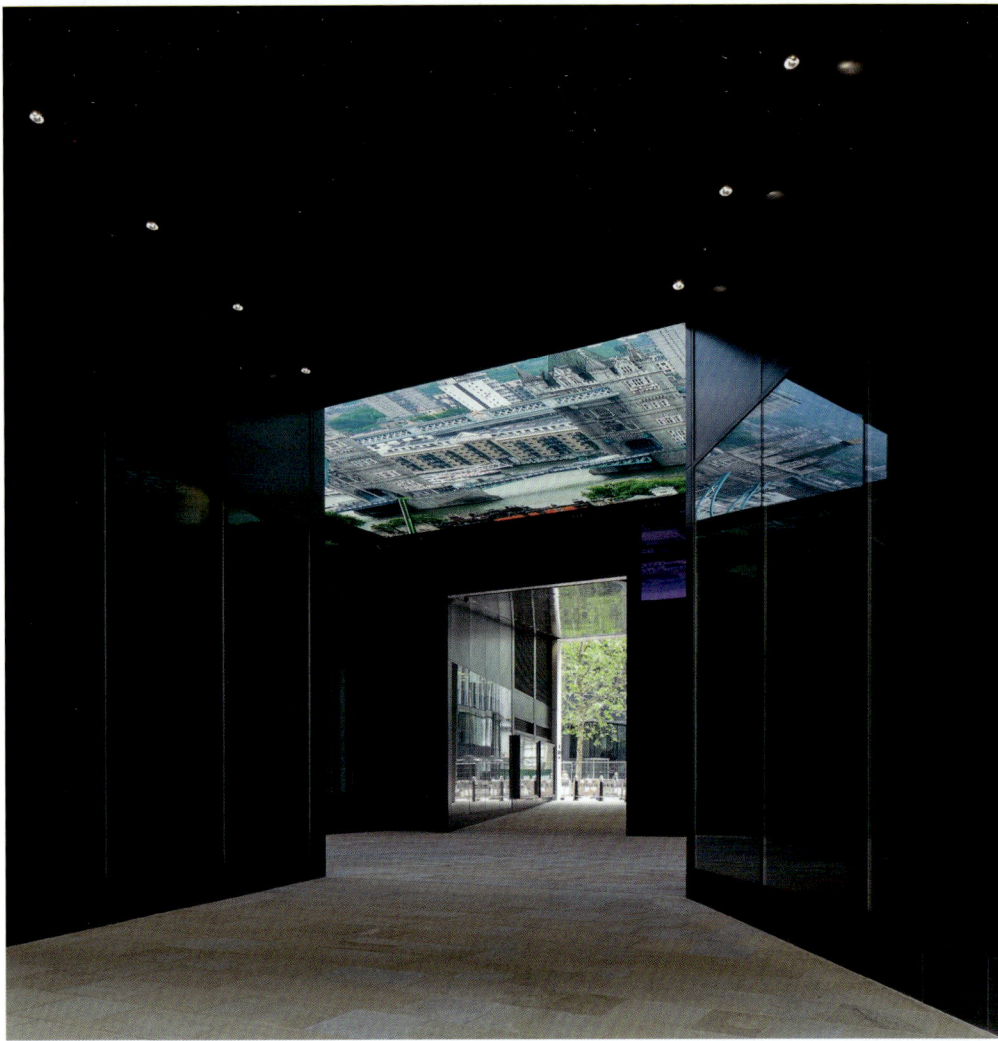

While the quid pro quo barter mechanism of planning gain resulted in the felicity of a public roof terrace, it is the consummate intelligence and skill with which the architect has conceived and executed the entire scheme that makes the difference.

Not wanting to add yet another all-glass office building to the City, whose pathological accumulation of cold greennesses is seen by Parry as a kind of cadaverousness, the architect has created an ensemble that is clearly about enjoying life. One is naturally drawn to things that live: the main body of Fen Court has a clear corporality that we experience with our bodies while the whiteness of its glazed terracotta reflects light down to the street, the civic space of the 'banking hall' engages us both visually and emotionally with the staging of images on its soffit, the crown's neon flicker bewitches us, and the generous, life-through-plants-and-people roof garden can be enjoyed up in the sky.

At last it has been proven that an alternative modus operandi is possible: corporate architecture can do the impossible and escape its lazy kowtowing to capitalist greed and the demands of the individual. It can serve the common good in its offer of inspiring buildings and the highest quality of civic space. In this way architecture, in regaining both its responsibility and its role as a cultural artefact, can encourage public life and social interaction and so support the very idea of the city.

Right
Fen Court's angular facades contrast with the curved forms of the Walkie Talkie.

Left
Ground level pedestrian route through the building; seminar room and workspace interiors.

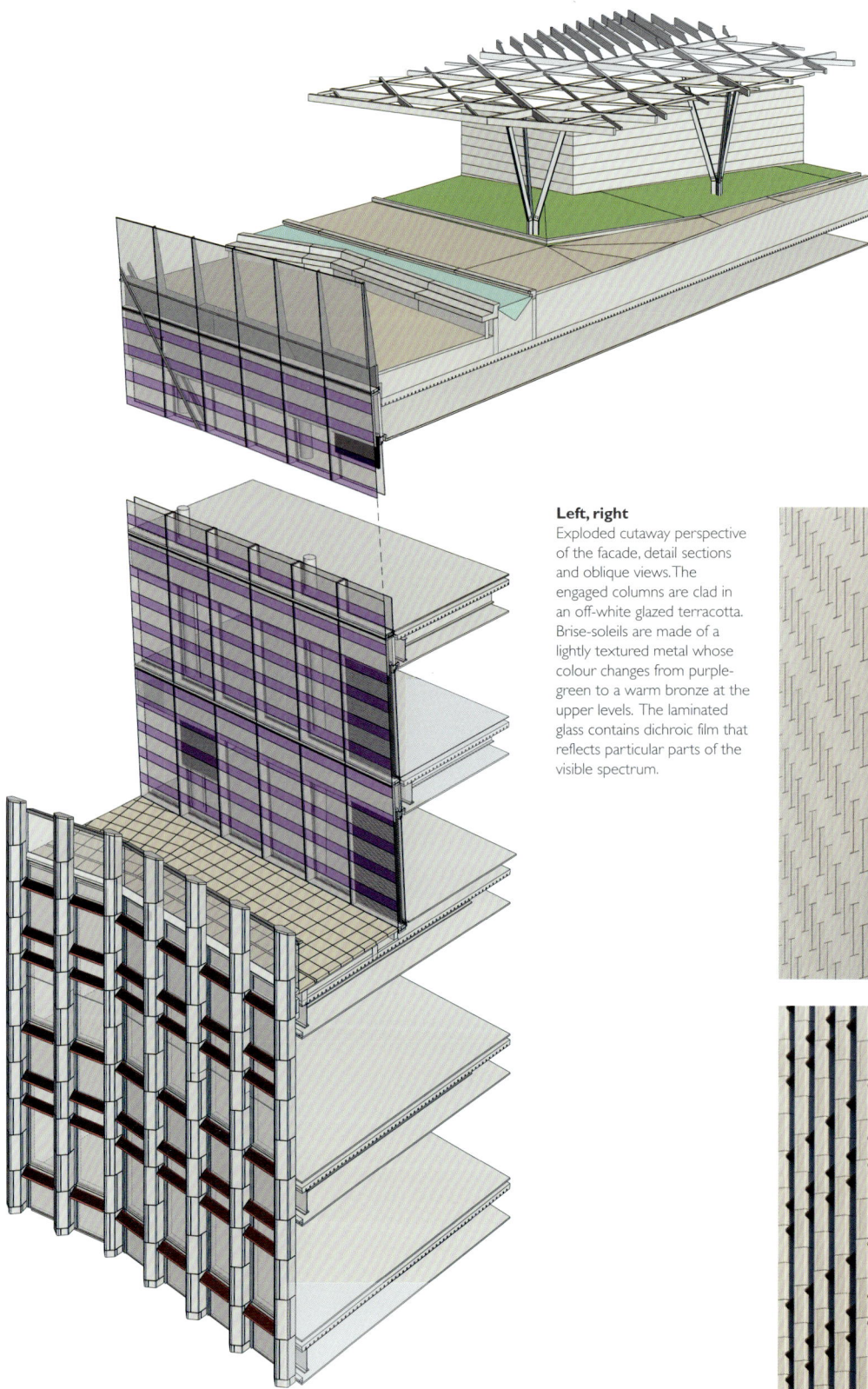

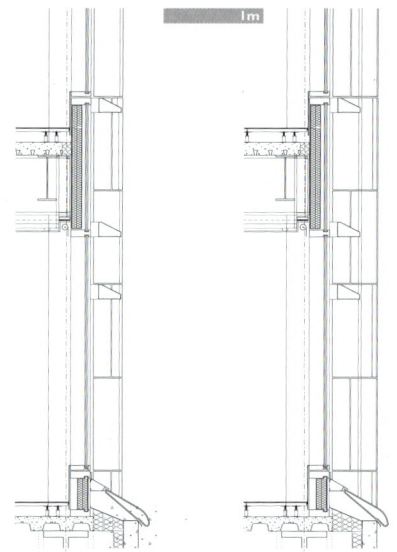

Left, right
Exploded cutaway perspective of the facade, detail sections and oblique views. The engaged columns are clad in an off-white glazed terracotta. Brise-soleils are made of a lightly textured metal whose colour changes from purple-green to a warm bronze at the upper levels. The laminated glass contains dichroic film that reflects particular parts of the visible spectrum.

Two Cities

Deborah Saunt in conversation with Eric Parry

Eric Parry Practicing as an architect in London, you find an extraordinary cultural shift between Westminster and the City. You need to be something of a chameleon, because for historical and cultural reasons they are so entirely different. Although London has joint infrastructure systems and so on, somehow the difference between its two historic cities is maintained.

Deborah Saunt Yes, and it's important because ideally when you are negotiating with a client, you are also conversing with or talking to the city, not just as a political entity but also as a cultural entity. You are trying to situate work back into the identity of a particular zone.

EP It is extraordinary to me that neither place has a written 'rule book' on plot ratios or adjacencies or heights; there are conservation areas and the bizarre constraints of viewing corridors, but individual projects can be discussed in terms of their merits, and one has a role as architect to arbitrate between the desire of the planners, who react to maintain something they see as of great value, and the developer, who tends to want to maximise what can be achieved on a site.

And actually that discourse is incredibly open. It involves the personalities who happen to be in charge within the local authorities at the time, and this can inevitably change. You start on your journey as an architect by walking into a room as a complete innocent, not knowing who the characters are, and bit by bit the theatre of this dialogue emerges. Naturally over time people move off the stage and you're left with a different set of circumstances. But even as we become familiar with new faces, we try to maintain a position that is professional, not one of friendship, meaning that I never go out of my way to know who we will be dealing with. Discussion with planners is something to be started anew with each project, just as it is with a new client.

DS Both the City and Westminster are settings in which you can't do the same thing twice — both want a response that is particular and bespoke; in fact I've never known the appetite for this to be so strong. It's a really fortuitous period to be an architect who is interested in making architecture that is particular and contextually derived.

There is a common preconception that the Great Estates are very conformist and enforce consistency; the stucco-fronted London square is the image. But actually those parts of the city for which they are responsible are a complete hodgepodge of influences. Both the City and Westminster are brilliantly heterogeneous.

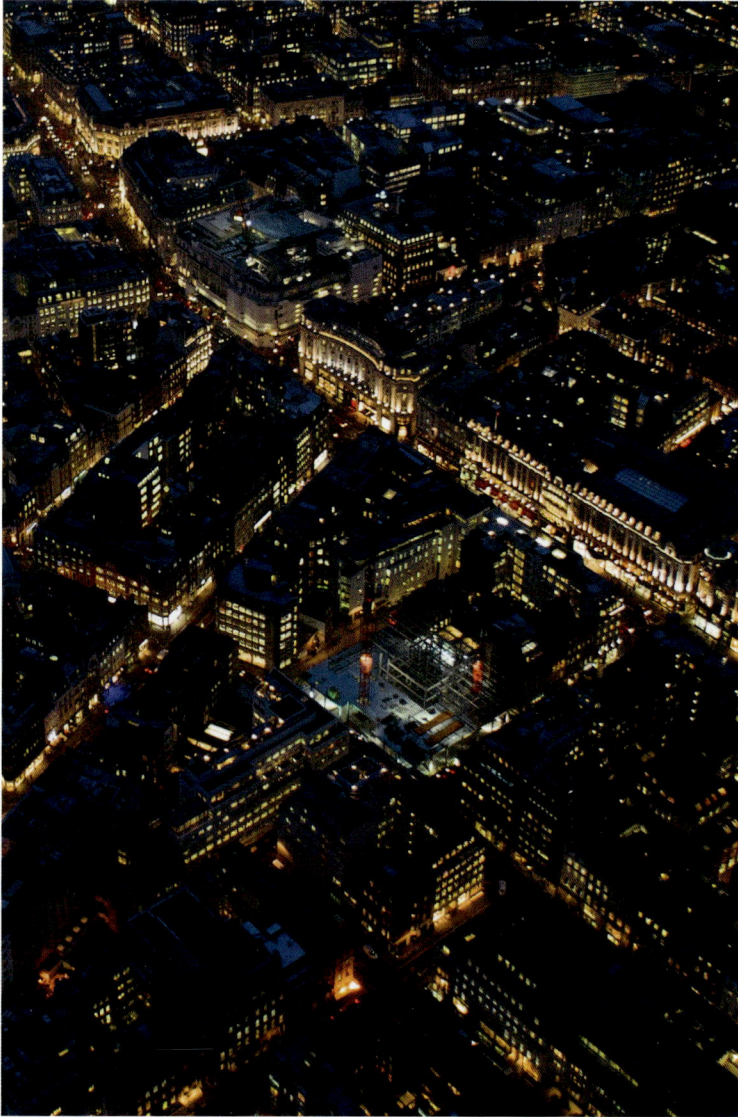

Your own work is very diverse; you're not simply rolling out a product. When my practice DSDHA started working in Westminster it became clear that the local authority wanted to 'collect' beautiful examples of different types of architecture rather than impose a standard template, which is a very different approach to that adopted in other places. But there's also a counterpoint to that; we heard mutterings that they didn't want any more generic architectural projects in a language that wasn't specific to Westminster.

The 'city fathers', be they planning committee members or officers, look to architects to be city-makers, and somehow to divine the real character of a place. The local authority is caught up in the day-to-day tumult — there's always change — and they look to architects to lay down or record some kind of moment. They seem genuinely reassured by good work.

EP I think that's particularly true of Westminster. In the City, Peter Rees, who was chief planner from 1985 to 2014, used to describe his domain as a vegetable garden which could be almost completely remade over a cycle of 20 years. The last thing that planners want is a status quo that can't be changed to suit a changing market or demand.

In the City of London, however, there aren't residential adjacencies, like in Westminster, that can create formidable problems in terms of rights to light, and residents who can often resist change. Another issue is conservation. It's interesting to see buildings like Richard Rogers' Lloyd's building being listed, but in the City these iconic buildings actually run against the general drift of change as a constant. Westminster would find that philosophy problematic, so the architectural and planning approach there is much more about urban repair.

The Great Estates are powerful forces of continuity and control underlying a lot of the territory. They were manifestly changed by bombing in the second world war, however, and some of the opportunities today arise from the sense that the replacement buildings of the 1960s can be erased and that one can start again.

DS In Mayfair we've been amazed to discover how little original historic fabric actually exists. Everybody thinks of it as fine and well-preserved, all three- and four-storey townhouses, but much of that has gone.

Mayfair is somewhat similar to the City in the sense that it is 'self-policing' — not many people venture into Mayfair at the moment; it somehow has put people off by its morphology and streetscape, and footfall is therefore low. I've looked closely at it in an effort to discover how you can have such a big area of city where so few people go. My own preconceptions were that Mayfair was very 'solid' and hard to navigate, but like the City it is incredibly permeable, and has begun to change much more than one would imagine. We recently made layered maps of Westminster to reveal this surprising dynamic, and this forms part of our argument when we propose quite radical new buildings. We 'prove' that the city isn't fixed, that it is an organism that is changing, and planners' appetite for that is usually positive.

EP It would be fascinating to take the maps that were produced of wartime bomb detonations, and see what this opened up in terms of redevelopment. Savile Row sits at a point where the grids of two Great Estates clashed, and was almost completely enclosed before the war. Then, following the bombing, you get the construction of the Central Electricity Board headquarters — later the head office of English Heritage — which was replaced by the building we designed, 23 Savile Row. If we'd been constrained by the pre-war plan, it would be a completely different story. Bomb damage allowed larger buildings, such as the very good police station, to crop up amid this grain of terrace houses with working, lower-ground floors. And that's the case with many of the Westminster sites on which we've worked.

In the wider area there was also significant change in the inter-war years. One thinks, for example, of the extraordinary scale of the Marylebone Road around Baker Street, where there are apartment buildings that are really gutsy — as though London was beginning to look across the water to the United States in terms of what apartment buildings might be. That era has left its mark as well.

Our St James's Square project is interesting in that respect because it replaced a building, completed in 1939 and some seven storeys high, which we have reduced to reflect the historic square. The new is actually more cognisant of the scale of the old than the building it replaces.

Regent Street is another example, where much of Nash's early nineteenth-century work has been erased by Reginald Blomfield, Richard Norman Shaw and others.

DS It's regarded as deeply historic but it's only 100 years old.

EP And it's an example of how — alongside bomb damage — the length of leases is a driver of change in Westminster, creating a tidal cycle of development.

DS And that cycle now has an international dimension with Norway's sovereign wealth fund owning a share of Regent Street.

Westminster's fortunes have varied considerably in terms of its desirability. Is it true to say that only in the last 15 years has it seen itself as a business hub? Maybe just as the development of Canary Wharf made the City more conscious that the historic centre could evacuate and lose its business focus, so that has also had an effect on the more gentlemanly arrangement of the West End. Until recently it wasn't really promoted as a business centre, but more as an elegant, cultured urban centre.

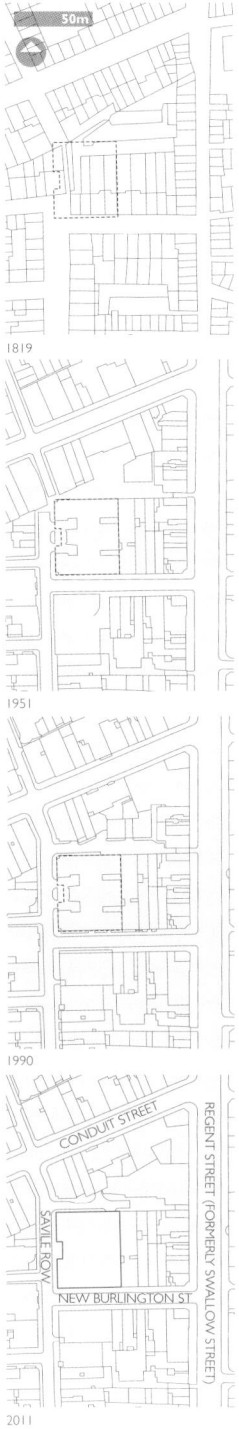

Left
To provide an increase in residential space equivalent to that in office space, the development of One Eagle Place included separate apartments on Jermyn Street.

For some time Westminster has been conscious that although the borough couldn't provide big flat-floor office space, what it could do is provide the best address — Oxford Circus is still regarded as the geographical heart of London by commercial agents — and the best quality buildings, and the highest levels of sustainability.

When we first became involved in the area — the door magically opened for us by accident with a project in Soho — we were told by politicians that any building we designed would inevitably represent Westminster as a newly rediscovered place to do business.

EP There is a longstanding set of working practices in Westminster, from the creative agencies in Soho to the parliamentary spin-offs in Victoria Street, and now with the huge growth of the financial world within the borough, there are the hedge funds that find it eminently more civilised to be in the West End. And with that, you get not just the traditional art market in Dover Street, Cork Street and so on, but also international dealers arriving, and looking for space near the hedge funds. It's to do with convenience, with being able to pop down to your art dealer as you would to the betting shop.

DS I'll never be able to look at Cork Street in the same way again.

EP The incredible intensity of these sorts of occupations means that an art dealer can't exist out on their own. Ideally, they have to be somewhere like the West End, near the punters.

DS Digital technologies have allowed the hedge funds to exist outside the traditional financial district, but they all still cluster together, and consequently all the art galleries cluster together.

EP I can't see insurance companies suddenly turning up in St James's Square; Lloyds and all those key players are in the City, and they traditionally meet and do their deals over coffee in the territory around Leadenhall. Hedge funds are much more boutique, and like the galleries they've got clients who are often more individual than corporate. So the City retains that sense of corporate gravitas while the West End offers a much smaller and more discreet scale.

The recent change in Victoria Street does change things in Westminster, because you can now get big floor plates in the borough. They are confined to particular territories, to protect the working practices of other areas which have such a marked character.

DS Westminster is something of a maverick in planning terms, which has inevitably brought it into conflict with government policy, such as over its stance against allowing the freedom to change a building's use from office to residential. By resisting that in Westminster they are actually holding on to the mixture of the city and not allowing it to turn into a solely residential dormitory. If the city centre is just somewhere people eat, sleep, shop and maybe go to the theatre, it loses the sense of urgency that work brings, and the flood of people coming in and out. A hotel district would never have that beating heart.

EP The balance that has been struck in terms of mixed-use — of residential quantum being a response to the uplift in office space — has been very enlightened. To take our 50 New Bond Street project as an example, it's a classic office scheme of offices and retail, above which, on Maddox street, is residential. So there's a terrace that was once given over to small offices in what were formerly domestic settings that has been placed back into mixed use.

That was also the case with our One Eagle Place project. We had an urban block into which we were able to insert a quantum of residential along with retail and office space. The office entrance is very discreet, and then there's a large opening that is retail. That's very different to the way the drum is beaten in bigger corporate buildings. In this neck of the woods, around Savile Row, New Bond Street and Piccadilly, the mix of uses encouraged us to revitalise blocks in an interesting way.

DS It's very different to the City, though, where the planners seem to do everything possible to deter residential uses.

EP Absolutely. There are ghettos of residential in the City, which are much sought after and rather brilliant, but these only house about 9000 residents in total. With the flow to Westminster of smaller commercial operators — and potentially some of the bigger ones — its planners perceived that they should offer exactly what you were talking about — that life goes on beyond six o'clock and the City is a place to drop by at any time of the day. So big efforts have been made at Cheapside and to some extent around Paternoster Square, with clubs, retail, food and bars. It's extraordinary to see how that the 'liveability' of the City has changed over the last 25 years.

DS In spite of the intensity of central London, in adding new buildings sometimes you have to be quiet, which is something I like about working in Westminster as an architect. When a project starts you're really not at all sure what its voice is going to be; you have to wait and listen and research and draw and converse with people to see where the significance lies. The antithesis of that is when people say 'We like your building on South Moulton Street, can we have one of those?'. We're always battling against people who want to commodify architecture in that way. We explain that we're making a part of the city and we don't know what it's going to be like at the outset of the project. We've learned that they can be reassured by bringing them to our model shop, or showing them the process through the piles of drawings. But our clients are always quite surprised by how long it takes, especially as Westminster likes to be involved in the early conversations about whether a building's character is background or foreground. How long does it take you to mature a project, to go through these iterations?

EP It depends, but the good thing at Westminster is that because the process inevitably takes quite a long time, and there will be pre-meetings and then meetings and discussions, things can marinate quite nicely. A world without English Heritage and the planning process would be a disaster because everything would be precooked and reheated, and a new project would not have that process of refinement or the capacity to change and find itself.

DS I find that very few architects are willing to change, or are not agile in response to each other when contributing smaller parts of a greater whole.

EP This brings us to the individual and the collective. In the early 1990s, the Temple Bar project in Dublin produced a healthy competitiveness between practices, but also a fantastic spirit of collaboration. In London we tend to do piecemeal exercises, but their lessons are rarely translated to the bigger scale of streets. High-rise residential towers are springing up but they don't know how to cooperate at ground level. There's an absence of grown-up collective thinking.

DS That's it entirely. The way architects work with each other corresponds to the idea of streets. Perhaps it helps if your practice is itself based in a jostling urban building: you get used to being neighbourly — independent, but enjoying the conversation and not seeing it as irrelevant chit-chat. To make a good city, we have to be able to talk.

EP Education is important too. Among things that characterise work in those schools which play up the idea of the architect as prima donna is an absence of scale — in terms of how you make a window in a wall — and a terror of repetition. I love the consistency of Gower Street, but that would now be anathema in many schools. The question is how to bring to contemporary architecture the sense of the city that is larger than the sum of its parts.

DS Are any of your buildings in Westminster actually freestanding?

EP Not in Westminster, although we do have freestanding office buildings at King's Cross, Finsbury Square and elsewhere. There's a widespread sense that 'urban repair' is not as architecturally fulfilling as designing freestanding objects, but when you look at it from an urban perspective, what is really critical is the kinetics of the street, and what you can put into the base of a building to play its part in the wider setting — what you described of people pouring onto the street and enjoying the conviviality and excitement of being among strangers.

Aldermanbury Square in the City is a standalone building, where all the other neighbours have been forced into a street. Getting up high there and looking down, I could see that the roofscape is in crisis — a realisation that actually was the beginning of our project on Fenchurch Avenue, which has a public garden on top.

DS Is the very constrained nature of the Aldermanbury Square plot by virtue of the history of that site?

EP The square was a post-war construct. The Brewers' Company formerly occupied the middle of it, but moved to one side when it built Brewers' Hall in 1962. Our building is at the end of the square and seeks to create connectivity with Wood Street, on the crossing of the historic Roman fort.

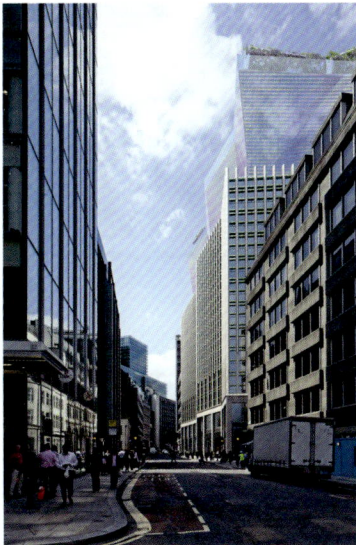

Above
Sketch of Four Pancras Square at London's King's Cross Central, and visualisation of 10 Fenchurch Avenue (now Fen Court), a 15-storey office building with retail use at lower levels and a roof garden.

Right
5 Aldermanbury Square, viewed from the elevated London Wall.

Opposite

Excavation around St Martin-in-the-Fields in the City of Westminster to create new access from street level to enhanced public and social care facilities in the crypt.

EP I empathise with that. In my experience the best 'armament' that one can have as an architect is to be so loaded up with creative energy, and a desire to build, that you can face down the inevitable steamroller of stuff that drives you towards mediocrity. So the best possible architectural education is one that leads students astray, opening the world of dreams and possibilities as wide as possible, because as soon as you leave school you are going to be faced by all of the things that try as hard as possible to erase all of that.

After my third year in architecture school, at a tough time in the 1970s, I worked for an engineer called Des Hennessey who ran a society called Underground London. Every time we got on a tube train to go to site he'd tell me about what piece of infrastructure was above our heads. I cherish the memory of his understanding, as an engineer, of what it was that made the city.

DS Underground is uncharted territory; there's no single three-dimensional map, and no single source of information about what's there. Much of it is covert. Your project at St Martin-in-the-Fields, for instance, is almost entirely underground. How was that?

EP It was wonderful. I sit on the Fabric Advisory Committee of Canterbury Cathedral and its archaeologist described to me the revelation that he'd had years ago, rattling through Trafalgar Square on a double-decker bus, that the St Martin-in-the-Fields site must have been important in the Anglo-Saxon world. Lo and behold, when we began to excavate there were two areas that Nash hadn't mucked up with his crypts. On Duncannon Street a Roman brick kiln was discovered. And in the front, just beyond the porch, were 28 bodies, one of which has been dated to 410AD, which was the year the Roman legions left. It was in a Roman sarcophagus but oriented in a Christian way. Others then were Anglo-Saxon. That threw the history of their presence in this place back 300 years in one fell swoop. And that, combined with the finds that were recorded during the period of building the Nash terraces, create a very interesting map of Anglo-Saxon and very early Christian London.

Likewise, at Finsbury Square we found loads of discarded cork shoes that were Elizabethan, which showed that cork was used as a material for footwear much earlier than was previously supposed. Everywhere there is this wonderful sense that the city is a million-piece, three-dimensional jigsaw that just keeps on getting richer.

DS Many people have remarked on the steps of St Martin-in-the-Fields, and the way that from them you can begin to read London's topography. Around the corner you've made these pavilions, connections to the subterranean spaces. They really do ask people to stop and consider the nature of the ground on which they stand, and very seldom in the city do you get asked that. At Savile Row, too, the base of the building gives a reading of the topography.

Because we're doing more and more urban design and landscape work in the city, this has become a passion. In every project we make, we're trying to connect people with the ground. Architecture's ability to communicate is now thought about in the context of the isolating effects of digital technology. I've got beautiful photographs of people who come out of tube stations and walk about 30 metres before they look up, because they are checking their devices. I've become increasingly aware of how important it is that people should feel here and now — that our buildings should make them sense the specificity of a place.

EP The question of London's specific qualities is interesting. All the projects we've discussed are, in my mind, part of either streets or squares, and if I'm thinking of what animates a street, or the characteristics that one admires in historic buildings and spaces, and the questions of where formality or informality are appropriate, the reference is to the experience of the traditional European city. London itself has always been knitted into that culture, not least through mercantile connections. If you go round the corner from New Bond Street, you have Hanover Square, and the church where Handel was a parishioner for 25 years — it is incredibly European in that sense. St James's Square was very much the result of a period spent by Henry Jermyn in Paris. It is the Place des Vosges drawn through Inigo Jones. And diplomats and others took bits of London back elsewhere; there's a continuous swing between London and the cities of Europe that leaves its mark on both.

DS London has always been very accommodating of new ideas and influences. Even today, you can see it just reading the roll call at Canary Wharf. It has always been an entrepôt of ideas and exchange, led by the market, including the market for ideas. Cambridge, by contrast, is a place of knowledge exchange, but not not financial or cultural exchange, and is very static.

EP Without mercantile influence, evidence of Cambridge's monastic foundations is still very apparent. In fact, that points to another fascinating aspect of London's history — the amount of fabric that was once monastic estates. We worked with the Charterhouse in Clerkenwell, which was once a monastery and is now an almshouse, to open it to the public with a new museum. Looking at its history, you realise how much of London's fabric was at one time monastic — inaccessible, secret — and how that has dissolved as though by acid.

DS The fragmentary nature of London — the fact that it has not been subject to large-scale replanning — is something people enjoy about it. There are many things side-by-side that don't 'fit', and there's an accommodation of contradiction. That's maybe why many of us don't particularly like the singularity of 'pencil' buildings in the City that try so resolutely to be perfect, model-like, and reference only themselves. They are not doubtful enough, not conversant enough. In that respect I enjoy the windows onto the alley behind your St James's Square building, whose design is in dialogue with the much older windows of St James's Church on Jermyn Street.

EP That brings us onto the crafting of buildings, and how things are put together. If you go to some of the big envelope contractors, mainly sitting in Switzerland, Germany and Italy, and you look at the map of where their work is, they are spread around the world and include dozens of buildings in the City of London. I look out from the balcony of our office and see cadaverous green glass taking hold of the entire City. A good bit of Portland stone is actually pretty grey, but it shines like gilt in this sea of greenness. Like the automotive industry, some approaches to construction simply assemble parts gathered from here and there. That is the opposite of what architecture is about — the unique situation.

We shouldn't be too pessimistic about it however; some of those City envelopes are pretty good, relative to Hong Kong, for example, where it is unbelievable how thin everything is. Rents in the City and Westminster are high enough to allow investment in the crafting of buildings. And partly because of the difficulties of getting planning consent in both the City and Westminster, there is actually the room to build things in interesting ways, with depth. Our planning system has a lot to be said for it; although in a general sense there isn't a very joined-up conversation between people with aesthetic or constructional expertise, there are plenty of planners who have got into thinking in detail about materials — not least because they've been ripped off so many times by the promises of architects that aren't delivered.

In Detail

Biba Dow in conversation with Eric Parry

Biba Dow We are standing outside 30 Finsbury Square, at the start of a tour of your speculative office buildings in London. This building marked a shift for your practice in terms of the scope and scale of work, and all of the projects that we're going to see develop an idea about an architecture that is generous to the city, holding and connecting spaces on an urban scale. The depth and composition of the facade at 30 Finsbury Square gives it a commanding position within the square, holding the corner and providing stasis in a public place which can feel more like a thoroughfare.

Eric Parry Although the buildings that we're seeing today were all speculative — which is the toughest brief you can get in terms of the impersonal, and all of the expectations of it that have accrued over a long time — I would argue that the best defence against the mercenary tendency of some developers is to be forearmed in order to fight the corners that need to be fought for architecture. That's what we see in the sculptural qualities, the tectonic qualities, and the response to context in each of these buildings.

City of London

City of Westminster

500m

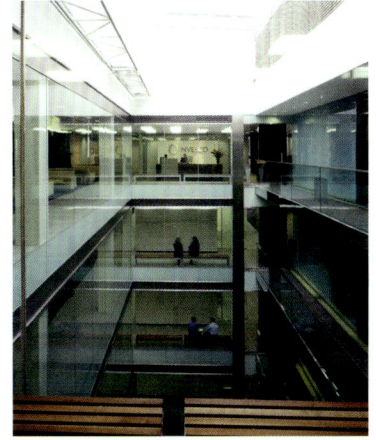

Left
The street entrance to 30
Finsbury Square is discreetly
acknowledged by an apparent
rotational shift of the stone
piers to enhance their shadow
and emphasise depth.

Above
The facade of Portland stone
piers, set in front of the glazed
envelope on Finsbury Square
contrasts with the flush
character of the rear elevation;
the top-lit, linear atrium.

BD What was your thinking about the relationship of your building to the square?

EP There's a central entrance but no canopy: just a twist of the piers to get a deeper shadow, and that's your introduction to the building.

And the openness at the corner — where piers on alternate levels are oriented in different directions — is a beautiful thing. You get that 'flipping' effect, which is a bit of an obsession of mine.

On the back elevation, we have a degree of eccentricity. The window is pressed right to the outside, so it's all about flushness. And here you do get a complete mismatch between the structural grid at 1.5 metres and the fenestration, so the position of the windows is slightly erratic.

I persuaded the client that we should think about the square and its effect on the building, and that we should commission the landscape architect Latz & Partner to prepare a scheme for it, which they did — although the council was reluctant to adopt something proposed by a private developer.

The idea of the building is that it has a 50-metre-long facade and a relatively deep plan of 35 metres. In the middle is an eight-metre atrium to bring in light. It rises from the back of the reception like the leg of a sock, and draws the connection to the landscape up into the building.

So you arrive on an office floor looking back towards the square, and get this fantastic open plan with no structure in the way. There are some good views of the square through the stonework too, as though it were a loggia.

Thirteen years after installation the interior finish looks just as good. I've always liked the naturally-lit loos. They're cheerful. Most of the money went into the stone facade, but the loos are one of this building's small pleasures. We're told by commercial agents that the first thing prospective tenants do is check the toilets, and they dismiss buildings with bad facilities. Architects may not prioritise it, but occupants do.

EP This is 60 Threadneedle Street, just appearing behind the Stock Exchange tower.

Hammerson bought a building that was on the site, but which was connected to the tower next door. Another architect had suggested pulling the two apart, and the adjacent tower was subsequently extended outwards by about five feet on all sides and reskinned. There was a horrible little route through between the existing buildings, but the separation of the buildings made a proper passage, which I used to define an urban block.

BD The dense grain of the City of London emphasises adjacencies and glimpsed views, and we have just walked here from Old Broad Street where the first sight of the building is of its curving corner, diagonally opposite the curved corner of the Royal Exchange. The new passage, Threadneedle Walk, pulls back and reveals more of the curved corner.

EP Looking at the context, where there are all these wonderful corners, most obviously spinning off Soane's Bank of England, it seemed to me that the City was so much about these conditions that a sweeping facade with rounded corners allowed this building to relate to Threadneedle Street on one side and to Throgmorton Street on the other, where the building form cuts back to create terraces in response to its scale.

On the lower side of the building, the double-height order picks up on Soane's wall at the Bank of England — one of the great, iconic walls in architectural history.

The new passage slopes down from Threadneedle, so on Throgmorton Street, where the ground floor is at its highest, we inserted a mezzanine level.

The Threadneedle Street facade faces south, and the idea was to use the solar shading to create a lyrical line that cuts back to indicate the entrance to the foyer, which is single-storey but has a rather grand scale.

If you stripped all the aluminium from the facade, this would actually be a glazed building; the facade is about 95 per cent glass, which gives good natural light inside. Over that, the metalwork just provides shade to counter solar gain, and gives a depth to the facade so that passers-by don't have desks pressed up against their noses in the public realm.

There's a very clear order of 1.5-metre units forming larger bays of three metres and six metres. They came assembled as three-metre elements, put together on site as six-metre sections before the 'eyebrows' were locked on and they were dropped into place.

Left
60 Threadneedle Street viewed from Old Broad Street and Royal Exchange Avenue.

Above
Eric Parry's facade study for 60 Threadneedle Street.

Right
Evolution of the context of 60 Threadneedle Street:
1 Bank of England
2 Mansion House
3 60 Threadneedle Street

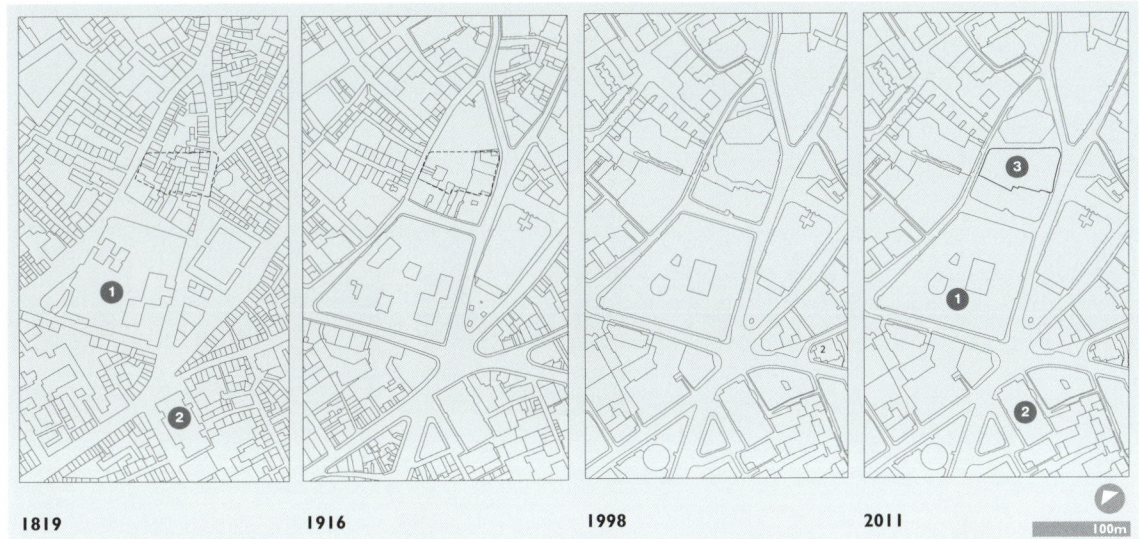

1819   1916   1998   2011   100m

223

The building is within the Bank conservation area, so using dark metal wouldn't seem an obvious thing to do, but patina on bronze can be absolutely jet black, so in a way it is very traditional. At the time we were designing this facade I was particularly interested in the work of the American minimalist sculptor Tony Smith, who achieved fantastic, very deep finishes, like a lacquer. I was keen that this building should have that kind of weight.

BD The blue-black colour is subtle and very unusual. How did you arrive at it?

EP An anodised finish, like Peter Foggo used at 1-3 Finsbury Avenue, can appear very dull. I wanted this to be more lustrous, to produce the reflections we can see on the soffits. We chose a painted finish, because with powder-coating you lose the effect of the pigment. The paint was sprayed under factory conditions, and it still has pretty much the same blue-black hue as it had on day one.

The first floor is a trading floor, and learning from nearby buildings where traders tend to shove rubbish up against the windows, we put a dichroic film on the windows as a foil to that anticipated mess.

The plan measures something like 40 by 60 metres. The core is pressed right back to liberate the floor plates, which are otherwise interrupted only by a few essential bits of structure — a pier here and there — and two atria to let light through. One of these comes right down to ground. The other, to the north, is cut out above the first floor. The cores pick up the geometries of the streets to find their natural form. They are finished in glass-reinforced concrete and canted to pick up the light coming from above.

The two atria have a role in the building's acoustic, fire and services strategies, but also give life to the office interiors.

225

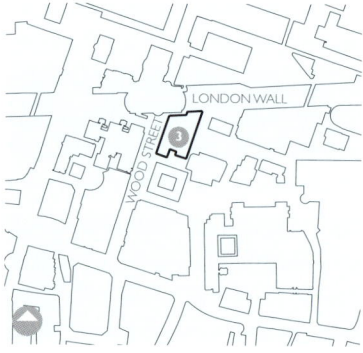

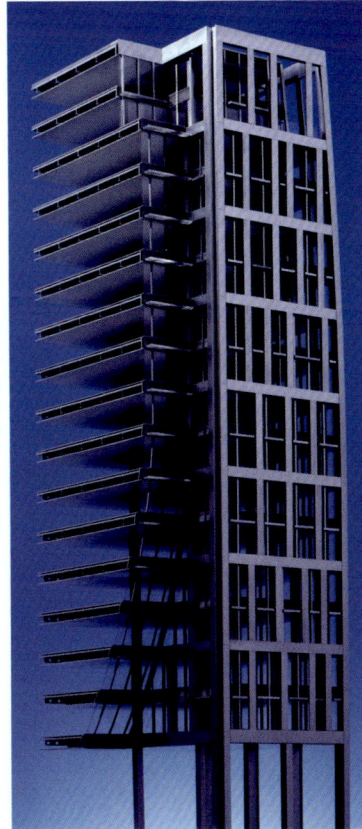

Left
5 Aldermanbury Square
viewed from the square.

Above
An inward curve in the facade
between the building's east
and west wings helps to admit
daylight to the undercroft,
which forms a pedestrian
route from Wood Street
(bottom) to Aldermanbury
Square.

Above right
Facade study model.

EP Number 5 Aldermanbury Square sits at the crossing of the cardo and the decumanus in the City's Roman fort, and replaces Royex House, built in 1962 as part of London Wall. We effectively doubled the floor area in the new building, but gave an undercroft which is 35 metres deep in order to liberate the space beneath the building and connect the square to Wood Street. The neighbours all face onto Wood Street in a conventional way, but I argued for this to be an individual piece because the best views from the upper floors are not east towards the street or west to the square, but to the south.

BD You had very specific ideas about addressing a wider site context here.

EP The idea is that there is a sort of geology to the base of the building, above which there is a piece like a Louise Bourgeois sculpture. The structural frame, at six-metre centres, is formed from weathered-steel boxes filled with concrete, which gives fire protection. During the course of the project, we found that we could push the structural design to get in another floor without increasing the overall height, so instead of two floors in the base we have three.

The building is divided into east and west wings, each 12.5 metres deep, to give a 10-metre break in between, where the facade curves inward to allow light to penetrate into the space below. From Guildhall Square, each of the wings appears the same width as one of the gothic pinnacles on the Guildhall. By creating the portrait-format double-height order, and breaking the building's 35-metre depth into two wings and a recess, we make a calm backdrop to the City's civic heart.

BD I find it interesting that in these buildings you combine the largest open plan that you can — which is effectively as neutral as possible — with an increasing intensity to how hard the facades and urban forms are working to make a richness and complexity.

EP The design of the envelope is predicated on the sculptural idea of expressing the structural grid. The skin is like a glove of carefully folded stainless steel elements, like billets, rising on a stacked joint on the structural bay. There are spandrels that bridge across at every other floor, and another baffle between, which creates a portrait-format ordering. These solar-shading 'eyebrows' indicate the division between floors whilst not joining the whole thing together. It's a recessive facade, like a three-dimensional weave, with a depth of about 500mm.

From the ninth floor the structure tips back to create an entasis. The cladding is faceted; all the pressings are 7.2 metres long, and were back-cut before installation to fit the radius.

Reflections in stainless steel are normally directional, but this is shot-peened so that it is non-directional and has a wonderful sheen to it — particularly as the building bends back; at the top it picks up the sky.

BD I love the precision with which you work with finishes and details.

EP In the reception area there's a relationship between geological concrete and diaphanous textile. The concrete was cast against real timber boards, but if you take a board straight out of the sawmill today it's damn nigh perfect, so they were blasted to give more figuration, and then laid in three different thicknesses to get more depth in the concrete.

We went to Paris to get the threads for the nylon textile wall, which was made by a master weaver in Frankfurt. It's like a landscape; a complex weave incorporating 'pillows' that catch the light.

We also designed the raft-like rugs that were knotted in Turkey, and the furniture. Instead of having standard Miesian benches, the idea was to make something that can be a seating area for meetings, or where you can stand and drink water from the dispenser, or watch the news on the media centre. The flooring is a beautiful cold grey granite from Boston. And for the lifts we lit the void, so that as a lift ascends it casts a shadow on the glass, giving a brief kinetic experience to someone waiting in the lobby.

For the landscaping of the square, on the building's sunny side, the idea was to create a light canopy of pollarded plane trees, which has grown very nicely to make a place of calm in the city. The seats are a type called the Lookout Bench, which I designed for Clerkenwell Design Week many years ago. You can see which ones are most popular by how polished they have become. Below the building there is a water wall with a lower and an upper level feeding a gargoyle, and the sound of water helps to drown out the noise of traffic and air-conditioning.

Learning from Giuseppe Terragni, I wanted to make a black soffit to the undercroft. A 35-metre soffit sounds daunting, and if it were in glass we'd have needed visible fixings everywhere. In order to make it appear jointless, we used a polished granite with a reverse detail. The stone is heavier than glass, but safer.

Right
Designs for foyer carpet and Lookout Bench, by Eric Parry, and view of the stone-clad soffit to the undercroft leading onto Aldermanbury Square.

Opposite
Bespoke furniture, lighting and textiles within the foyer at 5 Aldermanbury Square.

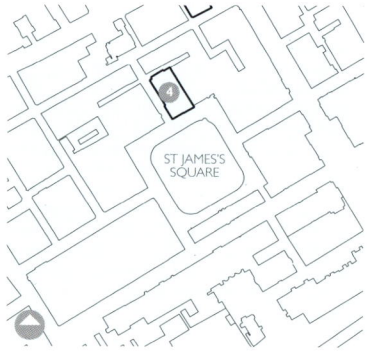

EP Here we are in St James's Square, where your building enjoys a very special position, both central and on a corner.

EP The square was laid out in the late 1600s with 23 houses, all with a 200-foot depth to a mews at the back. On this corner site was a 1939 building which was taller than the others on the square, and next door was one designed by Lutyens for three bachelors — lawyers to the king — who had apartments on the upper levels and a shared territory below. It was later the headquarters of the Royal Fine Art Commission.

Our project was 11 years in the making. The first iteration was for offices on the corner site, which would use the Lutyens building as space for boardrooms. We got planning permission but lost the job when it was bought by a developer who ran into financial difficulties, and the site was acquired by our eventual clients.

They decided that the Lutyens building should remain as a single house, so the corner site is now an office building extending 200 feet along Duke of York Street and wrapping around the back onto Apple Tree Yard. It's a single-aspect office with a linear core against the party wall, and encloses a private courtyard to the rear of the Lutyens building.

The fantastic thing about Lutyens' building is the flushness of its casement windows — so brave and brilliant. They are drawn right onto the front, and recall a period before the Great Fire of London. The piece of our building facing onto the square, the 'house' within the scheme, is also set with a sense of flushness.

BD I find it fascinating to see the increasingly intense scrutiny you pay to detail as you have developed this extraordinary body of work across London.

EP I felt that a dark brick would be the way to respond to Chatham House, across Duke of York Street, which is more red than a standard London stock. We chose a very hard brick from the New Forest to form a self-supporting nine-inch-thick skin.

For the windows we developed a white frame which is welded, so it is continuous. Each window is built with a slight cant, so the reflection of trees in the square is broken. It is a similar effect to that produced by the differently set panes in the Lutyens building.

I wanted to use render for the lintels, and to celebrate the first floor there are these big blocks of porphyry stone. Offices tend to have very repetitive sections, but here I was keen to create a piano nobile, so the first floor is much more generous than the others.

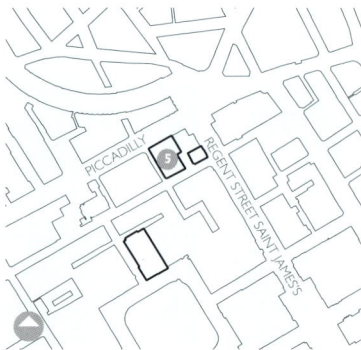

EP One Eagle Place extends from Piccadilly to Jermyn Street. There were three small buildings here, one of which was rather good; we got permission to replace the others. So overall we have one retained facade, one rebuilt facade, a new stone facade and a new ceramic facade — all created by skilled contractors from different companies.

BD How did you read the site?

EP The retained corner building on Piccadilly was in conversation with Alfred Waterhouse's National Provincial Bank opposite, but it had been butchered and the whole lower part covered. It was a bit nondescript but well crafted. We took it away stone by stone, stored it off site, and then brought it back, lifting the whole facade by just under six feet to create floor plates that would work with the new buildings. We rebacked the stonework in brick and added a new stone base, and the facade now has a fantastic life ahead of it.

With the ceramic facade, the idea was to pick up on where Richard Norman Shaw and Reginald Blomfield got to with cornices at this sort of height. I put forward six artists for consideration by our client, The Crown Estate, and Richard Deacon was selected. Through a long collaborative process we arrived at his 39 piece-cornice; it's the first time that his work has developed out of the body of a building in the same material. The colour could have been hand-applied, but in this instance we painted 30 colourways and applied them with transfers in a double firing. We took crockery technology from Stoke-on-Trent and put it on steroids.

The Piccadilly facade is like a face with make-up — it celebrates the artificiality of colour. The white ceramic is north-facing so it picks up reflections, particularly of Piccadilly Circus. Light flows across it. The red blush was applied to the window cheeks by transfer. It was designed using frits that are closely clustered in the depths of the cheek, and break apart as they come around onto the front face.

BD How did you detail the facade?

EP The wall is almost one metre thick. Within it are T-shaped steel elements, encased in precast concrete, that create a very stiff, rigid background to take the ceramic, which is lime-jointed so not a conventional rainscreen cladding. There's a slight 'smile' at the bottom of each window, because straight lines would have given a rather tense appearance.

Left
Existing facades on Piccadilly prior to the redevelopment.

Right
Construction of One Eagle Place incorporated the creation of a wholly new ceramic facade on Piccadilly, and the dismantling and reconstruction of a stone facade on the corner of Piccadilly and Eagle Place.

EP Until it was bombed in the second world war, Savile Row was just a small way through between two great estates. Our building at 23 Savile Row replaces one built after the war as a power-generation company headquarters. It is a very small site, but with the developer pressing one way and the planners pressing the other, the idea was formed to create a very simple rhythm, where the structure is actually within the wall, leading to a very clean interior.

BD Your building opens up space over the entrance, a space for art which also brings relief from the street.

EP It has a recessive facade, with string courses, and then every inset window is topped by a three-metre-long piece of Portland stone. In the light you get a very strong stratigraphy on it. And then there is a play with a very dark base of Indian basalt and an anodised aluminium window surround which is very light-absorbent and highly finished; I always thought of its big black framing in reference to London taxis.

Above the set-back, where there are fantastic terraces, there are two levels clad in anodised aluminium. The window frames are also extruded aluminium. It's often the case with an aluminium extrusion that the detail is all on the inside, to give it strength, but it ends up looking like a block of timber. Here, the idea was to extrude the thing the other way to make a ridged surface that creates shadows.

BD How did you commission the sculpture?

EP As we look north along Savile Row, the Joel Shapiro sculpture casting itself out of the facade is incredibly powerful. I figured on collaborating with Joel at the start of the process, and we worked six years and through two ownerships on the building to get it there. It's his first suspended sculpture, held off six cables, and it dances out of the facade, free of the building.

There were fantastic conversations with Joel on patination, and how dark the sculpture should be. It is almost pink — or golden — and quite matt. The amazing thing about it is that all of its pieces were cast in one. Timbers were sawn and beautifully joined, and then used to form the inverse of sand-cast elements that were all joined in situ in one piece. It's almost like a bit of Japanese carpentry. It was cast in the United States, so Joel could oversee its production in the foundry, and it arrived on site in two pieces.

Right
North facade of 23 Savile Row on New Burlington Place.

Opposite
Entrance facade with suspended sculpture by Joel Shapiro.

23 Savile Row

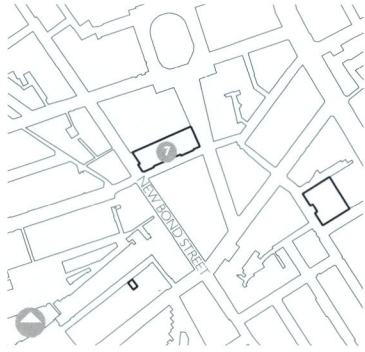

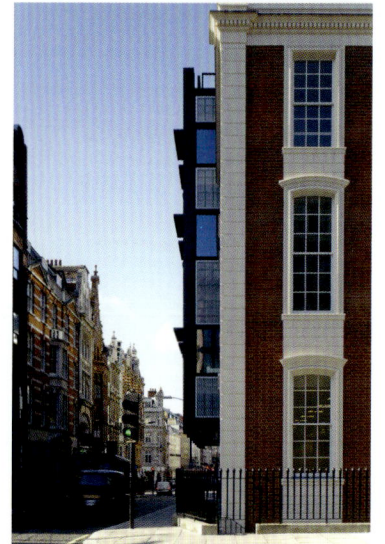

Left
Three faces of 50 New Bond
Street: green faience and oriel
windows on New Bond
Street; restored Regency
terrace and projecting upper-
storey extension on Maddox
Street, and restored red-brick
facade on St George Street.

Right
Fabrication and installation
of faience cladding for
50 New Bond Street.

EP At 50 New Bond Street we had
a plot of around 90 by 30 metres,
running between New Bond Street
and St George Street, and forming
one side of Maddox Street. There
was Hanoverian housing on
St George Street, to which we
added a top floor, but the rest is
absolutely original.

BD You have used materials to
articulate different parts of this
dense site that connects several
different buildings.

EP On Maddox Street, the Regency
terrace was originally houses,
and was then turned into offices.
We put the residential back, with
small retail units below. A listed
building that had burnt down was
poorly rebuilt in the 1970s, with
a toilet block and staircase that
came right down to the pavement.
Our replacement cantilevers over
the pavement in order to open up
the experience of the street, and
the view west towards Grosvenor
Square. Underneath is an artwork
by Antoni Malinowski called
'A Flow of Colour'. You get the
glass block facade above, and a
hand-set Murano glass mosaic
below.

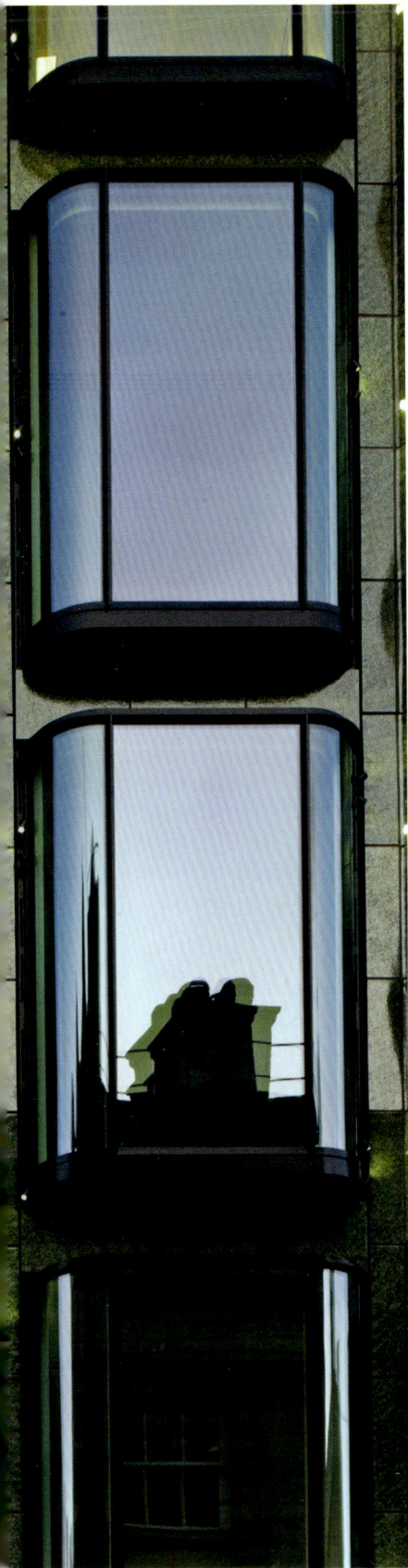

EP The retained corner building on New Bond Street was once the Pinet shoe store. My grandmother had tiny feet and liked nice things, and the only shoes she could get to fit were display samples from Pinet in Liverpool. So when I came to this building I had that memory in addition to the sense that New Bond Street has always been an amazing world of crafting and making things, from leather to jewellery. That led me to think that the new piece, next door to the Pinet building, should have a 'crafted' elevation which also picks up the faience in the facade of its older neighbour.

In the new piece there was a requirement for an open shopfront alongside a small entrance to the offices, which is enabled by a big vierendeel truss at first-floor level. At that level there are smaller oriel windows to allow for the bottom boom of the truss.

The trick with the facade is that viewers understand that the ceramic elements are cast rather than extruded because of the 'knees' — the inflections that give a wonderful sense of plasticity. We worked with a light artist, Martin Richman, to make a programmable illumination that adds life to the material.

The ceramic pieces are fixed back to aluminium panels on a steel frame. There are some movement joints, but we learned from our experience at Eagle Place where a very rigid structure allowed really tight lime-mortared joints.

BD Thank you, Eric; these are beautiful projects. In seeing this sequence of buildings I feel a strong sense of momentum that comes from your sustained interest in the craft of architecture — an interest both in the making of buildings, and the making of cities.

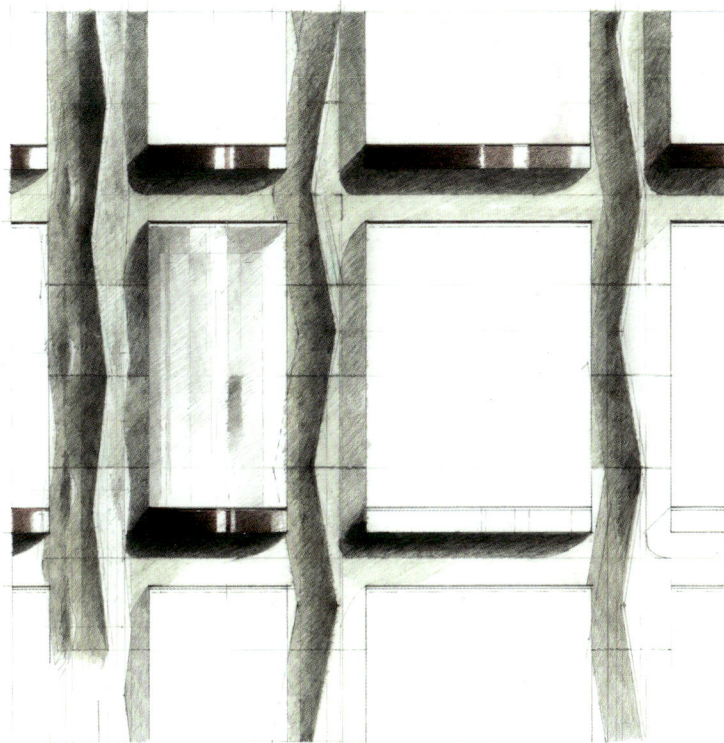

241

Art and Architecture

Vivien Lovell in conversation with Eric Parry

Eric Parry Our first encounter was with the Seven Dials project in Covent Garden in the early 1990s, before the conflagration that put paid to our plans. It was a real revelation to have this wonderful parade of artists — including Tim Head, Anish Kapoor and Shelagh Wakely — come to talk about the potential of the commission and what it might mean.

I was working a little with the Arts Council at the time, but the process of having a fantastic spectrum of possibilities was the first time I'd come across that way of operating. I don't know how you'd come to it because Seven Dials predated your art consultancy Modus Operandi. How did you get started, and what was your motivation in becoming a critical agent of change in the world of public art commissioning? And I would also like to ask you about the broader question of public art — about its genesis and where it is now.

Vivien Lovell At the time we met I was the founder-director of PACA, the Public Art Commissions Agency, which was based in Birmingham and one of very few public art organisations in the UK. It was partly subsidised by a grant from the Arts Council, but in time policies changed and funding for all public art agencies diminished. On moving back to London in 1999 I founded Modus Operandi as an independent consultancy focusing on permanent and temporary art in architecture and the public realm.

I trained as an art historian and had always been engaged with the history of patronage and commissioning art in relation to architecture and public space, and the ways in which patrons procured art. As well as artists being directly appointed for commissions, invited and open competitions have a long history; the competition entries for the bronze doors of the Florence baptistry, for example, still exist as evidence of this.

Today, there are many ways of encouraging artists' creativity, but it's usual for several to be invited to propose a concept design. For many artists a public art commission might be their first involvement with architecture and the public realm, but even for runners-up it can be a valuable experience, as diverse approaches by artists new to the field build up a matrix of possibilities. By involving architects as well as artists early on, when new schemes arise those architects may be more open to collaborations. And indeed clients — who may initially have been obliged to commission public art as a planning requirement — are often encouraged by their first positive experience to commission artists on a voluntary basis, even prior to a planning consent.

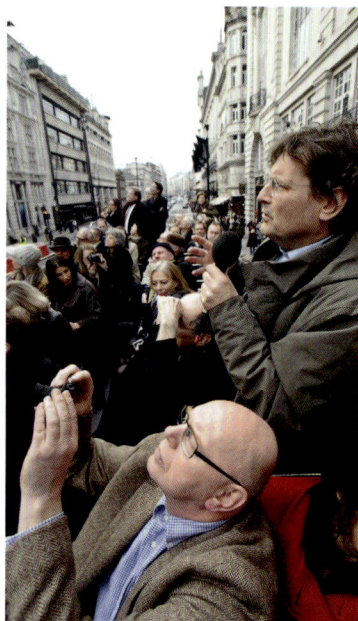

I've been working in this field for more than 30 years and it continues to be incredibly exciting, with new generations of artists, architects and clients who are increasingly open to public art commissions. Public art has come a long way from the tokenistic sculpture in the plaza. There are now so many ways of approaching it, from process- or performance-based work, socially-engaged practice, as well as artworks within architecture and the built environment — glazing, water and sound, for example — and the whole realm of temporary work. Defining public art is tricky as it's a moving target. It is also a field of activity requiring continual advocacy. That's a strength that curators can bring to the table, alongside a strategic approach and a deep knowledge of artists who are creating new work.

EP As you say, the changing character of patronage in the post-war period is incredibly interesting. One feels the public sector has lost its voice, and at the same time you can see the ascendancy of private speculation as the prime mover for urban fabrication. You tend to get many disparate voices participating in the sphere of urban making, but what often gets lost is the bigger vision that might once have been part of a municipal masterplan.

The sort of projects we are talking about generally feel to me like a very communicative thing between the silent edifice of the building and the public. Therefore they are very much to do with the public realm, and not just the decoration of buildings — a way of making these interventions accessible; some kind of common ground. Yet the effect is often piecemeal because of the way planning works and cities are made. There is an interesting larger question: how does one begin to make more of the public realm as a territory for the citizen (something developers tend not to be very interested in)? What determines where the gallery is located, where the sculpture park lies, where art in the public realm lies, and how that comes together in something other than a surrealist game of juxtapositions over which no-one has control?

VL You've put your finger on a really complex question. Often what is deemed to be 'public space' is actually privatised space with public access — try taking a photograph in Canary Wharf or Broadgate without attracting the attention of security guards. So what is public space, truly, and who is in control of it? We live in a time when local authorities are selling off public parks that were commissioned by the Victorians for the public good, just to make ends meet. To their credit the most responsible of the private estates — The Crown Estate, Grosvenor, Portman, for example — and developers such as Canary Wharf and Argent, have taken on the mantle for creating high quality public realm projects which incorporate public art.

Above
Eric Parry Architects' renewal and extension of the grade-one-listed church St-Martin-in-the-Fields incorporates the work of several artists, in a programme developed and curated by Modus Operandi.

A new East Window, by Shirazeh Houshiary, was installed above the altar in 2008. Mouth-blown clear glass panels, etched on both sides, are held within a stainless steel lattice. The panels graduate from a more transparent periphery to a denser centre, with a light ellipse forming a focal point.

Above right
Parry designed furniture and a stone altar for the Dick Shepherd Chapel within the church's new lower lobby.

Top
The upstand to the undercroft lightwell forms a pair with the entrance pavilion on the plaza. The balustrade to the upstand is encircled by a verse by poet Andrew Motion in polished stainless steel lettering, designed by Tom Perkins.

We've seen an erosion of the sense of public space, and along with it many associated institutions and initiatives. In the UK, the Property Services Agency, which used to stipulate art for the Crown and County Courts, no longer exists, and neither do the fixed-life Development Corporations and Garden Festivals which in the past controlled large-scale projects with public art budgets.

The Arts Council no longer has a public art policy per se, although years ago it lobbied Parliament, but failed to gain agreement for a 'per cent for art' on a national basis. City and county councils are still largely in control of highways and in theory could apply public art budgets. But for the rest of the public realm it is very often the private sector that pays for the art, and local authorities who gain what they can by imposing planning requirements. Public art is usually at the bottom of the list of Section 106 requirements, whereas it should be at the top, alongside public space.

We therefore have a pretty difficult and fragmented scenario in the UK at the moment. Yet there are some imaginatively curated public art commissions programmes in relation to various regeneration projects such as the Queen Elizabeth Park, Stratford Waterfront and the Royal Docks, as well as public art in the health, education and transport sectors.

EP When did the idea of a 'per cent for art' originate? The New Towns building programmes must have had it.

VL It first arose in Germany and Sweden in the 1930s, and in the UK in 1947 with Leicestershire County Council's school building programme, with both newly commissioned and acquired artworks. New Towns such as Peterlee and Harlow applied a Percent for Art from the late 1950s — as did Cardiff Bay Development Corporation in the 1980s, along with many local authorities influenced by Arts Council policy.

As most public art commissioning is nowadays funded by private developers, the agenda and starting points have changed. We now begin projects by gaining an understanding of the client's motives in commissioning art: is it mere box-ticking to meet planning conditions or is it aspirational, with artists appointed to bring something entirely visionary to the scheme? We may also challenge preconceptions of what an artwork might be. Plans for public realms still come to us with an 'X' marked 'sculpture', and our response might be to ask if the artist could design the whole space, or create an integrated work as part of the building fabric.

Your own track record of involving artists in schemes goes back a long time. I wanted to ask whether it was your time at the Royal College of Art, and the proximity of artists then, that led to an ease of dialogue? Later you designed studios for Antony Gormley and Tom Phillips. I wondered if you could talk about your encounters with artists in those early years?

EP It goes a little further back than the Royal College. My intention was to go to a university where a fine art department and an architecture department rubbed shoulders, and that was Newcastle. We used to have our tea and meetings with slightly unruly friends underneath Kurt Schwitters' Merzbau, so for me that became a kind of talisman of the way in which sculpture, or artistic endeavour, and built fabric could be pulled together. Ironically it later ended up in the art school gallery, courtesy of Richard Hamilton and Victor Pasmore. I was there from 1970 to 1973, when the faculty included a remarkable series of people who were not just sculptors but also great letterists, calligraphers and stained glass artists, so it was actually quite craft-based, quite hands-on. The artists Tim Head and Sean Scully were there.

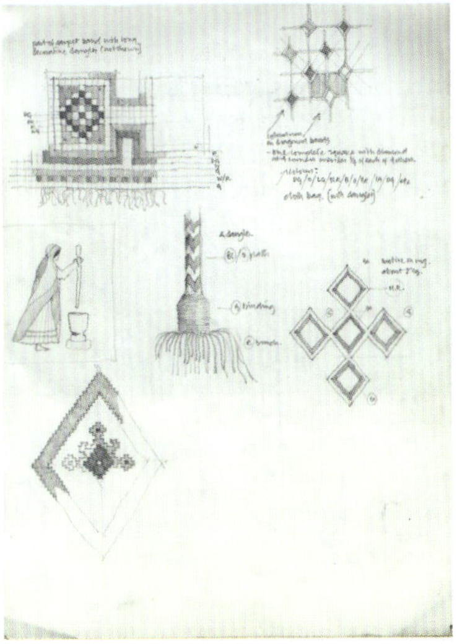

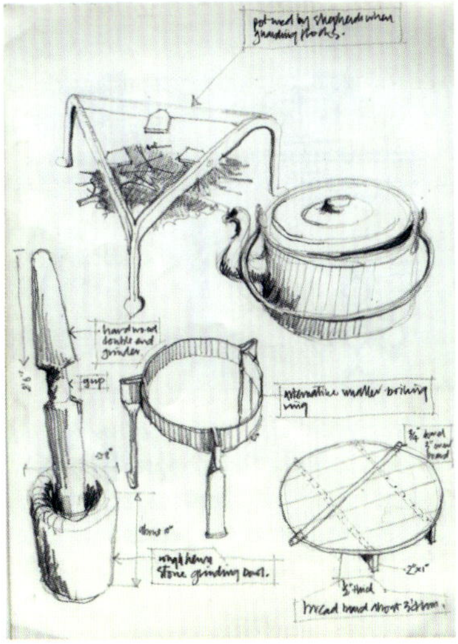

pot used by shepherds when grazing flocks.
hardwood double end grinder
grip
alternative smaller boiling ring
stone grinding bowl.
2"x1"

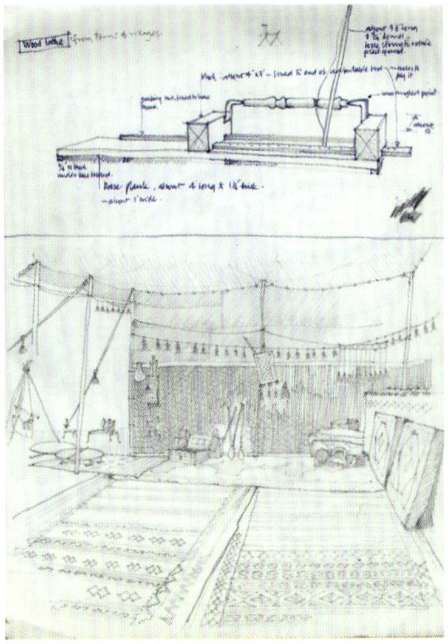

VL Absolutely — in each case it is a question of the optimum scale for the artist concerned. I remember going to Antony's studio when I commissioned 'Iron:Man' in the late 1980s (some years before the 'Angel of the North'), and seeing the full-sized piece reaching right up to the apex of the roof. I wondered then whether he had made it to fit just within the space, or if the space was made with this optimum scale in mind. There's a symbiotic relationship between the artist, the artwork and the space.

EP The interesting thing about the Arts Council is that it took me to visit studios. For instance I remember Antony in his previous studio, with his bread sculpture, 'Bed', which emerged out of his impecunious circumstances. That was also true of Shirazeh Houshiary at the time, and of Anish Kapoor. But they emerged from art school like well-formed pupae about to hatch in some extraordinary, unpredictable way. To have had the privilege of seeing that progression gives a perspective on the potential of those coming out of art school now.

VL It's important to take risks by creating opportunities for artists to change scale or material.

EP That's where I feel extremely comfortable in your hands; we can depart from my own territory of interests, and the artists I've watched develop, whose trajectory I know.

The relation of artist to architect is important because although there's nothing wrong in the potential of dislocation and separation between the artwork and architecture, there's also something interesting about the way in which the two can work together in a complementary way. It's missing a trick not to explore what an artist might do with the fabric of the building itself.

VL In relation to architecture and art it seems that there are several overlapping strands of approach. First, there's 'real' collaboration that stems from a shared concept, possibly from a shared intellectual dialogue, and that might result in art either integrated with the building or acting as a foil to it. I'm thinking here about the kinds of collaboration you have had with Richard Deacon or Joel Shapiro: art which amplifies the architecture but is distinct.

Then there's a second strand — art which has a more functional role; it might be decorative, or have a narrative or liturgical function, or even an acoustic function, as in the case of tapestries, for example. There are examples in your own work, such as at Aldermanbury Square, where Bob Allies referred to the combination of architecture and textile hangings as a 'gesamt-kunstwerk' — a complete work of art. There you were absolutely in control of the commissioning; it was partly your work, partly a collaboration. Or indeed the east window at St Martin-in-the-Fields by Shirazeh Houshiary. By definition the window has a function, but in that instance it goes far beyond function. Open to interpretation on the part of the viewer, it links interior to exterior; it has attracted new visitors to St Martin-in-the-Fields, and it even forms a key image in the church's communications material.

Some architects are more at ease with craft than art, especially when the craft has a distinct function in the operation of the building. But you've been amazingly brave with commissions like Joel Shapiro's sculpture at Savile Row and Richard Deacon's frieze at One Eagle Place. Could you say something about those approaches to commissions — one where art is more distinct and one that it is more integrated?

EP St Martin-in-the-Fields is fascinating because although the changes that we made to Gibbs' interior are quite radical, and create the proximities that make the social and liturgical operation of the church possible, you wouldn't notice them. The thing that people do notice is the East Window. The interesting thing is that the window touches so many chords — technical, liturgical, memorial, sacred — that it required an enormous consultative process. It's an extraordinary thing and dependent on many individuals. But all the conversations with the church's art panel — where I have been involved for a decade — have been fascinating, whether the installations under discussion were temporary and informal, like the Christmas crib, or formal and permanent, like the altar.

St Martin-in-the-Fields is more than a singular thing; it is a complex dialogue of parts that add up to something greater than any of them: Gibbs, Nash, a myriad of social organisations, all the artists, and the ritual. When some people decry the artificiality of art that is placed on a building, I think of St Martin-in-the-Fields as showing the opposite. For me it is a touchstone: one can't call it 100 per cent successful, but it is exemplary in terms of the process.

That is at one end of the spectrum; turning to the silence of the commercial field, where you are usually making a building without a defined end-user, probably paid for by a fund, with a planning authority somewhere out there in the desert — maybe supportive, maybe not — the question arises of how one can effectively create a dialogue. On a project like New Bond Street, where you and I worked together, it begins to be possible to see it as responsive to different territories, and to have a series of lower key, very intense interventions, such as Martin Richman's light installation that plays with the architecture.

VL It works; he has succeeded in enlivening that really complex rich facade, which I think of as your artwork. I regard you as an artist-architect because you craft your buildings beautifully, and they are always incredibly well judged and proportioned, probably due to the fact that you draw all the time.

There are many ways of integrating art into buildings and on the New Bond Street project, the Maddox Street soffit was actually rather a gift of a site. You may not notice Antoni Malinowski's installation the first time you walk down the street, but it is there to be discovered. Crafted by Italian mosaicists who worked with Carlo Scarpa, the work is inspired by the hidden river Tyburn.

A while ago I took a group on a tour from the BBC building through to St Martin-in-the-Fields, and we dipped and dived off Oxford Street and Regent Street to see various commissions curated by Modus Operandi, and people were able to appreciate the many different ways artists have intervened in architecture. Art's role in relation to architecture is incredibly rich territory and yet it is not necessarily very overt, which I enjoy.

EP With the Maddox Street soffit, as ever there was dialogue but there was also chance. Antoni Malinowski had a bee in his bonnet about Murano glass and Venetian mosaic and cutwork embroidery, so there's that sense that the artist has something that they want to get out.

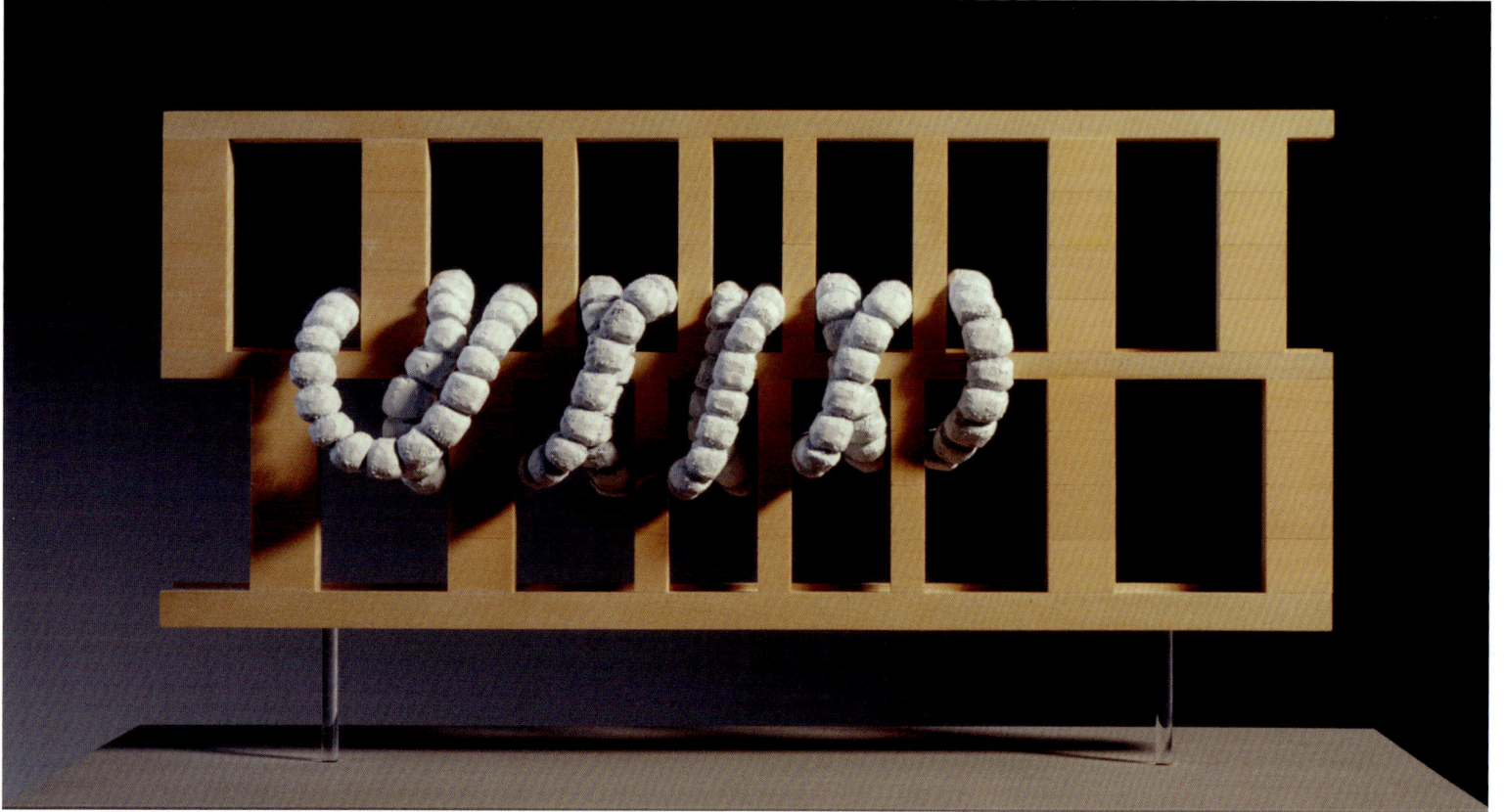

Left top
Unrealised proposal for
a sculpture for the facade
of 30 Finsbury Square,
by Richard Deacon.

Left bottom
Finsbury Square facade with
Richard Deacon's sculpture
incorporated; model of the
competition entry for London's
Millennium Bridge, by Eric Parry
with Deacon.

Eric Parry Architects' unbuilt
office building at 54-66
Gresham Street in the City
of London (2001–03) was
intended to feature a sculpture
by Anish Kapoor.

VL You've invited Richard Deacon and Stephen Cox to contribute to projects more than once. Could you say something about those dialogues? What are the common strands and concepts that have sustained your discussions over the years? You'd been collaborating with Richard Deacon for a long time before The Crown Estate scheme at Eagle Place, starting with the proposed sculpture at Finsbury Square that sadly didn't happen. I thought it was an excellent and very brave proposal, but frankly I wasn't surprised that the client didn't commission it, intervening so fundamentally as it did with the facade.

EP Richard and I had met before that, at the time of the Millennium Bridge competition, for which we made a proposal. When I invited him to contribute to the Finsbury Square project, instinctively feeling and knowing our work he responded very quickly, but unfortunately the art was dropped. I thought that was slightly an act of treachery, though to be fair nobody should be singled out for blame. We had a determined project manager who, once he had discovered that we were trying to make the building out of loadbearing stone, supported the project where it might have fallen. But the client had committed to the artwork in such a way that they could slip out of it. I learned that if you're going to pursue the dialogue about incorporating art in a project, it is very important to make it part of the planning process, otherwise it is too easy for it to be value-engineered out.

But that project was extraordinary in the sense that I think Richard's take on it was entirely different to mine. He saw it as evoking something lost in the world of decoration, or ornamenting the body. He had this interest in African body ornament, and that's where the idea of a string of beads started. At the same time he was working with these amazing glazes on some big pieces in Cologne. I was completely taken by those glazes, and at about the same time I was also working at Wimbledon School of Art, where we made a wall of glazed bricks for the new art studios. Seeing Richard's take on glazes opened up an incredible world of possibilities in my mind.

VL Did he have an open brief?

EP Yes, and he came back with the string of beads idea. But actually there was a dialogue in its emergence because the elevation was very much a drawing together of strands to a particular point, and that patch of the facade was very much determined with the artwork in mind. The sculpture would have been a polychromatic, viscous thing to be read in conjunction with the rather mute and absorbent stone.

When it came to One Eagle Place, the thing that first sparked what we did was the extraordinary location. It had to replace three buildings, one of which was mildly interesting and well crafted, and because it is in a conservation area everything was incredibly highly charged. But flying in the face of other instincts, what seemed to me incredibly important was that it was a north-facing building, near Piccadilly Circus with its glitzy lights, and that the potential of polychromy and artifice should be grasped. I just felt that we should be working with the idea of the artificial and the man-made.

We also wanted to make something out of the body of the building. There was a question in my mind as to whether the real collaboration should be on the characterisation and the physiognomy of an entire facade, or whether there should be a framework within which there's an understanding of possibilities, so there's a charge at that particular point — the cornice, in this case. It's absolutely shared in terms of the exploration of the material, but the field for the art is defined by the framework.

VL Collaboration can take many different forms but here it concerns materiality and the sense of colour, the location having been prescribed. The materiality of Richard's proposal for Finsbury Square, which didn't come to fruition, has come back in here which is very satisfying. Was the red blush around the windows part of your contribution or Richard's, or shared?

Above

The sculpture for 23 Savile Row was developed by artist Joel Shapiro over a five-year period and completed in 2008. Comprising various rectilinear forms suspended above and projecting beyond the entrance canopy, it is held by cables and changes in appearance with the angle of view.

The untitled work is "an active engagement of architectural and urban space that will, I hope, be accessible because of its use of the figure and configurations that have a certain commonality in the public psyche", said Shapiro. It was cast in bronze, which retains the strong saw marks of its wooden mould.

Right

'Relief Figure Emerging' (2015) by Stephen Cox faces onto Apple Tree Yard at the rear of 7-8 St James's Square. The basalt relief was carved in India, where Cox has had a studio for 30 years. It draws on Gandharan Buddhist statues that were informed in turn by antique Greek sculpture. The emergence of the figure from the rock was also influenced by Michelangelo's Taddei Tondo (c1505), in the collection of the nearby Royal Academy of Arts.

Adjacent to the relief, below the building's two-storey overhanging bay window, are three blocks of dolerite stone bearing a carved inscription in tribute to Edwin Lutyens, in whose office on this site the plans for New Delhi were drawn. Their arrangement and form recall Buddhist stupa rails.

When working with artists, one is attempting to conjure something out of the context in a way. First of all that is an architectural response to it, and then one seeks a reverberation that might add to it. For example, the piece by Joel Shapiro at Savile Row represents to me a liberation out of an architectural order that I felt highly constrained by; I was fine to work through it, but it just needed that idea of the 'solo' — the artist as the individual — emergent from the 'continuo' of the architecture.

VL Did the direct selection of Joel Shapiro come out of a long deliberation and quest for the right sculptor, or did you know immediately that he was someone who could work with very formal elements but also the abstraction of a figure, almost dancing? What was it about his work that suggested him to you?

EP I first encountered Joel in a brilliant show that he made in Timothy Taylor's Gallery; he simply had a whole series of maquettes in this smallish space. When Savile Row came along, and knowing that I would have a canopy and a space above it, I wandered down to the site with Joel and Tim, and we just talked about it. Tim mentioned that the ground floor could make a great gallery, and although I designed it so that it could work equally well as a Ferrari showroom, it became Hauser & Wirth's London gallery. Joel's sculpture is a piece of such quality that it draws people who can appreciate it.

It is a joy to introduce these voices into the public realm — which is the case with most of the work we've discussed. To see what it has contributed one only has to imagine these buildings and conditions without the art.

VL So the role of each of the artists you've commissioned differs considerably in relation to each of the buildings — from art creating a singular foil, a statement in relation to the architecture, through to an integrated, possibly more quiet presence forming part of the building.

It's probably invidious to mention names, but who would be your ideal commissioning client?

EP One needs to start by going back to that question of how culturally significant is the territory you're dealing with. There's no single answer, but with St Martin-in-the-Fields, it was important that the consultative process was far and wide, and 'civic' in that old sense. Therefore the commissioning process needs to be one that somehow draws those voices into focus. It may be that actually no client has the capacity to engage simply with the context, with a free will that comes close to the artists' normal sense of 'no programme, no constraints'. So perhaps the ideal is a client who is hands-off, providing the artist with freedom to respond to the architecture: 'We're happy to have a conversation, but here's the cheque'.

The City Works
Directory

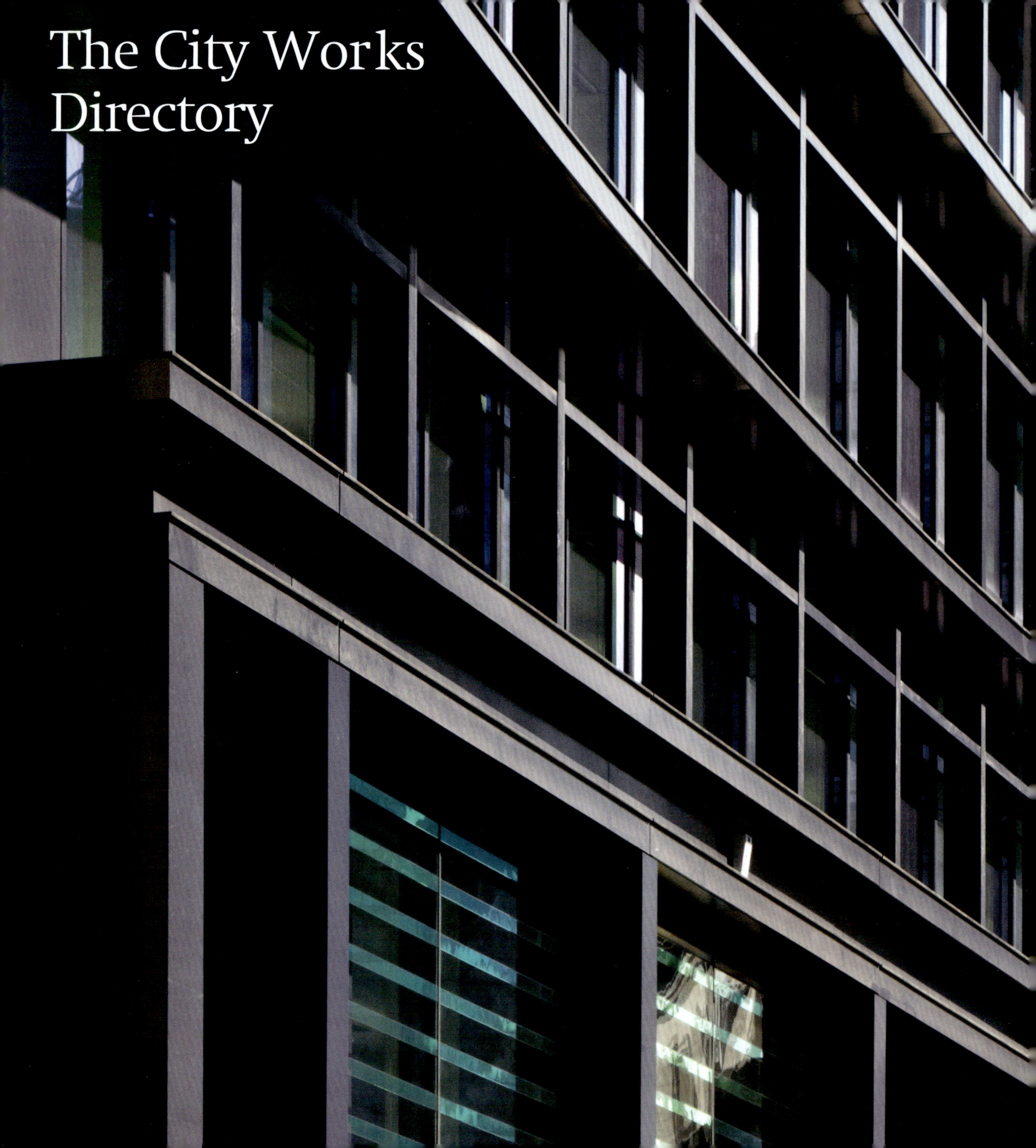

Ondulé Textiles

Weaving Contours with a Fan Reed

Norma Smayda with Gretchen White

Schiffer Publishing Ltd
4880 Lower Valley Road • Atglen, PA 19310

Other Schiffer Books by the Author:

Weaving Designs by Bertha Gray Hayes: Miniature Overshot Patterns, Norma Smayda, Gretchen White, Jody Brown & Katharine Schelleng, ISBN 978-0-7643-3246-3

Other Schiffer Books on Related Subjects:

Weave Leno: In-Depth Instructions for All Levels, with 7 Projects, Martha Reeves, ISBN 978-0-7643-5101-3

Hex Weave & Mad Weave: An Introduction to Triaxial Weaving, Elizabeth Harris and Charlene St. John, ISBN 978-0-7643-4465-7

Weaving Innovations from the Bateman Collection, Robyn Spady, Nancy A. Tracy, Marjorie Fiddler, Foreword by Madelyn van der Hoogt, ISBN 978-0-7643-4991-1

Designed by RoS
Photography by Nat Rea, unless otherwise noted
Type set in Chaparral Pro/Lato

ISBN: 978-0-7643-5358-1
Printed in China

Published by Schiffer Publishing, Ltd.
4880 Lower Valley Road
Atglen, PA 19310
Phone: (610) 593-1777; Fax: (610) 593-2002
E-mail: Info@schifferbooks.com
Web: www.schifferbooks.com

For our complete selection of fine books on this and related subjects, please visit our website at www.schifferbooks.com. You may also write for a free catalog.

Schiffer Publishing's titles are available at special discounts for bulk purchases for sales promotions or premiums. Special editions, including personalized covers, corporate imprints, and excerpts, can be created in large quantities for special needs. For more information, contact the publisher.

We are always looking for people to write books on new and related subjects. If you have an idea for a book, please contact us at proposals@schifferbooks.com.

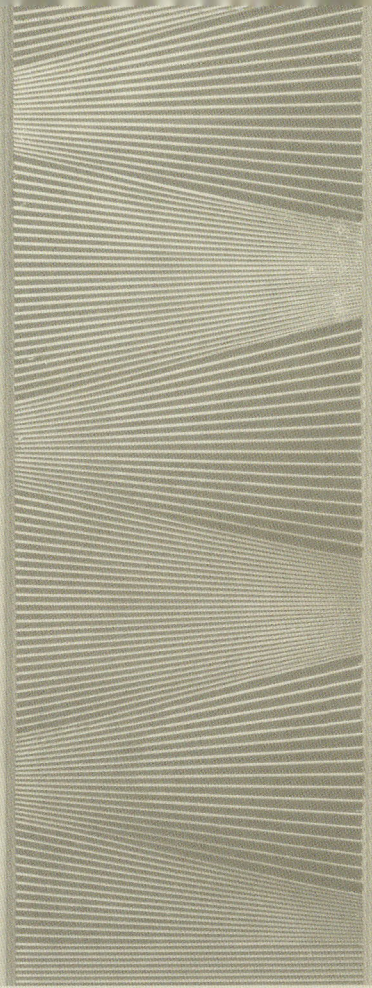

Dedicated, with gratitude, to the unknown craftsman
who created the fan reed.

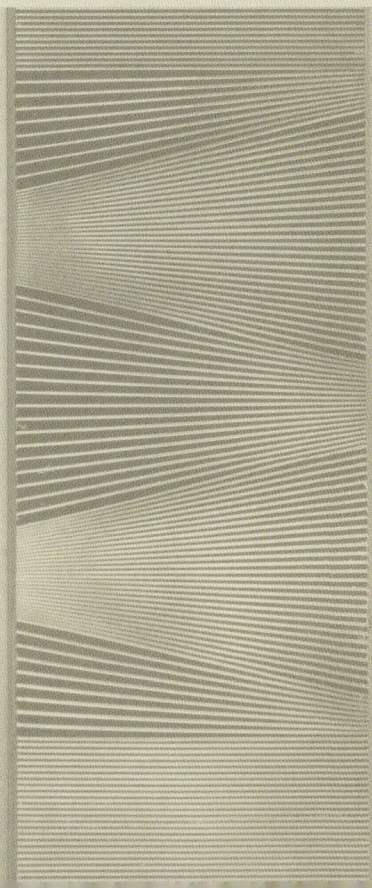

Life spins the thread time weaves the pattern god designed

The fabric of the stuff he leaves to men of noble mind

Carolyn Hazard

The Weaver, a bronze bas-relief sculpture by Daniel Chester French, 1920, located on the grounds of the South Kingstown Public Library, in Peace Dale, Rhode Island, was dedicated to Rowland Hazard and his sons, owners of the Peace Dale Manufacturing Company, a thriving textile mill in the 1800s.

Contents

Foreword

Many years ago when I started weaving, one of my first books, *Step by Step Weaving* by Nell Znamierowski, began: "Weaving can be defined simply as the interlacing of threads at right angles to form a web or fabric. However, it is much more than this in terms of the excitement and satisfaction that you will find in the actual process of creating a fabric."[1]

The weaver, bound by the many constraints placed on this simple definition—perpendicular threads, a need to have a cohesive fabric structure, available materials, loom size and features—often searches for methods to design more complex and original textile forms.

Curves and roundness in a system of perpendicular threads have long been sought by weavers. Patterned damask comes close to registering curves if executed in very fine threads in very small units. Weft-faced tapestry techniques can convey roundness. Deflected threads can create interesting visual effects. Warp distortion is more subtle, and using the ondulé reed to produce curved lines is a lovely way to create unique textiles.

It was a watershed moment in both my weaving and our business when Pat Foster in Great Britain (a contributor to this book) inquired about sourcing an ondulé reed to expand her weaving horizons. Hans, my husband and business partner, explored reed manufacturers worldwide and searched for suppliers—finally settling on a German reedmaker who supplies remaining textile mills in the area with custom reeds. From there, I received my first reed to test the concept so we could better serve customer wishes. Together with the reedmaker we tested ideas for suspending the reeds and developing effective mechanisms for raising and lowering them. That was the easy part. Designing with a new tool that is relatively undocumented has been a challenge.

To date, there have been sparse references to the background and use of ondulé reeds. Finally, Norma Smayda has translated her intense interest in developing textiles with undulations into what is the first publication to explore ondulé reeds, with rich examples from textile artists using these reeds, as well as tips for designing and weaving with the reed. I'm looking forward to exploring the ideas contained here and hope that you find new inspiration for creative handwoven fabrics using the ondulé reed.

Sara von Tresckow
The Woolgatherers Ltd.
Fond du Lac, Wisconsin

Winter Wonderland. Yardage of mohair, lurex, and textured yarns, woven by Sara von Tresckow; photo: Sara von Tresckow.

Acknowledgments

My sincere thanks:

To Augusta Uhlenbeck, Kadi Pajupuu, Judy Dumke, and Mike Friton, who responded quickly when I asked for historical information and descriptions of their unusual approaches to ondulé textiles.

To Larry Ackmann, for initial photography and the term "Proper Puckers."

To Cathy English, who offered encouragement from the beginning, and helped create the PowerPoint presentation for my first ondulé talk.

To Tom Smayda, for his enthusiasm for my weaving projects, especially those in ondulé, for generating ideas and drawings with AutoCAD, and for always being supportive.

To Polly Poulin, for her expertise with graphics.

To first readers Trisha Easton, Barbara Herbster, and Margaret Moone, for viewing the manuscript with a critical eye, offering insight, encouragement, and invaluable suggestions.

To Jeff Mee, for the supplementary beater-shuttle, for devising ways to mount my weavings for photography and for exhibit, and for his remarkable computer expertise.

To Tim Staley, for mounting two pieces for exhibition.

To Emiko Nakano, for locating Japanese information on the fan reed, and to Rowland and Chinami Ricketts for their translations from the Japanese.

To John Marshall, for so willingly sharing photos of his remarkable Japanese textile collection, and his knowledge of the pieces I selected.

To Hans von Tresckow, who helped immeasurably with his AutoCAD expertise to design my two hybrid reeds, answered many questions, and shared his knowledge of reed making (Appendix II).

To Margaret Arafat, Pat Foster, Amy Putansu, Karina Nielsen Rios, Anne Selim, and Jean Hosford, who greatly increased the scope of this book with their contributions.

To Sara von Tresckow, who introduced me to the fan reed and ondulé textiles, and has continued to offer encouragement and answer questions.

To RoS, for working her creative magic to design a book I am truly proud of.

To my editor, Sandra Korinchak, for her wisdom and good humor in guiding me through the publication process, and for answering all my questions, no matter how foolish.

To Nat Rea, photographer extraordinaire, who saw value in my woven work and worked tirelessly to show my textiles to their best advantage. His photographs bring the book to life.

And especially to Gretchen White, my "sewist," first reader, ready cook, advisor, and friend. I can truly say that without Gretchen's encouragement, perseverance, wisdom, and untold hours there would be no book. Gretchen "had my back" throughout this project.

There aren't enough adjectives to adequately express my appreciation to you all.

Section One

1| Prelude

"Why are you a weaver?" This question was the opening of an interesting discussion. One response resonated with me: "Because I like graph paper. The grid of warp and weft." This chapter is an introduction to the journey of my weaving life.

I was first exposed to handweaving while living in Norway in the mid-sixties. Seeing luxurious blankets labeled "HANDWOVEN" in a large Oslo craft shop made me wonder if that was something I could learn to do. I sought out the Monica Skolen Weaving School, took a summer course, and was hooked. That year I bought a small Monica table loom which has string heddles and a swinging beater. This loom is still in use in my weaving school. A few years later, again living in Norway, I located a large well-established craft school, Baerum Husflidsforening, and took many courses, weaving nearly full-time for a year. I bought what remains my loom of choice, an 8-shaft, 54" countermarch Glimåkra Standard, which has been upgraded to a 10-shaft, 12-treadle loom. Thus my weaving career began with the influence of Scandinavian design, colors, and yarns, and a thorough grounding in weave structures.

Living in Rhode Island, the cradle of American industrial weaving and hand-loom traditions, it is not surprising that the work of William Henry Harrison Rose, aka Weaver Rose (1841–1913), and Bertha Gray Hayes (1878–1947) would play a large role in my work. However, this might not have happened except for two fortuitous occurrences. In 1974, I returned to Rhode Island where I have lived since. When looking for used looms for my new weaving school, I bought a small Hammett loom found in a neighbor's barn. Included in the sale was a fantastic treasure—a packet of papers that, upon opening, turned out to be approximately 270 drafts, handwritten by Weaver Rose and other weavers who predated him.

Worlds Wander summer and winter table runner with an etching of Weaver Rose, lent by North Kingstown Free Library, RI. 38" × 17".

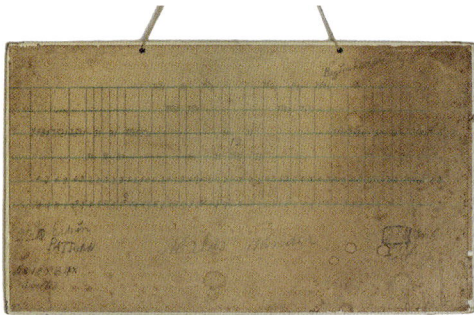

Weaver Rose's draft of *Worlds Wander*, a summer and winter threading.

Weaver Rose's poster for Bugbee & Brownell's Spices, the reverse side of his draft above.

Of course, I pored over them. I learned to decipher his notations, and wove many of his overshot, spot Bronson, and summer and winter patterns. The reverse side of a poster for Bugbee & Brownell's Spices was used by Weaver Rose to record a summer and winter threading he called *Worlds Wander*. The blue and white runner is my woven version of his threading.

Remembrance and Springtime Fancy. Linen table runner in a combined weave of *Remembrance* #7 and *Springtime Fancy* #46. 60" × 22", and two Bertha Gray Hayes sample cards.

Bertha Gray Hayes with some participants of the National Conference of American Handweavers, 1940. Bertha is second from left in second row.

Looms in Saunderstown Weaving School.

Star Log, designed on logarithmic graph paper. 31" × 29". 1977.

The second fortuitous occurrence was that I was entrusted with what became the Bertha Gray Hayes Archives, now belonging to the Weavers' Guild of Rhode Island. Again, poring over her notebooks and sample cards occupied much of my weaving time and resulted in my coauthoring the book, *Weaving Designs by Bertha Gray Hayes: Miniature Overshot Patterns*. I became immersed in her history and in her designs. The center photo on the facing page is of a table runner, in which I combined two of her patterns, and her sample cards from which I took her threadings. The effect I wished to achieve in this runner is one I've seen in Japanese kimono fabrics, of large motifs superimposed on twill weaves. The portrait on the facing page was taken at the 3rd National Conference of American Handweavers in Hartland, Michigan, in 1940. Miss Hayes is pictured second from the left in the second row. She attended, and was an active participant in, these conferences from their inception in 1937 until 1946.

In 1974 I established the Saunderstown Weaving School, with a great deal of help and encouragement from my late husband, Andrew Staley. My collection of looms continues to grow, and my teaching schedule has been enriched to include national conferences and regional workshops.

There are many reasons why I am a weaver. First, for me, is the ability to make cloth, being able to incorporate my own color and design choices. Verticals and horizontals impose neatness and orderliness, qualities I have always liked in weaving. One of my graduate school thesis projects, which was based on the geometry of overshot patterning, was designed using logarithmic graph paper, which forms a grid of decreasing sized rectangles.

11

Log Cabin with Bronson spots
table runner in cottolin. 28" × 11".

Pillow and two samples in cannelé.
Blue sample shows reverse side.
Pillow: 15" × 15".

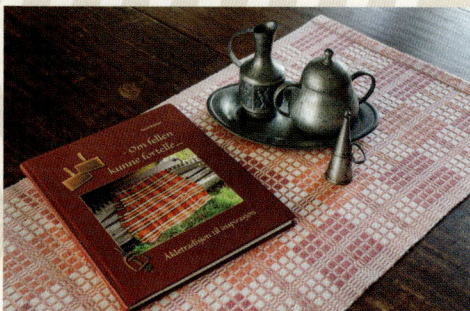

Monk's belt table runner in cottolin. 37" × 16".

I am attracted to the simplicity and order of log cabin weave, and to the added surprise of a spot in the center of each block. I also like the clean lines of monk's belt. As I became involved with the work of Weaver Rose and Bertha Gray Hayes, I was drawn to the charm of overshot patterning. Especially appealing were the curved or rounded motifs, as in the table runner *Remembrance and Springtime Fancy*. Equally pleasing motifs can be developed on five or six shafts in summer and winter, one of my favorite weave structures.

While in graduate school, among other studies I pursued honeycomb weaves, enamored of the undulating weft outlines. A weave structure I now prefer is cannelé, which has undulating wefts, sometimes with undulating warps as well. It has the advantage that both sides of the fabric, although not the same, are good cloth. The photo at left is of a pillow woven in cannelé, plus two samples. The blue sample shows the reverse side. Simplicity and orderliness, with a touch of something unusual, are what I strive for.

I, like other weavers, am attracted to weaving because I like both the stability and the fluidity of cloth. Consciously or not, weavers are drawn to the structure of the grid, of a tensioned warp and a more flexible weft. I know that I also like the ability to push against the grid, to see the lyrical quality in the curving lines that some woven designs provide. Curves offer a contrast to straight lines and rectilinear shapes. When combined in the right proportions curves can engage the viewer and become a WOW factor.

Only recently in my weaving career have I discovered the fan reed and ondulé textiles. In Sara von Tresckow's seminar, "Designing for Ondulé Reeds," given at Convergence 2010 (the biennial conference of the Handweavers Guild of America), I saw her samples of this amazing cloth. Graceful, sinuous lines of warp move apart, then together, in rhythmic waves. Amazing, because before this I thought that warp threads should be straight, parallel to each other, and perpendicular to the weft. Now I saw that they could move, form strikingly graceful undulations, and become shadow-like, woven into subtle hourglass and oval shapes. As the undulations develop, the warp is alternately

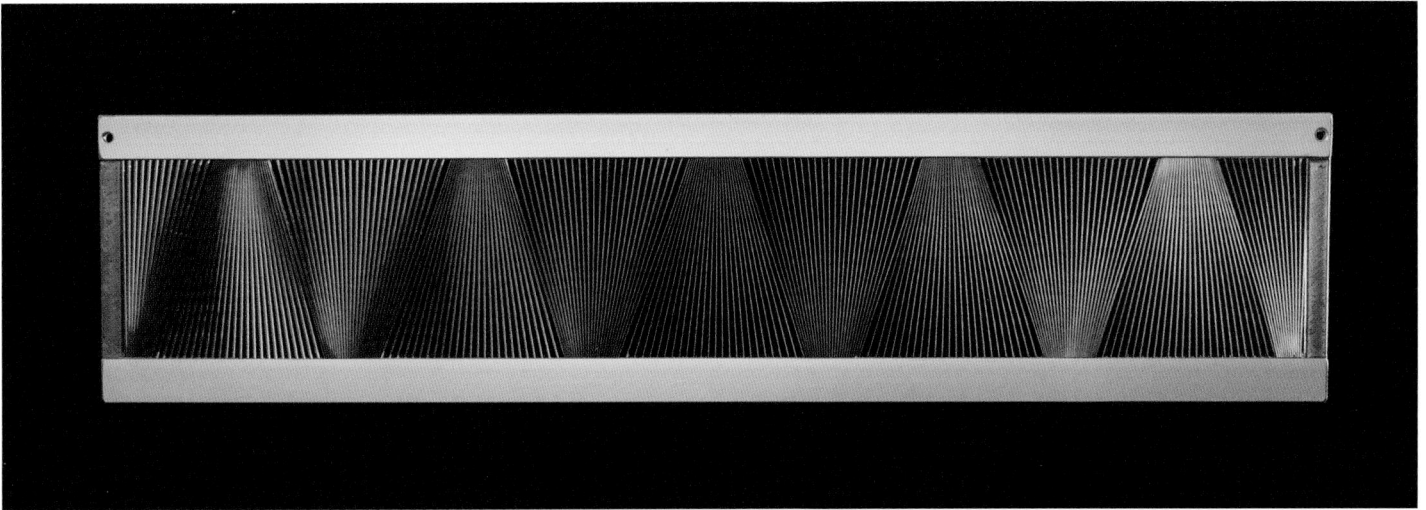

Lars reed. My first fan reed. 12.5 dpi.

spread out and densely crowded, forming areas that vary in texture from grainy and open to smooth and dense. I learned that *ondulé* is a French word meaning undulation, and refers specifically to textiles having curving warp threads. I had found a new direction for my weaving explorations.

I will refer to the reed as a fan reed, and to the fabric as an ondulé textile, having ondulé effects. The reeds in themselves do not undulate, but they cause undulations in the cloth during the weaving process. In the literature, however, we see both terms used: ondulé reed and fan reed.

Fan reeds are composed of wires to separate the dents, but unlike ordinary reeds where all the wires are parallel, these wires are grouped in fan-shaped sections. By incrementally raising or lowering the reed as it beats in the weft, some warp threads curve outwards or inwards from their straight paths.

Ondulé textiles are graceful in appearance and curvaceous, due to the undulations of the warp threads. These textiles are woven using fan-shaped reeds on both mechanical and hand looms. The purpose of this book is to show my work with fan reeds and the striking textiles that can be woven with them. The first section includes a selective history of undulating warp and weft, highlighting the work of Peter Collingwood and Theo Moorman. Lovely examples of historic Japanese textiles are followed by a look at the work of five contemporary ondulé weavers, each using the fan reed in her own style. These five—Margaret Arafat, Pat Foster, Amy Putansu, Karina Nielsen Rios, and Anne Selim—were chosen for the ways they have adapted their looms for the use of the fan reed, for the unusual materials they have chosen, and especially for the lovely and varied ondulé textiles they have created. They are serious fan reed weavers, leading the way to new creative expressions.

2| History of the Fan Reed

I have not found much literature relating to the fan reed. These reeds were first used in mechanized looms at the beginning of the 1800s in France. At some point a handweaver realized their potential and began to weave beautiful cloth with undulating warps. Japanese handweavers began using this reed early in the 1900s. Their textiles are glorious. (Chapter 6 shows selections from John Marshall's Japanese textile collection.)

I think it important to include the information I have found, especially since most of it comes from obscure sources. Some was supplied by Pat Foster and by Jean Hosford, who have also searched for a history of the fan reed. European and American history are covered first, followed by what I have learned of Japanese ondulé textiles.

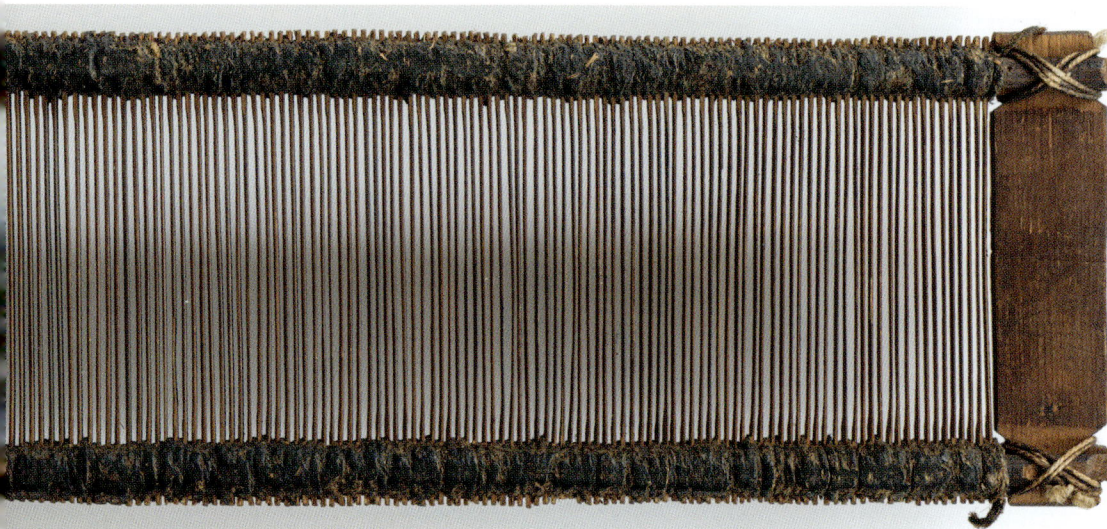

A cane reed, made of reed, tarred string and wooden half rounds. 14 dpi. 3.5" × 44".

The reed, held in place by the beater, serves two purposes. It separates the warp threads, holding them in place and parallel to each other. In addition, the reed is that part of a loom used to push the weft yarn into place with an even and consistent beat.

In 1726 John Kay, who was apprenticed to a reed maker at age fourteen, developed the first metal reeds, using polished wire, flattened iron, and brass. Before that, reeds were composed of reed or cane.[1] The cane was split and then bound between ribs of wood. Later, modern reeds were made of metal wires which were flattened, straightened, given rounded edges, then bound between two half round ribs of wood, held together with tarred string, and more recently, set into epoxy.

The earliest reference found for the fan reed is John Murphy's 1827 *A Treatise on the Art of Weaving* with his description and two diagrams for figuring shaded silks.[2,3]

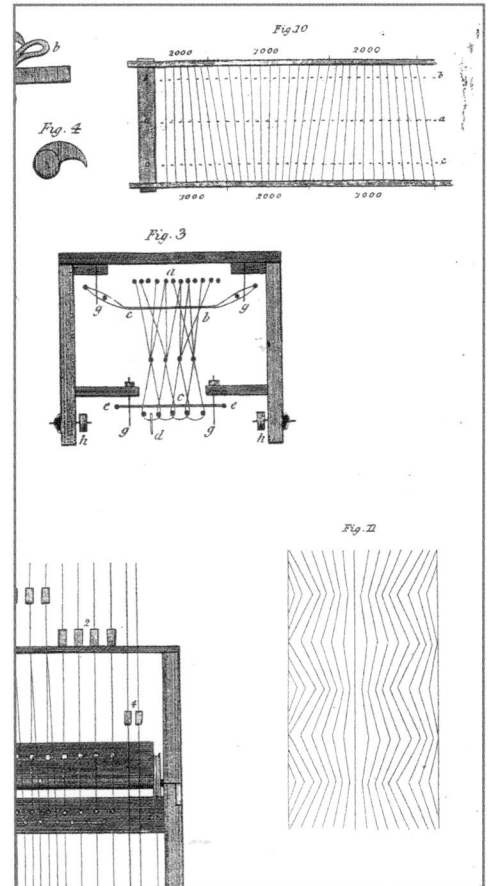

New Method of Figuring Shaded Silks. – A new method of figuring shaded silks has just (January 1827) been introduced from France, which is likely to give a pleasing diversity to this branch of manufacture. The figure is produced by a peculiar construction of the reed, and a vertical motion given it by the weaver's feet. The reed is made in alternate spaces, varying in fineness from one rib to the other; for example, from a 1000 to a 2000 reed; but those spaces which are of the fineness of a 1000 reed, in one side or rib, are of the fineness of a 2000 reed, in the other side or rib; the splits or dents standing obliquely, as represented at Fig. 10. plate 13. The machine in which these reeds are made is so constructed, that two turns of the wooping are taken round the rib between the splits in the coarser spaces, and only one turn where they are finer. The reed is about seven inches deep between the ribs; and, as already observed, has a vertical motion given to it in the lay, by means of a rack or other adequate apparatus, communicating with the treadles by cords; and consequently, where the finer parts of the reed come in contact with the face of the cloth, the warp becomes condensed, and shows much deeper in color: and the effect is the reverse, where the coarser parts of the reed strike the cloth. In other words, when the centre of the reed a a, Fig. 10. plate 13, strikes the cloth, the fabric will be uniform; but when it is raised till the line c c, for example, comes in contact with the cloth, the spaces marked 2000 will be finer in proportion as the line c c approaches the under rib, and those marked 1000 so much coarser than the medium sett; and when the reed is sunk till the line b b strikes the cloth, the effect will be the reverse; so that by gradually raising and sinking the reed alternately, the threads of warp will assume the waved appearance represented in Fig. 11. plate 13. It is evident, however, that this figure is woven by a uniform motion of the reed up and down in the lay; but where the motion of the reed varied, which might be effected by a rack and spring shifted by the weaver's hand, as in weaving lappets, a proportionate diversity of patterns would be produced; and probably an apparatus similar to the lappet wheel might be applied with advantage.

New Method of Figuring Shaded Silks. From Murphy's *A Treatise on the Art of Weaving.*

Plate 13. From Murphy's *A Treatise on the Art of Weaving.*

Ondulé weaving with a fan reed was developed in industry, with warp ondulé fabrics preceding those of weft ondulé. Another early text is *Falcot's Weave Compendium*. It contains a diagram for three fan reeds, (fan, parallelogram composed of two half fans, and half fan), showing various curves that can be obtained with each, as well as a mechanism used to raise and lower the reed. This mechanism of cog wheels and ratchets works when the shed is opened, and is controlled by punch pattern cards. As the reed rises or falls during weaving, the width of the fabric increases or decreases and a shaped edge is made. Ribbons were woven with curved edges. Falcot's figures 6 through 11 show the various curved and angled shapes that can be woven with the three pictured reeds (Falcot's figures 1, 3, and 4). Different reeds give different effects; Fig. 8 is produced with Fig. 3; Fig. 9 with the reed in Fig. 4.[4]

In 1898 E. A. Posselt described the fan reed and its use in obtaining novel effects in cloth.[5] A critical part of the operation had been further refined. As the beater is pushed back from the fell, it is moved to the height which gives a shed allowing the shuttle to pass freely across the web. As the beater is brought forward, it is lowered or raised to the position which will give the proper placement for producing curved warp lines. In 1906 H. Nisbet detailed other uses.[6] He described specialized reeds having only fans that expanded upwards, leaving voids where they contract at the base. These reeds were designed to produce perforations in the cloth, both horizontally and vertically. I can't help but marvel at the idea of being able to weave holes in cloth in predetermined spots using a fan-shaped reed, such as those shown on page 18.

Others continued to patent methods of raising and lowering the fan reed.[7] Later, F. Fielden patented a special ondulé mechanism that was said to be much easier to install and remove from the loom when no longer needed. This loom was also equipped with "leno motion" for weaving leno or "cross woven" effects.[8] When producing ondulé cloth, leno is an important technique to keep warp ends at the edges of the fans from wandering. Charles Labriffe, a well-known textile teacher in Roubaix, France, wrote *Manuel de Tissage* in 1928, describing the difficulties of weaving plain weave with a fan reed which had ratchet wheels to raise and lower the reed. He pictured two reeds: one is a single large fan with wires spreading out from a central base position, and the second with parallel wires sloping in one direction only. He emphasized that leno is necessary to hold the warp undulations in place after finishing.[9]

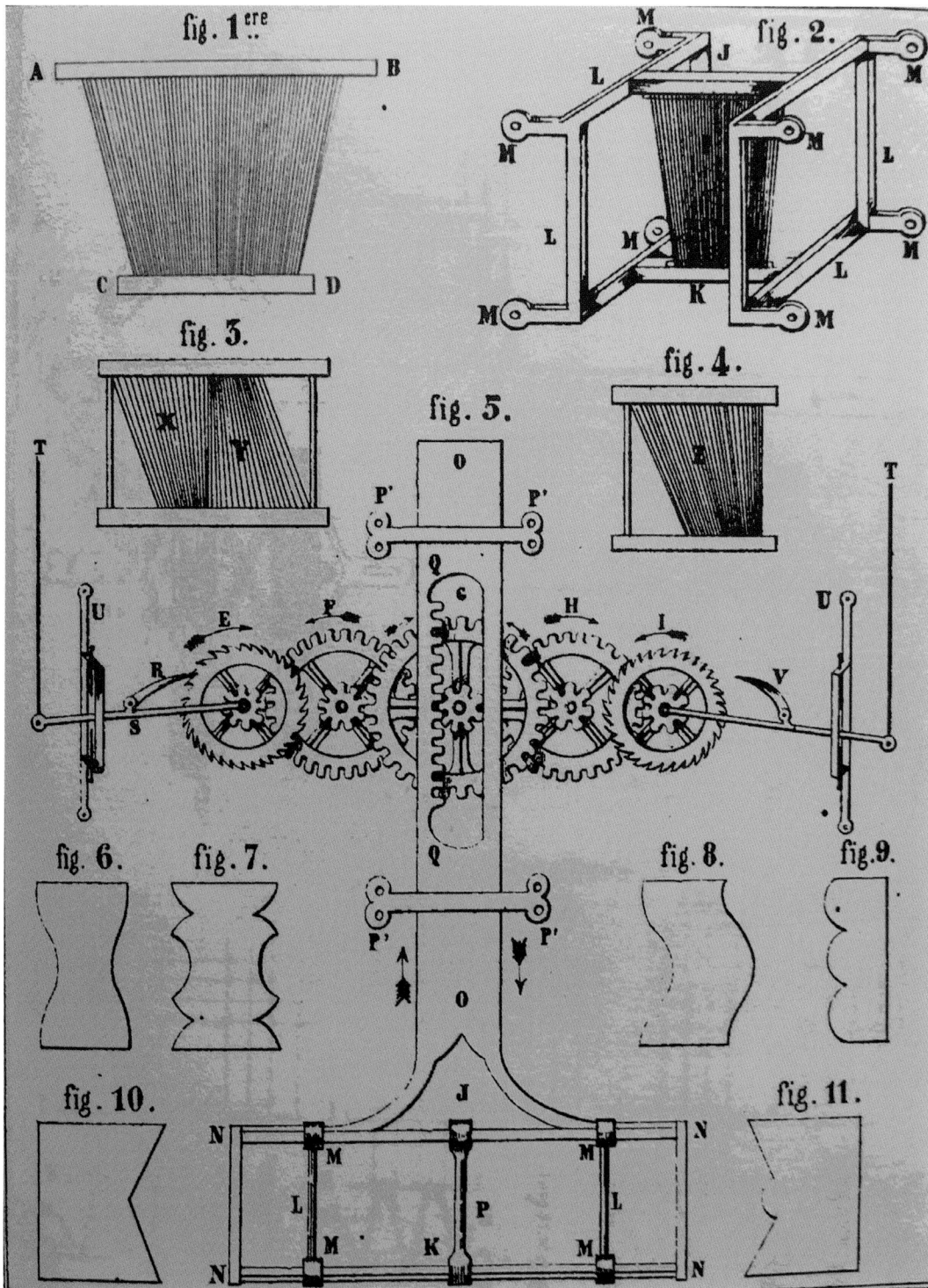

Plate 221. Peigne Conique from *Falcot's Weave Compendium.*

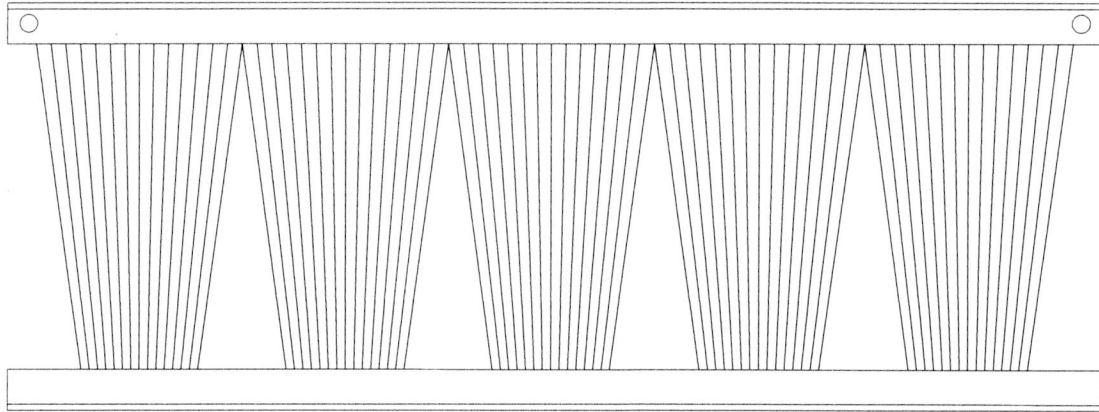

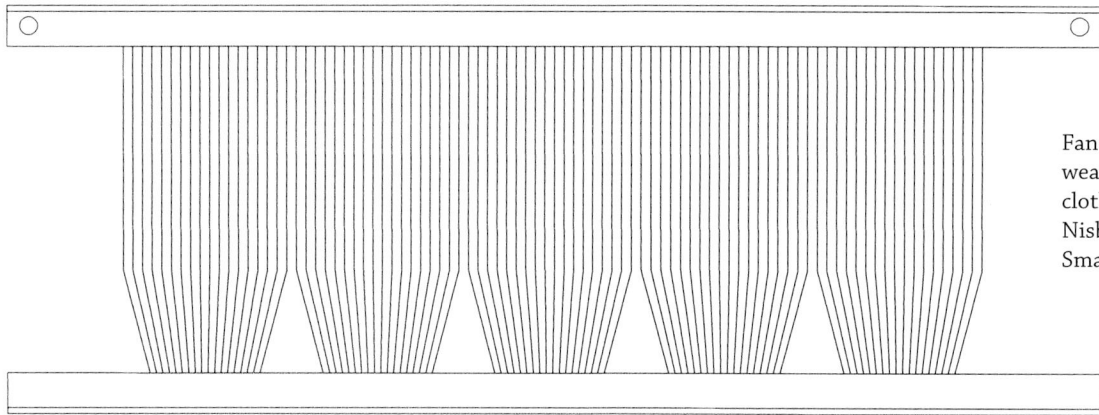

Fan reeds designed to weave perforations in cloth. Adapted from H. Nisbet; figure: Tom Smayda.

Z. J. Grosicki edited *Watson's Advanced Textile Design, Fourth and Seventh Editions*, 1913. Ondulé fabrics are defined with a description of a typical fan reed, of a fan reed with wires all slanted the same direction, and of the mechanism for raising and lowering the reed. Also, a weft ondulé effect is described, produced by the use of easing bars to tighten alternate sections of warp ends.[10]

In the early 1930s New England mills were manufacturing ondulé fabrics, but as they were expensive to make, production soon ceased. John H. Strong in *Fabric Structure*, 1947, included descriptions of both warp and weft ondulé, and said that warp ondulé was never produced on a large scale but that dictates of fashion could bring it back at any time.[11] Curtains and drapery, scarves and shawls have been woven using this reed. Small fan-shaped reeds were used industrially at the start of the twentieth century for making "slipper uppers and other small shaped pieces."[12]

At Clemson University, W. E. Tarrant experimented with less costly ways to weave weft and warp ondulé to benefit industry, by simplifying the weaving processes without complicated attachments.[13]

18

The Burcklé or trapezium reed, made today, consists of a single fan that is used to determine the width of a bout of threads and is used exclusively on industrial warpers. This allows for a small adjustment in warp width by raising or lowering the warp in the reed. The Officina Meccanica Bulgaro, an Italian company that manufactures equipment for industrial looms, makes a movable fan reed. "This application, applied on a Dornier Loom, is composed by a movable reed holder that can hold a special reed with inclined dents which, with a suitable movement, force the warp yarns to change their density. The reed-holder is motorized and it is possible to programme the movements through an industrial computer. The width and the movement direction of the reed are variable at every machine 'beat.'"[14]

Fan reed mechanisms continue to be developed. Patents over the last century number in the hundreds for reeds, reed variations, and mechanisms for raising and lowering the reed. The goal is to weave shoes, socks, shaped curved sleeves, elastic fabric, and more. As recently as 2007 Rongde Ge applied for a patent for "a method for weaving curved warp yarns and a woven fabric." This includes a lifting and descending mechanism that holds the fan reed, and which allows the warp to present a gradual change and an orderly arrangement in the fabric.[15]

Thus, fan reeds and ondulé fabric as produced in industry have been referenced over the years. The information in Nisbet is the most detailed, and in Tarrant the most exploratory. Even with the advantage of online searching for obscure information, it has been a challenge to learn about the origin of the fan reed and its place in history. One clear difference between industrial weaving and handweaving was the early development of mechanisms for raising and lowering the beater, and for holding the fan reed vertical to the fell of the cloth.

In Japan, obi and kimono were woven using the fan reed from the beginning of the 1900s. Its popularity decreased after World War II, with some mills moving to China and other mills closing. Mills in Japan have had a hard time competing with less expensive Chinese goods.[16]

At least one Japanese weaver currently uses old looms to weave with the fan reed. Takeda Masatoshi collects industrial looms from the early twentieth century and has developed a small industry making ondulé textiles. His Factory Oriza produces scarves, shawls, and caps in plant-dyed cotton, silk, linen, and wool.[17] He has even produced warp and weft ondulé in the same fabric, using a reed that combines both. He weaves this with leno, adding specialty heddles to obtain a better shed and to hold the warp threads in place.

Emiko Nakano, a textile artist from Kyoto, sent material from two books, which was translated from the Japanese by Rowland and Chinami Ricketts:

> Yoroke-jima or ondulé stripe is a kind of striped weave that falls into the category of complex weaves. The reed is laid out in a fan pattern, and spreads out the warp yarns into areas of different densities. Yoroke was invented in France and first woven in Japan around 1901 or 1902. Before World War II it was popular in silk and cotton weaves.[18]

> Images [in *Technique of Handweaving*] include a fan reed; a fixed weft yoroke or wave reed; an adjustable weft yoroke reed, which can be rotated to spiral sideways; a notched loom attachment to manually raise or lower the reed; and examples of both warp and weft yoroke cloth. By beating at the top or bottom of the reed the warp yarns can be spread out to create ondulé patterns. Fewer warp yarns create a smooth pattern while more densely packed warp creates a stepped effect.

One of the challenges of this type of weaving, when done with a warp yarn with no stretch, is that the shed opens more on the section of the reed that is more widely sett, and less on the more dense portions of the reed. In order to correct for this, Nishijin weavers from a textile district in Kyoto use a mechanism called a "fumise." This is a type of temporary additional heddle, like that used when weaving leno, that has its own tie-up, which allows the weaver to add additional downward pull on the more densely packed yarns to create a better shed.

On professional looms there is a built-in cam that allows the reed to be adjusted up and down to create a smooth transition of the wave pattern. On handlooms the same effect can be achieved by adjusting the beater up and down with a device that is attached to the loom.

The reeds for weft yoroke are very dimensional, and the pattern of the weave is determined by the shape of the reed. This requires a special attachment to position the reed in the loom. The loom is set up as one would normally for plain weave, but care must be taken to leave enough play in each weft shot to compensate for the path the yarn will travel along the face of the reed.

Adjustable weft yoroke is a unique type of weaving in which the path of the weft yarn changes with each pick. This is done with a special reed and a geared carved metal or wooden template that revolves behind the reed, pushing the dividers in the reed forward to create a wave pattern. The template rotates during weaving, with one full rotation being one repeat. Doing this type of work requires specialized equipment. That said, if you are using a heavier yarn, a similar effect can be achieved by using a bamboo toothpick, a comb, or a carved shuttle [See photo on page 23 of Jeff Mee's contemporary supplementary beater-shuttle]. When using a heavier yarn the weft tends to move a lot more; it was suggested one can dilute wood glue and apply it to the weft yarn during weaving to hold the yarns in place.[19]

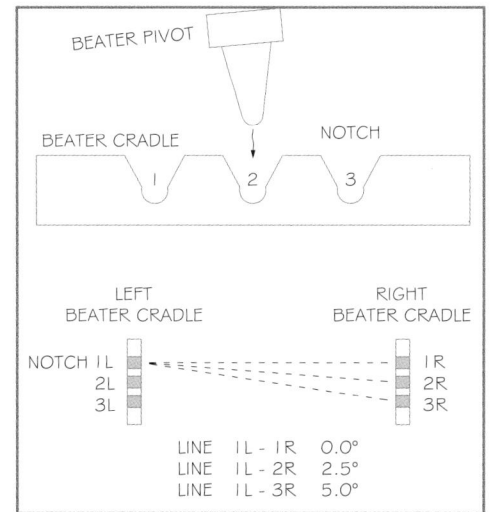

3| The Contoured Weft

A loom, because of its construction, produces a textile with weft threads crossing warp threads at right angles. Should the loom become out of square, a poorly woven textile will result. Some weavers, thinking outside the box, view this as a step towards creating textiles unusual in warp or weft, as did Peter Collingwood.

Judy Dumke wrote "An Angle Fell" in *Complex Weavers Journal*, June 2011, after having seen a DVD of Collingwood and what he called the Angle Fell.[1] He discussed this as a precursor to the development of his macrogauze hangings. The angle fell is the angle at which the reed hits the fell of the cloth as it beats in the weft. Dumke's loom, with an overhead beater, lent itself to exploring this possibility. A distortion of the fell of the cloth is caused by having the reed hit the fell closer to the breast beam at one selvedge than the other. With an overhead beater and three places on the beater cradle to pivot the beater, she was able to explore five different angles for the reed to hit the cloth and produce different angles of the weft. The drawing at right shows the beater and cradle positioning (top is a side view, bottom is an overhead view), and the angles possible. The photo at right shows her sample, woven in twill, with weft curves added by the use of a pin. Varying the beat could add another factor. Dumke says her work was just an exploration. Several of the references call this "breaking the rules." She prefers to think of it as "testing conventions."

Without an overhead beater to achieve this, the reed could be removed from the beater, and held by hand, with the weaver determining the exact angle for the angle fell, varying it to the weaver's taste. I wove a sample as Dumke described, and found the slight irregularities in weft angle beating only looked like poor weaving, and I, too, found no inspiration to pursue this further. Marianne Straub[2] also shows angle fell distortion with zigzag weft striping.

A sample of angle fell, woven by Judy Dumke; photo: Judy Dumke.

Weft ondulé, sometimes called "cross-over" ondulé because it is the picks of weft that assume a wavy character, was described by H. Nisbet[3] as being developed in one of two ways. The first is by means of the Erdmann Reed, so named after its inventor. This shaped or curved reed has vertical wires that form a serpentine line from end to end and produce undulations in the cloth. See the photo on page 59 of the nami or weft ondulé reed used by Karina Nielsen Rios.

A second means of causing weft distortion "may be produced in looms furnished with ordinary reeds, by dividing warp threads (immediately after leaving the warp beam) into groups according to the length of the wave required, and by passing alternate groups of threads over one bar, and intermediate groups over a second bar. By slowly oscillating both bars in contrary directions, a gradually varying degree of tension will be imparted to warp threads, whereby the two divisions of threads will be alternately tautened and slackened. This will cause the picks of weft to assume more or less wavy lines, according to the disparity between the tension of the two divisions of threads."[4] We can see this effect happening by mistake in our weaving when we have an unfortunate few (or more) warp ends that have become tangled and are suddenly under more tension than the rest. The weft does not lie straight across the fell, but forms an indentation in the cloth. The opposite happens if some warp ends are too loose, and the weft lies beyond the fell at that place.

Incorporating this idea, Collingwood tied unused treadles with cords to groups of warp threads for eccentric tensioning. Depressing a treadle tightened a group of warp threads, causing wavy picks. Harriet Tidball[5] shows an early example of his weft ondulé, in which he used eccentric warp tensioning through rocker bars. A beautiful example of his angle fell weaving is pictured in Irene Waller's book, *Textile Sculptures*.[6]

Weft ondulé continues to be explored by a number of weavers using a variety of techniques. Straub[7] describes honeycomb treadling on a cell weave to produce densely woven cells surrounded by single distorted weft picks. Tidball gives numerous examples of using weave structures to obtain undulating wefts. A technique used by fiber artists in the 1960s was to place an extraneous object such as colored glass, a sea shell, or a seed pod in the shed, and weave around it, pressing the weft in by hand. Once the cloth was off the loom, the object could be removed, leaving a permanent space, or left in place as part of the finished piece. Fiber artists Luella Williams and Ted Hallman wove hangings in this manner.[8]

Japanese weavers use a supplementary undulating beater and shuttle combination that is designed as one tool and called a nami or namiosa. The top photo on the facing page shows a contemporary copy of a nami made by Jeff Mee, and weft undulation in fabric on the loom.

Kadi Pajupuu is a textile artist and inventor, working at Tartu Art College, Estonia, where she has developed equipment to assist in producing curves in warp or weft. Her Stepping Reed, designed to make waves in the weft, is built with bicycle spokes, pipe clamps, and plastic tubes. Those spokes, when placed forward of a horizontal rod in alternate sections, beat the weft into curves.[9]

Experimentation with weft ondulé is continuing today at Nike. Using a shaped reed, sports footwear innovation engineer Mike Friton is currently exploring curved weft hand-woven fabric with the goal of weaving a seamless shoe in its entirety, reducing waste and costly make-up time. The length of his reed buckles into a wave formation, while the wires are equally spaced vertically. This fabric will not have the usual bias stretch, and will be more malleable to form the toe of a shoe.[10]

Top: Supplementary beater-shuttle, used in weaving an undulating weft pattern. Shuttle by Jeff Mee.

Stepping Reed designed by Kadi Pajupuu, used in weaving wefts in curves; photo: Ole Akhoej.

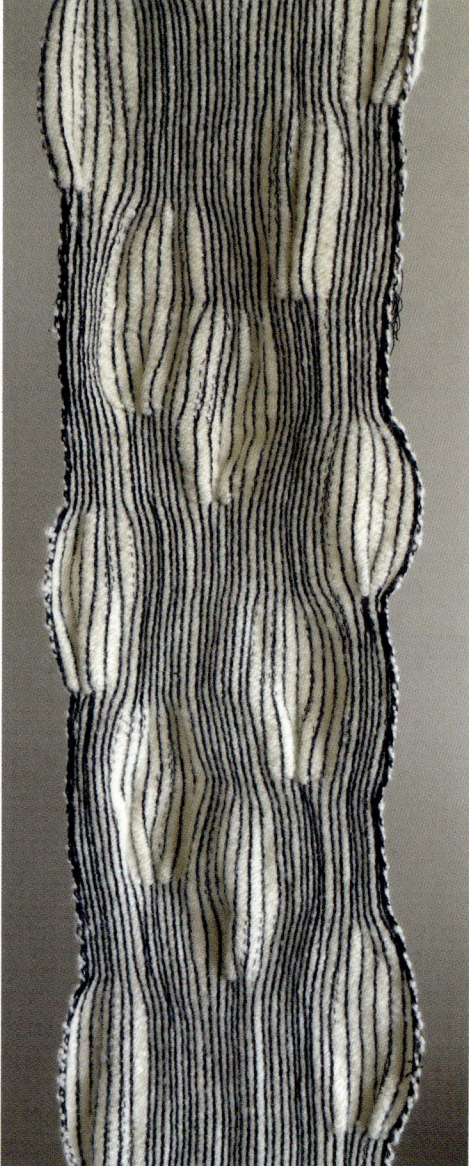

Weaving by Juula Pardi, using a 5-Module RailReed; photo: Ole Akhoej.

4 | The Contoured Warp

Several Scandinavian weavers are combining the Japanese aesthetic and mechanical adaptations with their fan reed weaving. Åsa Pärson and Japanese-born Kazuyo Nomura both weave ondulé textiles, and both have studied at the Swedish Technical School of Weaving in Borås, Sweden. Pärson first used the fan reed in Borås and continued her studies in Japan at the Kawashima Textile School, where she used both the yoroke (fan) reed and the namiosa (weft ondulé) reed for her textiles. Back in Sweden she is now designing ondulé textiles for industrial production in Japanese mills, where there are still some looms equipped with fan reeds. Pärson also designs fan reeds for her own use. She weaves with fine yarns, experiments with weave structures, and especially likes the effect of light playing on satin weaves. She weaves on a large countermarch loom with an overhead beater, much like my Glimåkra, using her Swedish fan reed and two Japanese hybrid reeds.[1]

Kazuyo Nomura has lived and woven in Sweden for several years. Her fan reed was made to her specifications at the Markaryd (Sweden) reed factory. The Markaryd reed manufacturer also produces fan reeds for industry, where they are used in winding on warps. Nomura at first suspended her fan reed with Texsolv cords. Later she acquired a loom with a beater that makes it easier to raise and lower the reed. She weaves exhibition pieces in damask with linen, rather than in plain weave with cotton or silk as is traditional in Japan.[2]

Kerstin Froberg from Bergdala, Sweden, writes of weaving with the fan reed. Using a countermarch loom with an overhead beater, she drilled additional holes in the vertical swords of her beater to raise and lower the reed even more, and sometimes uses every other hole for a more dramatic curve. She works with different fibers and different weave structures, sharing her successes and failures. She mangles the folds or the wrinkles that occur naturally in ondulé textiles.[3]

An article in *Vävmagasinet* reports on active weaving groups in Denmark, where interest in the fan reed has spread from Borås, Sweden to Zealand, Denmark. There a countermarch loom was set up with a fan reed for members to use at their weaving center.[4]

24

Perhaps there is a resurgence of interest in this technique in Japan, as Nakano suggests. In 2016 Japanese weaver, Yukiko Yokoyama, had a solo exhibit at the Tenri Cultural Institute of New York, showing her dramatic, billowing ondulé textiles. We know that there is a connection between contemporary Japanese and Western weavers. Danish weaver Karina Nielsen Rios and Swedish weaver Åsa Pärson studied warp and weft ondulé in Japan, and Japanese weaver Kazuyo Nomura now weaves in Sweden. Use of the fan reed in Scandinavia and Great Britain may be facilitated in part because weavers there often use a countermarch loom with an overhead beater, making it easier to gradually raise and lower the reed. A counterbalance loom is more commonly used in Japan.

Suzi Ballenger had an open top reed made to her specifications by Gowdey Reed Company, located in Central Falls, Rhode Island. Once the weaving is underway she removes the top baulk of the reed and systematically moves groups of warp threads sideways, enabling a warpwise undulation. Because the warp is threaded in heddles, warp threads must be kept in the correct threading sequence; hence they cannot cross over each other as Collingwood does in his macrogauzes. Open top reeds could once be purchased for any denting from 4 to 25 dents per inch (dpi) and any length requested, but this selection is no longer available. The photo on page 27

RailReed, designed by Kadi Pajupuu, used in creating warp undulations; photo: Ole Akhoej.

shows two open top reeds. The older one has 6 dpi, and was handmade by removing the top baulk and replacing it with a grooved wooden rib to hold the wires in place. The second has 12 dpi and was made recently by Gowdey Reed Company. In both cases the top baulk is held firmly in place by the top of the beater.

Kadi Pajupuu found weaving with both the fan reed and the open top reed too constricting or too complicated. She developed the RailReed, a device to make the process of warp undulation easier. It is a sliding reed consisting of sections made from bicycle spokes. The sliding modules can be adjusted individually. The warp threads can be moved sideways, changing the fabric width and varying the sett to create interesting forms or folds in the fabric.

She also uses rigid heddle sections, made to her specifications, so she can cross entire sections of warp yarns. The rigid heddles are made with especially large eyes, and they and her Stepping Reeds and RailReeds are designed for use with her heavy wool yarns.[5]

Monika Correa, a contemporary fiber artist from Mumbai, exhibited at the Pucker Gallery in Boston, Massachusetts, July 2014. She produces large monochromatic fiber pieces, removing the center portion of the reed, leaving those warp threads the freedom to move unrestrained. A combination of natural warp movement and, possibly, hand manipulation accentuates the airy quality of her work. Later she may return to the normal woven grid. Her works are less structured than textiles made using a fan reed.[6]

L. Thomas in *Smart Clothes and Wearable Technology* discusses the value of the woven structure on shaped smart clothing. A project called A-POC, "A Piece of Cloth," involves Jacquard woven double cloth that requires minimal sewing to produce finished garments. When weaving double weave with the fan reed it is possible to make seamless tapered tubes. Thus, in garment construction there is now the opportunity for less make-up time and little or no fabric waste.[7]

Photographs and information about the work of the weavers mentioned above can be found in their blogs and in magazines.

Two open top reeds, one handmade, the other made c. 2014 by Gowdey Reed Company.

An interesting plainness is the most difficult and precious thing to achieve.

Mies van der Rohe

5| Two Innovative British Weavers of the Twentieth Century Pave the Way

Peter Collingwood

Peter Collingwood developed methods of manipulating warp and weft to produce curves without using a fan reed. There is no indication that he ever used one. Collingwood's interest in warp movement led to his development of a method to shift his warp threads from side to side, producing his large macrogauze hangings.

He used rigid heddle segments, set into a special beater, and changed their positions within the beater to get the diagonals he wanted. He did not use regular shafts and reed. Instead, at the back of the loom, he weighted many individual warp sections, each corresponding to a rigid heddle. He then raised and lowered the heddles in the beater, hung on springs, to get the two sheds necessary for plain weave.

Narrow rigid heddle sections are now readily available in varying slot and hole spacings (5, 8, 10, and 12 spaces per inch). On my Glimåkra loom I am able to get two sheds by moving the loom's swords vertically from position 1 to position 8. The photo on the facing page shows my effort to duplicate the technique Collingwood used in creating his macrogauze hangings.

Woven textiles typically consist of biaxial threads, interlaced at right angles. However, there are a few examples where this is not the case. Triaxial weaving consists of three sets of threads that interlace at 60° angles. This produces a light, strong, and flexible fabric. NASA developed a power loom to produce these textiles. In *The Maker's Hand*, Collingwood describes the unusually beautiful triaxial pieces woven by Isamu Miyajima on a handloom developed for this purpose. As Collingwood says, "Mr. Miyajima has provided splendid confirmation of my belief that there are still things to be invented in textiles at the low-level, non-computer, end of technology."[1]

Collingwood, in discussing the effect the Industrial Revolution had on textiles, commented that new machines could do with greater speed and precision what human hands had already been doing for millennia. The inventions brought about a change in the amount of yardage woven in a day,

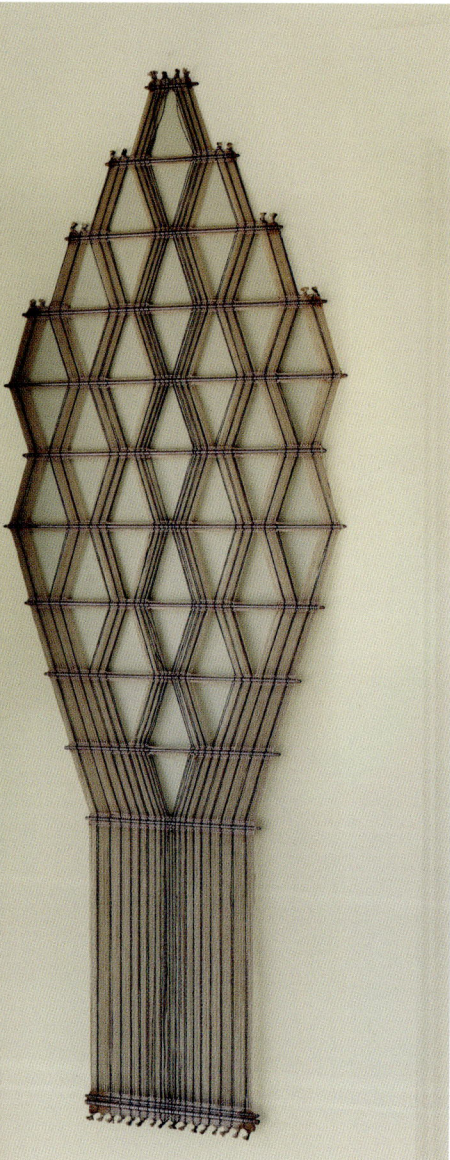

Macrogauze Hanging by Peter Collingwood, in linen and wood. 46" × 16.5".

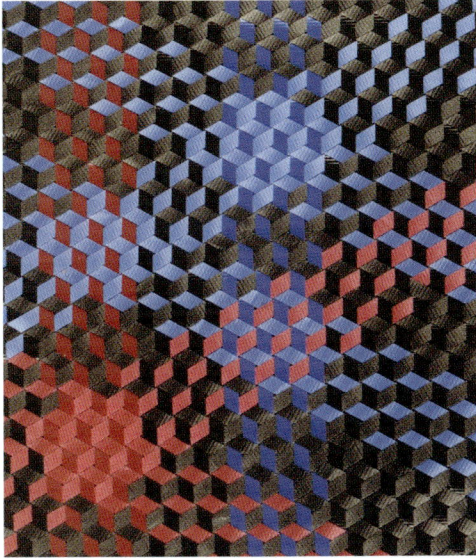

Triaxial weaving. *Fireworks*, Elizabeth Lang-Harris; a curling ribbon prototype. Photo courtesy Schiffer Publishing.

Simple reappears when complex is exhausted.

Peter Collingwood

not a change in its type or quality. "I believe strongly that there are discoveries still waiting to be made of quite another type, unconnected with picks per minute. As examples of this type, already in existence, I would include Mr. Miyajima's beautifully simple loom which gives triaxial interlacing and perhaps my own shaft-switching system. Both offer the handweaver possibilities denied him before, not in the realm of speed, but in structure and personal control over design."[2] To this I would add Collingwood's use of rigid heddles to create his macrogauzes, and the use of fan reeds by handweavers.

Seven rigid heddle sections with a "macrogauze" weaving in progress.

29

Theo Moorman

This book, a lovely and loving tribute to Theo Moorman, a famed British weaver, contains many examples of her work with the fan reed. *Seashore*, c. 1986, shown on the book's cover, is composed of many graceful fan weavings attached to the final piece.

Theo Moorman developed a simple fan reed in the 1960s,[3] which she used in weaving many of her small hangings, as well as for elements incorporated into her larger hangings and church textiles. Her book, *Weaving as an Art Form*, became a source of much inspiration for me. As an MFA student in visual design at the University of Massachusetts-Dartmouth, I had a teaching assistantship which included the welcome responsibility of working my way through her book, weaving samples for the textile department's reference library. This enabled me to concentrate on what we now know as the Moorman technique. "A loom can be a simple frame or an elaborate multiharness structure. The elaborations add to and subtract from design possibilities. For example, a beater and reed are needed for weaving a length of cloth, but if we discard these things we are immediately free from the restrictions of the rectangle."[4]

I first used the Moorman technique to design and weave curtain material for faculty office windows at UMass-Dartmouth, and then in projects for my thesis. I was fortunate to meet Moorman some years later at the New England Weavers Seminar and hear her lecture. I have one of her small fan weavings.

Other thoughts of Moorman's I find particularly inspirational:

"The comparatively recent emergence of the artist-designer-weaver, emphatically one person, seems to me to constitute a major breakthrough in

Book cover: *Theo Moorman 1907-1990* by Hilary Diaper. Photo is of her woven hanging, *Seashore*, c. 1980.

30

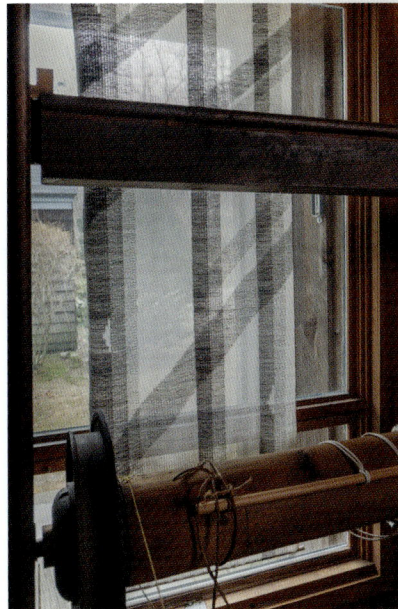

Fan weaving by Theo Moorman, linen, wood, stones with crochet caps. 20" × 2.5". c. 1981.

the history of the craft . . . . A wall hanging in a room fulfils the same essential function as a drawing or a painting, even though it is far removed from either in appearance. It is intended to please and interest the eye and arouse thoughts and emotions in the mind."[5]

"A design concept for a piece of weaving seems to me to derive from two main sources. On the one side we have the physical content of the work, that is, the materials, the equipment, and the techniques available. Coupled with these is the practical objective or use for which the article is intended. On the other side, we have the mental and emotional content, the spark which lights up and brings to life the physical content. I think of these as two converging streams. It is at the point where they mingle and become a river that the design in its entirety comes to life in the mind of the weaver."[6]

"I believe that a woven hanging should always show something of the unique qualities of the craft."[7]

Moorman's first fan shapes were woven by fastening narrow warps to the center of the cloth beam, threading them, and then spreading or fanning them out evenly on the warp beam. She wove narrow hangings which she weighted with interesting stones.

She describes how she refined her technique by making a specially prepared fan reed, using very simple materials. She claimed she was not a carpenter and anyone could make this reed. To make the reed she used seven pairs of wooden skewers, each pair tied together at each end. The skewers were laced close together at one end and fastened between two wooden slats. At the other end, pairs of skewers were spaced 1 cm. apart and glued onto a dowel. Her warp was composed of forty-two ends of fine mercerized cotton (80/2), threaded to plain weave and sleyed seven ends per dent in the six dents or spaces she created.

"It was not fixed in the beater, but was suspended from the top of the loom on cords which could be easily adjusted in length. Weaving was started with the reed in a high position so the warp threads were forced closely together, forming a narrow web. The reed was then lowered by gradual stages so that the warp was constantly widening."[8] An attractive stone was hung as a weight below the reed. She sometimes threaded her warp to a 4-shaft double cloth and wove pockets to insert flat pebbles.

Linen curtain in Theo Moorman technique, designed for faculty office, University of Massachusetts-Dartmouth. 60" × 23". 1977.

6| Japanese Ondulé Textiles
from the Collection of John Marshall

John Marshall, a reknowned American fiber artist with a special love for Japanese textiles, first went to Japan in 1972, at the age of seventeen, to be apprenticed in traditional doll making. This process included studies in a wide range of dyeing and weaving techniques. Since that time he has specialized in the katazome (stencil) process of silk dyeing with natural dyes and tsutsugaki (cone drawing). He designs and sews one-of-a-kind clothing, using katazome to color the fabrics.

He has generously shared eighteen photographs of textiles from his personal collection. These textiles date from the mid- to late Showa era, specifically from the 1960s to 1980. Mizuori, translated as *water weave*, is created by manipulating the warp and/or the weft with a pick, in a primitive technique called bruising. Nami-ori or wave-weave is done with combs or undulating beater bars. Marshall reports having seen, but has no sample of, a Japanese textile in which the reed is both a fan reed and a wave undulating beater bar. All photographs in this chapter are by John Marshall.

Weft beater manipulated silk. A very fancy, but still casual kimono. Notice the eccentricities in the undulations. This may be achieved with a comb, but is more commonly done with a set of beater bars. Each has a slightly different severity of undulation, and they are used sequentially. The sequence may be reversed to move the peak of the undulation. The bars may be gradually shifted to change the line-up of the waves.

Weft beater manipulated leno silk. This is an example of the use of the beater bars described above. There only needs to be five bars in this set, starting with a straight one, then a slightly curved one, and so on. An occasional straight weft thread helps to stabilize the fabric. This is a detail of a summer obi, the leno weave helps to keep the threads spaced without bruising.

Weft beater bar warp face silk. Unlike the previous example, only one curvaceous beater bar is needed here. The peaks and valleys do not line up. This is achieved by shifting the beater to the right or left and contributes to the stability of the fabric. This garment is an obi that may be used year round.

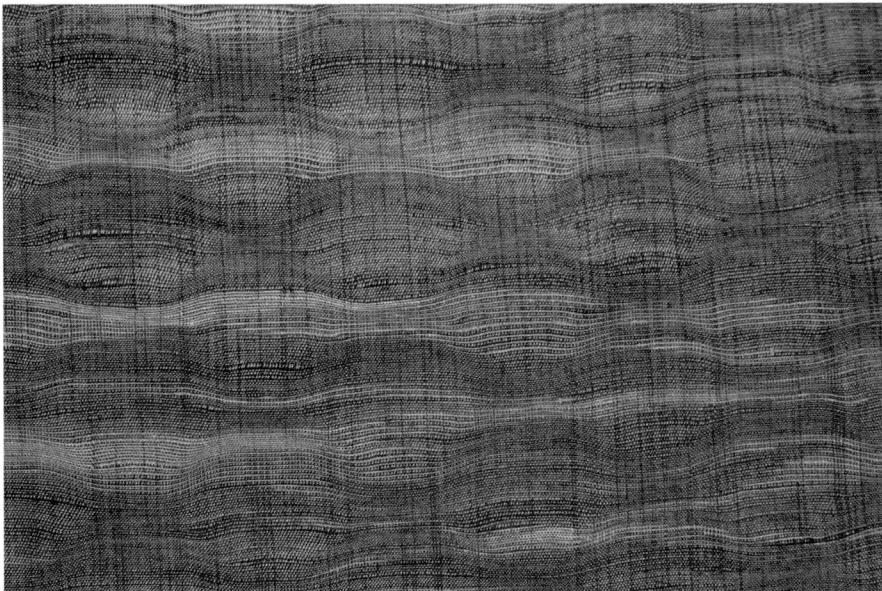

Weft compound beater bar silk. This cloth shows the same technique as described above. Casual, semi-formal kimono. The slubs in the weft distort the undulations a bit and this, coupled with the variations in color, give a greater sense of spontaneous earthiness to the weave.

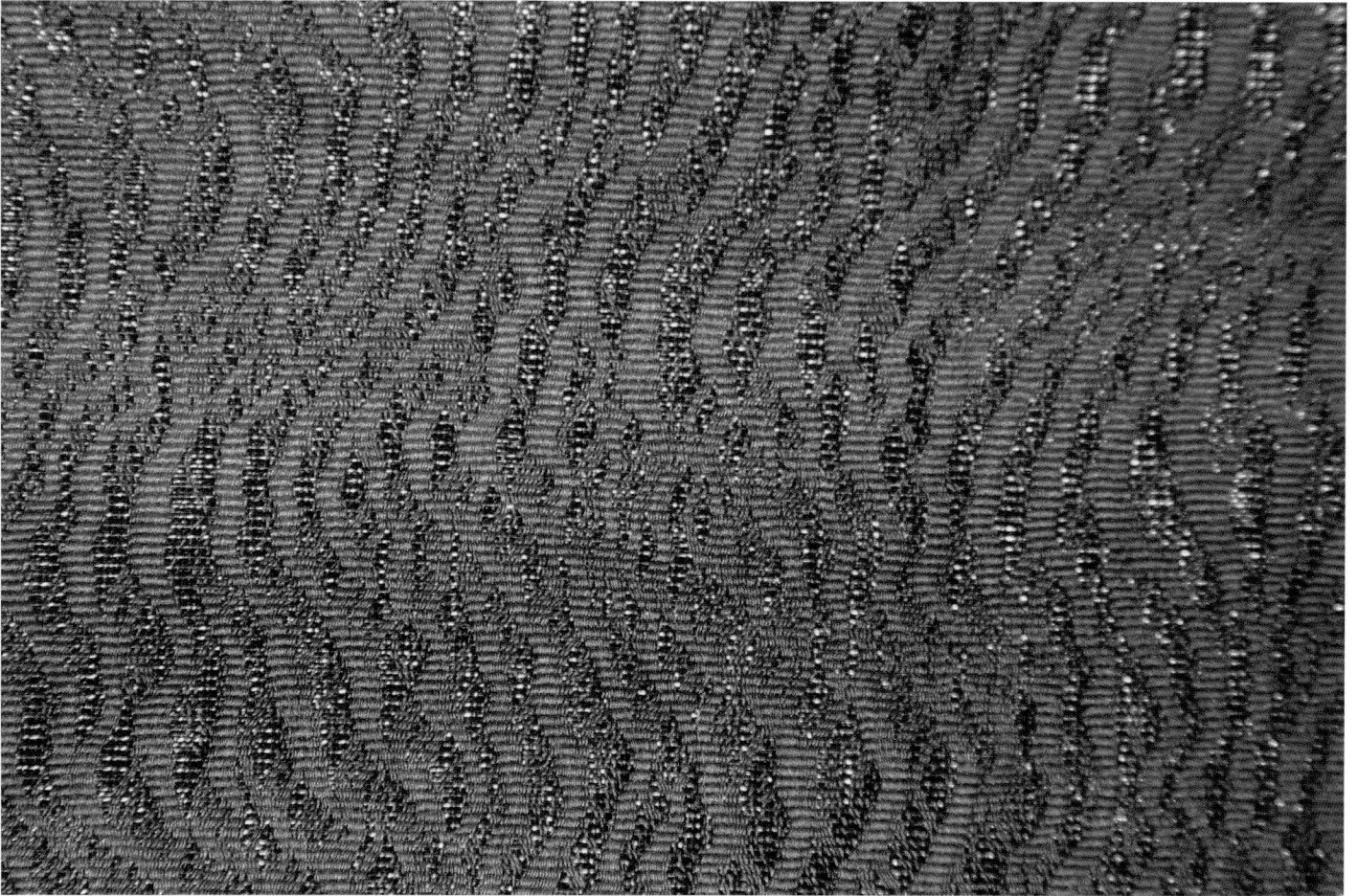

Warp face bruised silk. Loosely woven warp
face with filament floss silk. Normally a warp
face hides the weft, but in this case the
bruising allows a gold weft thread to peek
through here and there. Semi-formal kimono.
Bruising achieved with a comb.

Bruised warp with grass blades in silk. This is a silk haori top or jacket, worn over the kimono by a woman in the summer months. Spaced silver warp threads add a bit of sparkle. The bruising is most likely done with a Japanese comb.

Bruised weft with supplemental tapestry weave. The weft is woven very loosely and bruised using a Japanese comb. The oarsman is a supplemental weft tapestry weave. This is a detail of a contemporary fukuro-obi, a wide sash worn over the kimono by women. This one is for summer use.

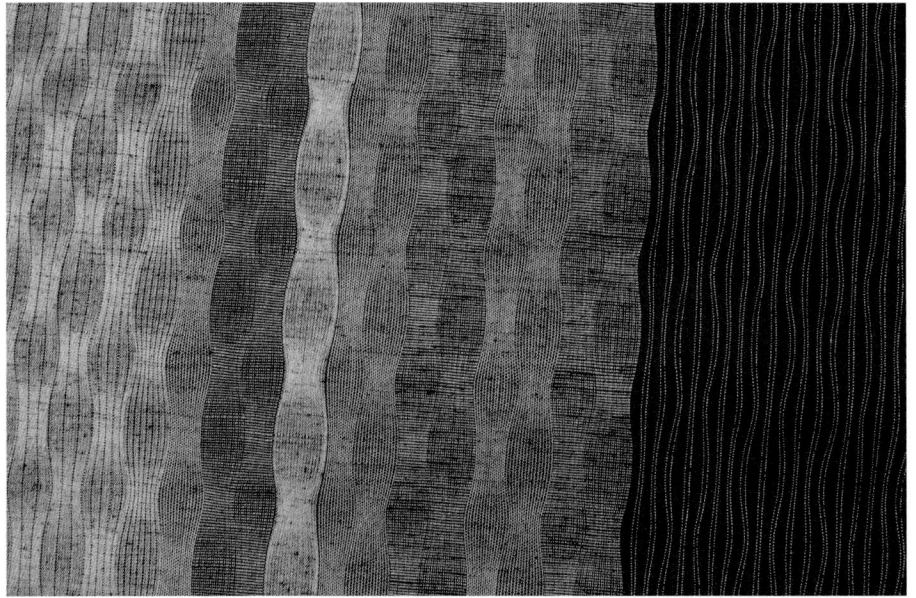

Fan reed silk utogitsumugi. This is a bolt of very fine spun silk, a portion of which is ikat dyed. Utogi is the region in which it was produced.

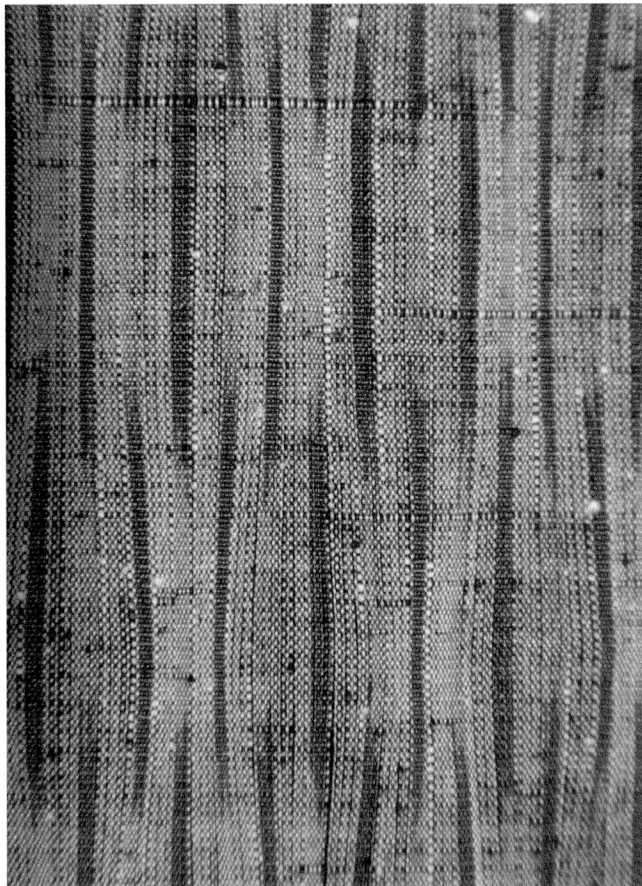

Fan reed silk ikat. The kasuri (ikat) threads are dyed before threading the warp. Spun raw silk (tsumugi). An everyday, casual woman's kimono.

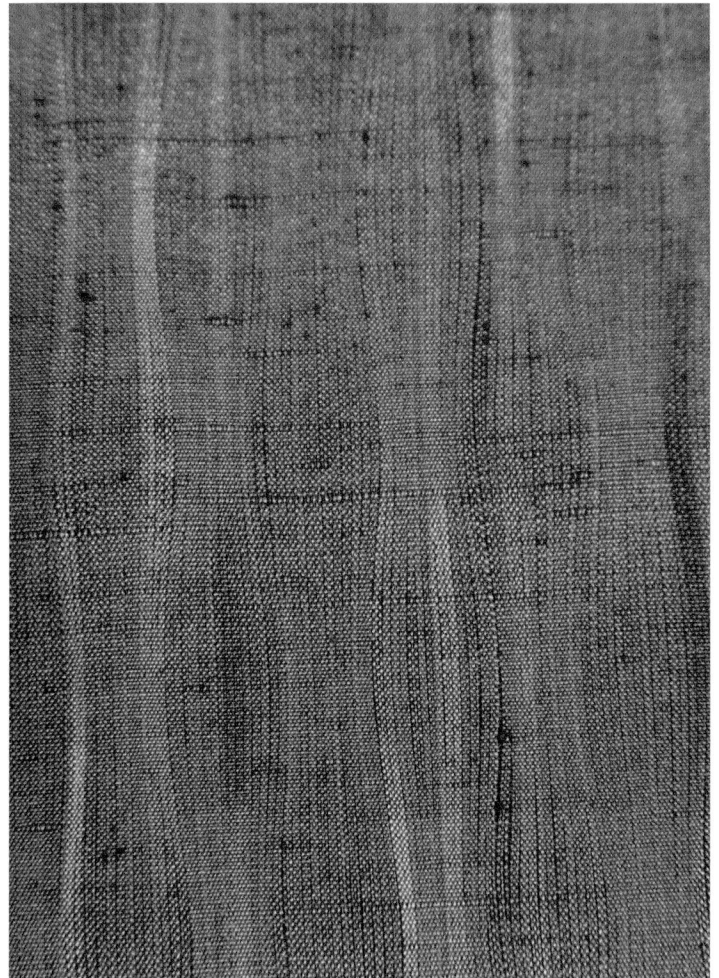

Fan reed silk ikat. Similar to the cloth shown at left.

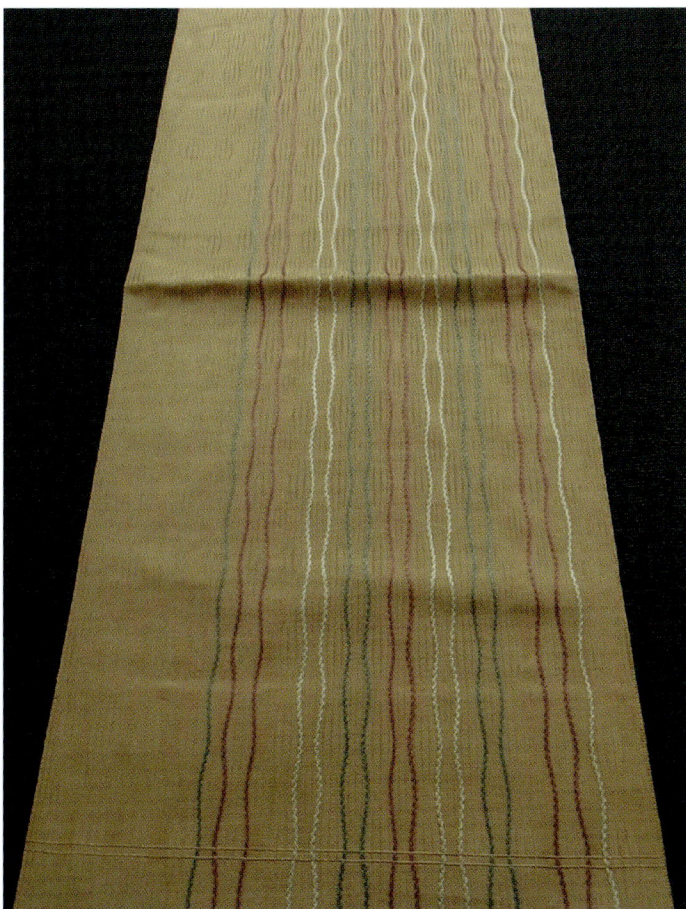

Nagoya-obi. Silk, woven using a fan reed. The undulations are accentuated by the addition of slightly thicker and more colorful warp threads.

Sprang silk. Floss silk with 18K gold weft accents. Fukuro-obi with sprang ondulé. Once tied, this section would appear in the back of the wearer as the center of a simple knot called an otaiko. Sprang is an old Japanese technique as well as a Scandinavian one.

Fukuro-obi. Silk, handwoven using a fan reed.

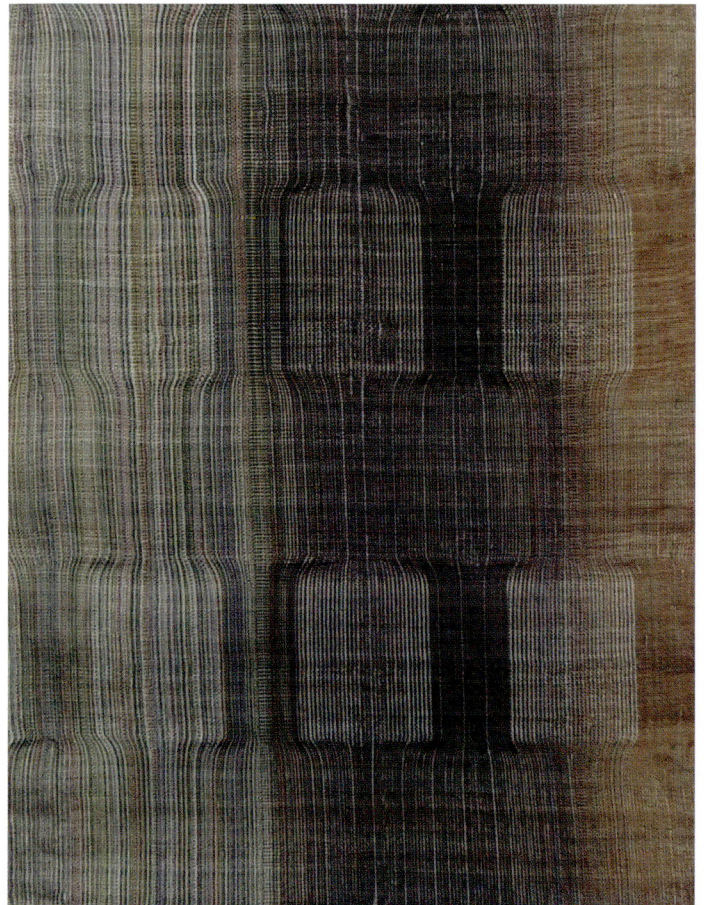

Detail. The startling rectangular motifs are created by an unusual use of the fan reed.

40

7| Five Contemporary Fan Reed Weavers

We each bring individual experiences and aesthetics to our work with fan reeds. In this chapter five invited artists, speaking in their own voices, describe their journeys with these reeds and the textiles they have produced. It is exciting to see what they are doing. No effort has been made to unify terminology.

Margaret Arafat; photo: Sam Arafat.

Margaret Arafat from Texas, a weaver since 1997, designs and weaves mostly functional items. She is a "structure person," focusing on how to manipulate fiber to her specifications, especially since she began using fan reeds.

Weaving with an ondulé or fan reed brings unexpected challenges. It's not just that the mechanics of handling the reed add uniqueness to the weaving process; it also means even more thought goes into each project. No matter how carefully one chooses the structures, colors, and fiber there are several variables that must be considered which make the process a slow one.

Where do I want the piece to begin and end in the reed? If I begin in the middle of a fan, the sides of the cloth will be straight. Begin at the first dent of a fan, and the sides will undulate. Will the number of ends in a pattern-repeat fit easily within a single fan? How frequently do I want to move the reed up and down? Is the pattern going to look pleasing as it's distorted by the reed? Will the weave structure even be evident? The more I work with this unique tool, the longer the list of questions grows.

The Floor Loom: When using an ondulé reed, I dress the loom front-to-back, or hybrid method. Sleying a fan reed off the loom is the most efficient. Once I take the reed to the loom, it is set in place with a couple of alterations to the usual process.

Except for holding the reed stable while sleying and threading, the beater is either moved out of the way or removed from the loom. On my 8-shaft, 42" Schacht floor loom, I remove the top bar from the beater, pin the beater in its upright position, and set the reed in the groove. The reed is suspended from a pair of wood clamps attached to the castle using Texsolv cords threaded through holes at each end of the reed. Alligator clips fixed through the open areas of each cord hold the reed in place, allowing it to hang freely, yet be moved up and down easily. At this point, the cords are allowed to hang slack, and the beater's pin is removed so it rests against the castle. With the reed closer to the heddles, threading is relatively simple. When threading is complete, the reed is taken out of the beater which

Floor loom set-up; photo: Margaret Arafat.

is moved forward so it sits against the cloth beam, out of the way while the warp is wound onto the back beam. Before winding and tying-on, reed-height is set at the vertical center point, or the point at which I want to begin weaving.

The Table Loom: *Dressing the table loom is similar, but it needs a modification of the castle-mounted setup on the floor loom. I use a 16-shaft, 24" Ashford table loom which has no tray on the castle, meaning the clamps must be affixed differently. I made a removable platform that I can secure to the castle with spring clamps. Its base is tailored so it does not interfere with the cords that raise and lower the shafts. The platform is tall enough that the wood clamps clear the treadling levers and can be moved up and down without restriction. Because this castle and its treadles have a deeper width than the floor loom castle, wood clamps with longer bars let the reed hang about three inches in front of the heddles, away from the levers.*

The Reeds: *I first tried an ondulé reed at Convergence in 2008. "Standard" or "full-fan" ondulé reeds come in 12- and 15-dents; mine has 15-dents per inch. There are eight fans in a $15^3/_4$-inch by 4-inch weaving plane, a single fan having 30 dents. When I used my reed for the first time, I marked $^1/_4$-inch increments onto both ends of it as a guide for raising and lowering it along the vertical height of the reed, or what I call the "reed-cycle." Fisherman's tape, marked in $^1/_8$-inch increments, is now affixed to both ends of my ondulé reeds.*

The November/December 2012 issue of Handwoven *included an article by Ellen LaBruce who wove a shawl with a band of tablet weaving within the body of the cloth. "Wouldn't it be cool to do that with an ondulé reed?" Well, it wouldn't happen with the one I owned: you cannot weave straight cloth and curved cloth at the same time with that particular reed.*

I pitched the question of having a reed with fans inserted into a standard reed to Sara and Hans von Tresckow from whom I purchased the original, and they checked with the reed maker in Germany. Done. I am now the proud owner of two hybrid reeds: a 24-inch reed with two fans inserted at about one-third of the distance from one end, and a 27-inch reed with four fans inserted in the same relative position. The remaining part of each reed has normal, vertical dents.

Table loom set-up, front view; photo: Margaret Arafat.

Table loom set-up, back view; photo: Margaret Arafat.

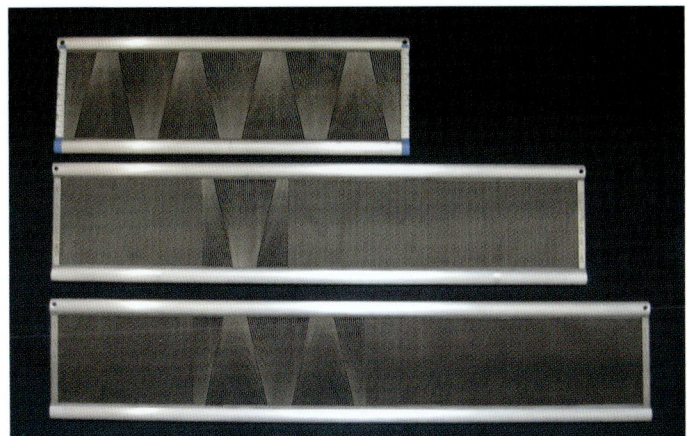

The reeds; photo: Margaret Arafat.

Full Attention Blues; photo: Margaret Arafat.

Weaving with the Full-Fan Reed: *While weaving the first samples, I learned how frequently to change the reed's position in ¼-inch increments to get a particular curve, what happens to the warp-tension as threads simultaneously spread and compact along the length of the warp, and the true value of proper wet-finishing.*

My first "real" piece was for the Fort Worth Weavers Guild 2011 Biennial Gallery Show. A black and blue scarf woven with 20/2 silk in a modified, 4-shaft herringbone twill to fit evenly within three fans, it satisfied the Show's theme, "Rhythm and Blues: The Music of the Loom."

To this point, each piece was woven with yarn at 30 epi. What happens when you use thicker yarn? Things change. I chose 60 percent silk/40 percent bamboo. The sett was 15 epi. Great, until you get to the narrowest point in a fan where sett almost doubles. Another lesson learned: check whether or not the yarn will go through this area of the reed. I used three inches of the four-inch reed-height, eliminating the upper- and lower-most ½-inch sections of the reed. Using a shorter span produced more subtle curves.

Weaving with the Hybrid Reeds: *Hybrid reeds offer challenges that the full-fan reed does not: deciding where the undulating areas will be used may be problematic. "Should the waves be within the body of the cloth or just on one side of it?" "Will there be different take-up between the area of the piece with undulations and that in surrounding, non-undulating sections?" The only way to answer questions about tension is to weave.*

The first piece on one of the hybrid reeds was designed for the 24-inch, two-fan reed with a one-fan stripe that had an undulating selvedge on one side of the scarf and a straight selvedge on the other. There is a green stripe undulating between a narrow black selvedge and the body of this silk scarf—curved along one edge, straight at the other. Tension differences are not apparent.

Black and Green; photo: Margaret Arafat.

44

Piccola Vespa, detail; photo: MaGee Grundmann.

Following that successful venture, I used the same reed, including both fans and the standard dents on either side. I wanted an undulating stripe surrounded by solid colored cloth.

Once again, the 24-inch reed was used for a fashion piece for an exhibit: a narrow scarf woven in Black Pearl, a luxurious white yarn made of 50 percent Tencel and 50 percent crushed pearls. I hand-dyed the yarn, painting sixty accent threads to fit within a single fan, and immersion-dyed the remaining yarn for the other warp ends and the weft. The original fiber had a luster that seems to be enhanced by the addition of color; it must be the pearls shining through.

The Fort Worth Weavers Guild needed sixty aprons for an installation to celebrate the Guild's 60th Anniversary. I wanted curves in my cloth, and wanted fabric that required only a bit of sewing. I was not concerned that the curves wouldn't be centered if I used the full reed-span, in fact, I preferred it. The draft is a simple 4-shaft twill and basket weave pattern: twill confined to the fans, with basket weave included in the three center fans, and basket weave alone in the sections on either side of the fans.

The potential of the work that can be done with all three of these reeds is virtually untapped, as far as I am concerned. There are more structures to try, more types of cloth to weave, all sorts of different materials to work with, and more experimentation to correct what hasn't worked so well. The only downside is that I began weaving so late in life and didn't learn about ondulé reeds sooner.

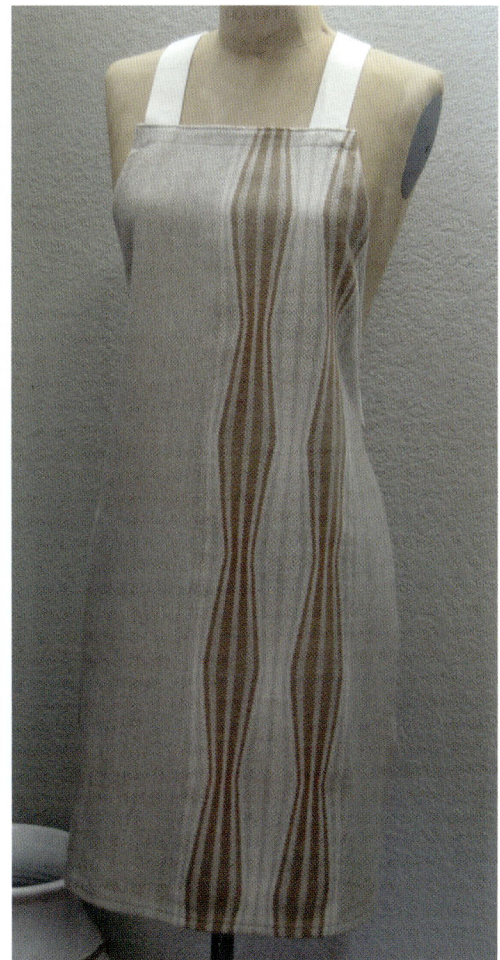

Apron; photo: MaGee Grundmann.

45

Pat Foster; photo: Pat Foster.

Pat Foster from Malvern, Great Britain, was the first to contact Hans von Tresckow at The Woolgatherers about designing a fan reed. She suggested widths of 1", 2", and 3" for the narrow base, median, and wide base of the fan, which is now standard. It has turned out to be a successful design.

Fan Reed Weaving: *The mechanism for the fan reed on the Louet Kombo is driven by winding a pair of wing nuts up and down. Since this is all manual, an Excel file is generated which specifies how many turns should be used. A smooth curve was used. There is no point in weaving fabric with a sharp rate of change of dent as the warp threads will just pull into a smoother curve. After experimentation with various curves, I settled on a cosine curve which could be squashed or expanded in length.*

Several pieces have been woven. One warped in cotton of many colors was not entirely successful. In my opinion, the white band is not effective. It is not straight-edged, as it is too wide. At the same time, it is too narrow from a design perspective.

All of these samples have been plain weave. If the weft is a different color from the warp, where the pattern is widest is a different color from where the pattern is narrowest. It was decided to weave some samples which involved using a pattern, and it was planned to have a pattern of lace in every "bulge" of the pattern, but this was not attractive when tried out and tabby was used throughout. It is interesting that the use of a patterned weave with a fan reed is not common and a two-shaft loom could be used.

Kerstin Froberg of Sweden has woven many different items using a fan reed. She was also responsible for a suggestion which I felt had to be researched. Her thought was that the reason why there were few nineteenth century samples in museums was that successive washings would gradually even out the warp effects and return the weaving to the appearance of having been carried out with a 'normal' reed. I tested this by taking a length of the cotton fabric shown in the photo on page 48 and machine washing it eight times at 104 degrees F (40 degrees C). Photographs were taken after each wash. There was no obvious difference between any of the photographs. The type of yarn used could have a serious impact. If the yarn was wool, then on first washing, the threads would mesh together and it is unlikely that there would be any shift after later washings. This might also be true of cotton, and the green striped sample did contain some slub cotton as well as being mostly unmercerized. However if a fine silk was used, the warp threads might well shift after washing.

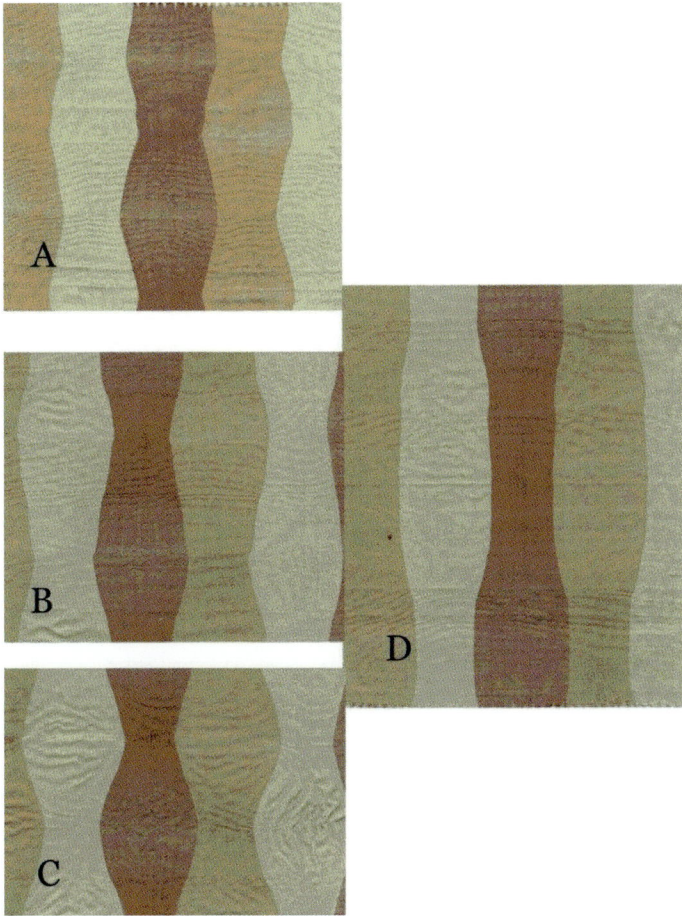

Top: Scarf with 70/2 silk warp and dark brown 70/2 silk weft. Below: The effect of three different wefts. A. Light brown 70/2 silk weft. B. Ecru silk noil. C. Dark 70/2 silk; photo: Pat Foster.

Various shapes for the same warp. A and C are derived from cosines, while B and D were hand drawn. A was selected; figure: Pat Foster.

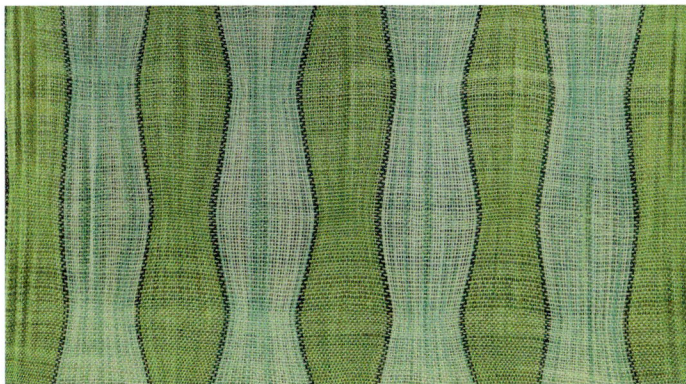

8/2 Tencel and fine wool warp and 8/2 Tencel weft; photo: Pat Foster.

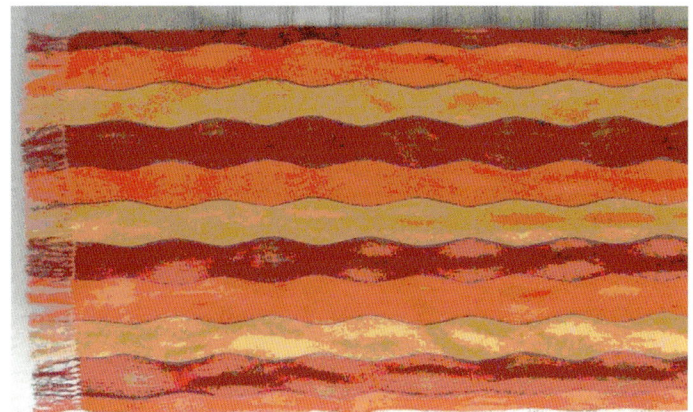

70/2 silk warp and weft with the curves outlined; photo: Pat Foster.

Detail of green and white cotton fabric; photo: Pat Foster.

Fan Reed Mechanism for a Louet Kombo Loom: *In 2006, there were no obvious suppliers of fan reeds. I located Hans von Tresckow of The Woolgatherers who was prepared to get one made for me if I designed it. It was based on being used in a Louet Kombo whose width was 27.6 inches (700 mm). The height of the reed supplied with the Kombo was five inches (2.5 cm) while the actual usable reed is 4.25 inches (10.8 cm). I decided on 15 dents per inch at the center and a fan width at the center of the reed of 2 inches (5.0 cm). The bottom width of a section was set at 1 inch (2.5 cm) and the top at 3 inches (7.5 cm). Experience in using the fan reed has shown that the narrowest section is unusable and the minimum and maximum widths are more like 1.2 inches (3.0 cm) and 2.8 inches (7.0 cm). The included angle is about 40 degrees and possibly this could have been increased, but these dimensions gave 11 sections across the reed width of 21.5 inches (55 cm) which would result in a nice cloth. The fan reed is mounted on a Louet Kombo loom which has a hanging beater.*

The figures on page 51 illustrate the process for adapting the Louet loom for ondulé weaving. The holder for the beater snaps into two holes in wooden diagonal side spars. These two pieces of wood are screwed into both the castle and the horizontal support structure and hold the loom structure together. Louet is a Dutch firm and uses metric dimensions.

A spare hanging beater was purchased and disassembled. This meant unscrewing the metal spars from underneath the lower holder. The two wooden holders (called Lower and Upper) are 1.4 by 1.4 inches (35 by 35 mm) in cross-section. The Lower wooden holder for the reed was cut in half lengthwise.

This was done on an accurate machine so that the cut faces were smooth and parallel to the original outer faces. Call the lowest of the two cut pieces Lower A and the upper one Lower B. Two of the three pieces, Upper and Lower B, hold the reed while Lower A supports the mechanism to move the reed up and down.

15 DENTS PER INCH

In the reed holder, as received from Louet, the metal spars (diameter 0.8 cm) have a short straight section by the reed and a longer straight section to the holders on the side spars. These need to be reversed so that the longer straight section is at the bottom. The short horizontal arms originally at the top of the beater were fitted into the slots under Lower A and drilled through both Lower A and the metal arm so that they can be bolted together later. Use an M4 (4 mm) drill.

In my case, the Louet Kombo is 27.6 inches (700 mm) wide and the fan reed was made 22.4 inches (570 mm) wide. The reed slot was square at 1.5 cm by 1.5 cm (15 mm by 15 mm). The wooden pieces, Lower A, Lower B and Upper, were clamped together in a vertical pile, lining up the ends and a hole drilled through all three sections at 2.6 inches (65 mm) from each end. An M8 (8 mm) clearance drill was used.

The metal spars were screwed into position. Into both 8 mm holes in Lower A, a 13.8-inch (350 mm) length of M8 studding was screwed with a nut and a locknut on the lower side and a nut on the upper side. A wing nut was then put onto both lengths of studding under Lower B, and Lower B was then threaded onto the studding. The fan reed was then inserted and the Upper section also threaded onto the studding. A length of cord was added running round Upper and Lower B and tied tightly so that the reed plus Upper and Lower B formed one unit which moved up and down on the wing nuts.

To move the reed up or down, the two wing nuts are given the same number of turns in the required direction. A small spirit level is kept handy to check that the two sides of the reed are in step.

The last step is that the wooden diagonal braces needed to be re-positioned. It is quite a good idea to clamp these to the castle while the mechanism is tested. If it is not correctly positioned, the mechanism will foul on the breast beam winder. When it is in a satisfactory position, the diagonal braces are screwed onto the sides of the loom. This adjustment is needed to make the warp stay in the same position in the reed as far as possible.

This viability of the system depends on the exact dimensions of the fan reed itself. If the length is much greater than 22.0 inches (560 mm), this method cannot be used on a 27.6-inch (700 mm) Louet Kombo because there will not be enough space to drill the hole for the M8 studding on which the mechanism moves.

ORIGINAL LOOM AND BEATER

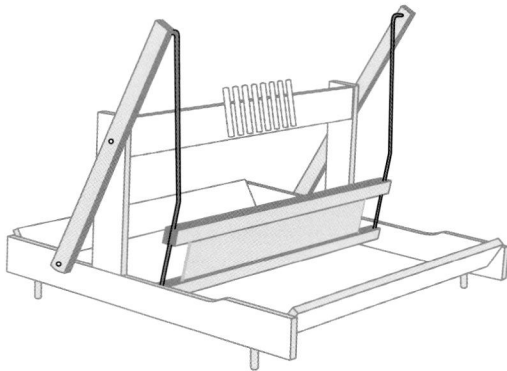

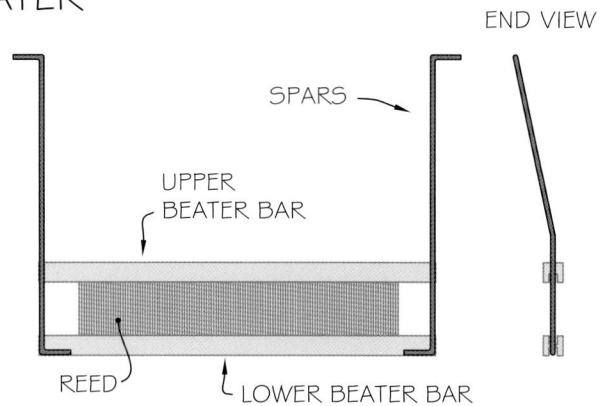

END VIEW

SPARS

UPPER
BEATER BAR

REED

LOWER BEATER BAR

Construction

1. Remove beater from loom and take apart.

2. Saw lower beater bar in half lengthwise.

3. Stack 3 beater bars and drill holes for threaded rods.

4. Flip and spin spars. Drill bolt holes through Lower A beater bar and spars.

5. Re-assemble beater and adjust diagonal braces as described in text.

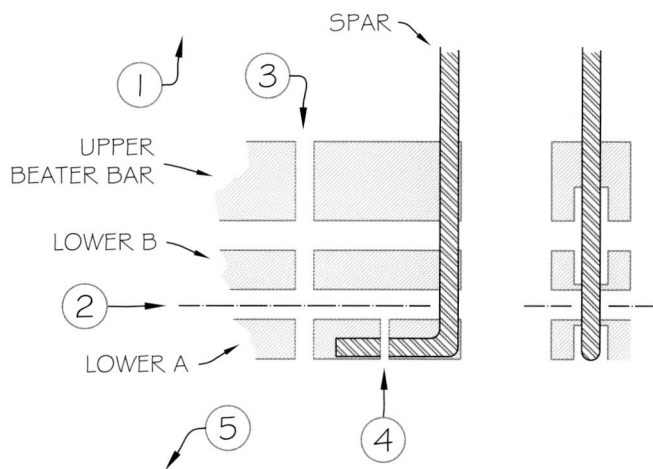

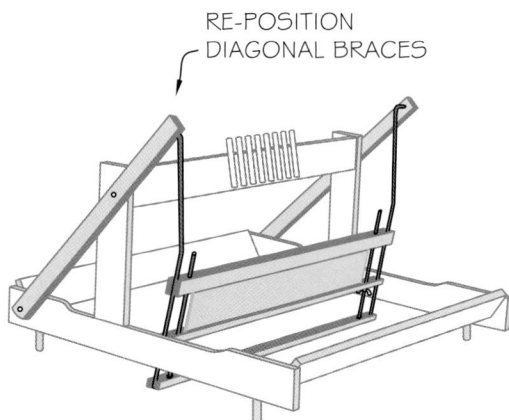

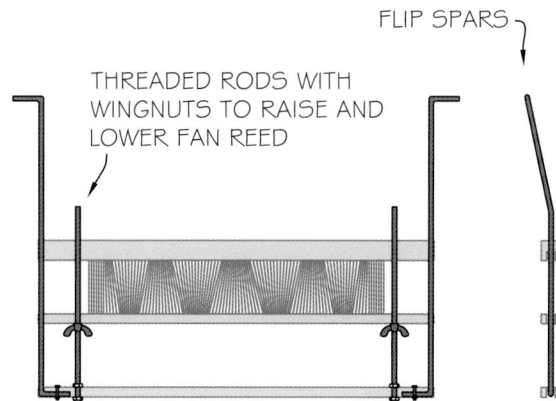

SPAR

① ③

UPPER
BEATER BAR

LOWER B

②

LOWER A

⑤ ④

RE-POSITION
DIAGONAL BRACES

FLIP SPARS

THREADED RODS WITH
WINGNUTS TO RAISE AND
LOWER FAN REED

COMPLETED LOOM WITH ADJUSTABLE BEATER
Pat Foster's method

Adaptation of adjustable beater for Louet loom; figure: Tom Smayda.

Amy Putansu; photo: Steve Mann.

Reed on loom; photo: Steve Mann.

Amy Putansu who grew up on the Maine coast, is a Rhode Island School of Design graduate and is now a full-time faculty member of Haywood Community College in North Carolina. She exhibits and teaches ondulé weaving internationally. She has two fan reeds from Japan and one from Germany.

I first encountered the concept of ondulé in Ann Sutton and Diane Sheehan's 1989 influential text Ideas in Weaving, *while in college at Rhode Island School of Design.* Ideas in Weaving *is responsible for many contemporary ondulé weavers, as I later learned while researching European weavers pursuing the same technique. In July 2002 I acquired my first ondulé reed via Japan after a decent national search of manufacturers. Not only is the fanning reed quite beautiful as an object, the possibility of softening the grid was so enticing that I made a concerted effort to pursue this path.*

It wasn't until I had reed in hand that the reality of this challenge set in: that of maneuvering the reed to, in fact, produce the desired results of waving warp. I have always been a dedicated Macomber loom enthusiast and this was the loom I modified to accommodate the reed. After several trials I arrived at the solution I still use today to produce the waving effects that the reed is known for.

Since that time I have focused on an investigation to truly control the technique and develop a material repertoire that not only is suitable for the mechanics of warp ondulé but also remains authentic to my artistic voice. I have used ondulé in combination with other favorite techniques such as double weave blocks, ikat, and clipped floats. Over the course of many yards of ondulé cloth I have observed and responded to the nuances of this manipulation and how tiny adjustments show up in the cloth. It is a dynamic relationship between weaver, loom, and threads.

I find the nature of this relationship between maker and material to be so compelling that in 2009 I abandoned all other methods of weaving and began focusing exclusively on ondulé. The opportunity to focus so narrowly but deeply has afforded me the realization of many technical and conceptual connections. Warp ondulé produces a rhythmic undulation that one can easily equate with the breath or ocean swells. I was raised on the northern sea coast which contributed largely to the visual language I draw upon today. In 2013 I began to stretch and frame my finished cloth, presenting it to the viewer under tension the way it is perceived during the making. In this way the cloth maintains the qualities that I experience while on the loom, and I approach compositions as if I am making paintings.

I have investigated a wide variety of yarns and learned that not all yarns can yield to warp ondulé beautifully or successfully. The technique requires strength in warp yarns because of the repeated and abnormal amount of abrasion. Fineness of yarns has been a signature quality in my weaving, and this quality lends itself well to warp ondulé to produce dramatic results of transparency and opacity. Strength and fineness combined point to a narrow field of fiber choices. Silk is most well-suited to meet these criteria and my favorite material to work with. I have also used polyester, and surprisingly, spun linen warps have suited my technique well.

When I was first presented with the problem of how to allow the fanned reed to meet the fell line at various heights throughout the weaving there was no instruction available. Each weaver who has pursued warp ondulé has singularly developed an original method, largely based on their loom-type. Obvious solutions included adjusting the height of the reed within the batten during weaving, or adjusting the height of the entire batten piece up and down. I made minor attempts at these, until it was clear that for me and my loom-type, it makes more sense to raise and lower the weaving itself, while the reed and batten remain in place as normal. All of my solutions have been designed for my Macomber 8-harness, 48" jack-type loom. While these solutions are very adequate they are only somewhat useful on other loom models because of the many factors of loom construction.

The first experiments used an additional beam placed upon the breast beam, beneath the weaving, raising it so the reed meets the weaving near the top of the reed. The beam would then be removed, lowering the weaving so the reed meets toward the bottom. These early developments did not include much of a transition between extremes and it was evident in the cloth. Additionally, the cumbersome nature of physically placing and removing an extra beam lead to the development of a stationary beam with hinges, what I now call a supplementary breast beam, that folds up and down with the simple release of the tension. This is the mechanical method I use today.

The subtleties of manipulating warp threads from highly crammed to highly spaced takes care of itself to some extent because threads move into the path of least resistance. However, to eliminate gaps in the weft when moving from the highest position to the lowest position, a more fluid transition needed to be addressed.

When observing the motion of the underslung beater as it relates to the position of the fell and how the reed meets the weaving it is apparent that the reed meets at varying heights naturally, depending on where the fell line is positioned. Using this to one's advantage in warp ondulé creates smooth transitions between the highest and lowest reed positions. Further subtleties are addressed by observing the nature of the jack-type loom and its rising shed which results in meeting the fell at a lower position in the reed. The opposite is achieved by keeping all harnesses lifted to beat in the weft: meeting the fell at the highest possible point when the beam is also in its highest position.

In my method of warp ondulé there are roughly a dozen different positions within each repeating unit. The process is a physical one in terms of repeatedly adjusting the tension, the breast beam position, and the position of the fell line. This very active style of weaving is as rhythmic and flowing as the aesthetic results that warp ondulé produces. I enjoy this level of constant engagement with all aspects of the loom and the cloth. Ondulé now serves as a backdrop for my artwork, it is the skeleton upon which I incorporate a variety of techniques to achieve a range of moods and expressions.

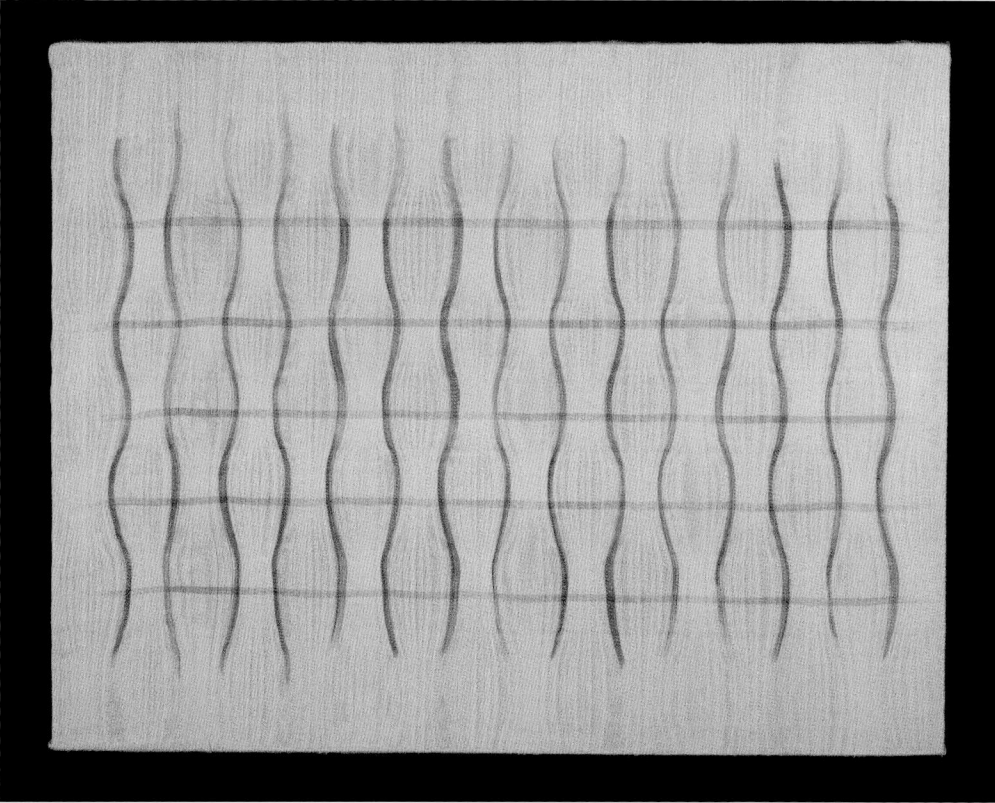

Grid. 25" × 31"; photo: Steve Mann.

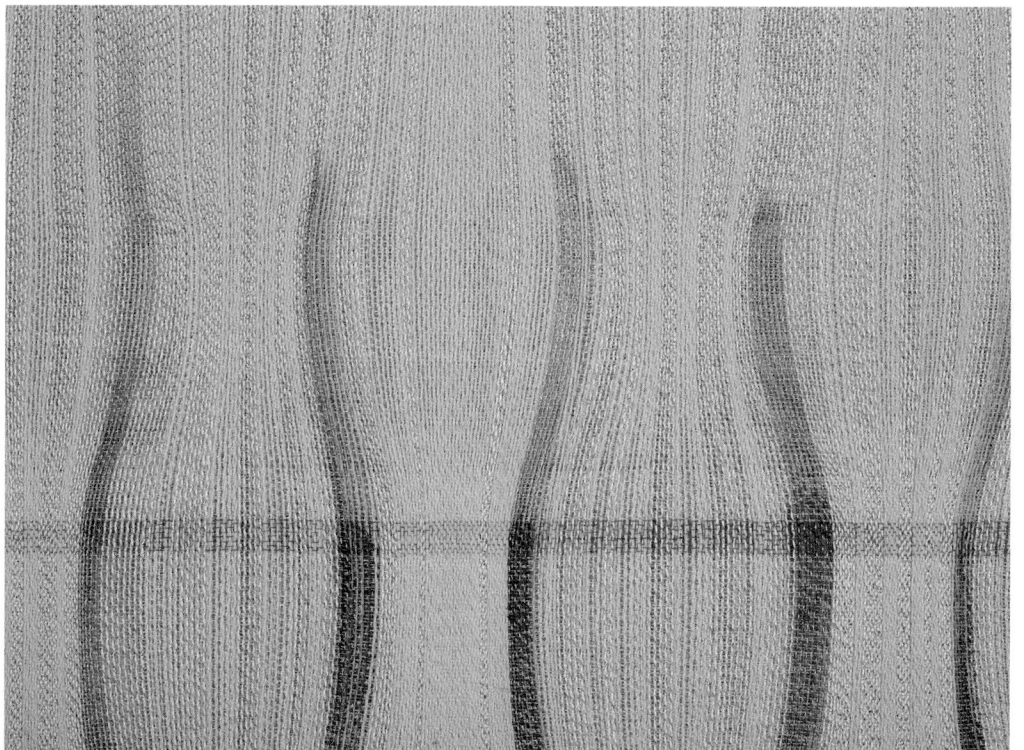

Grid, detail; photo: Steve Mann.

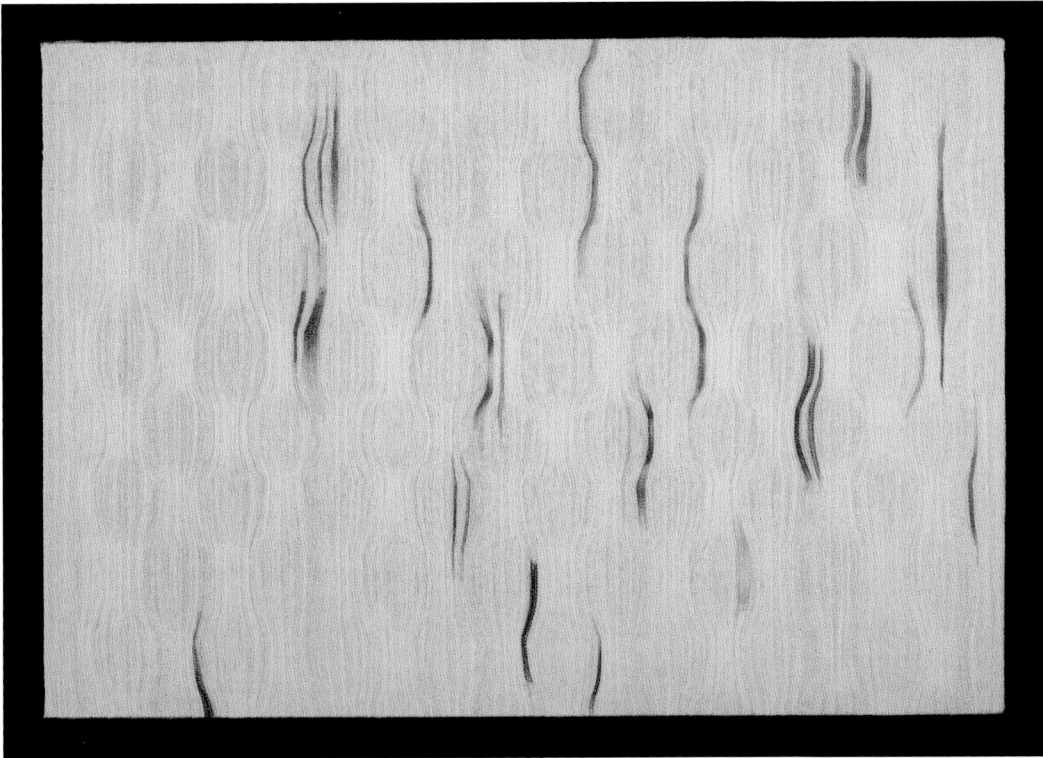

Smudged. 25" × 35";
photo: Steve Mann.

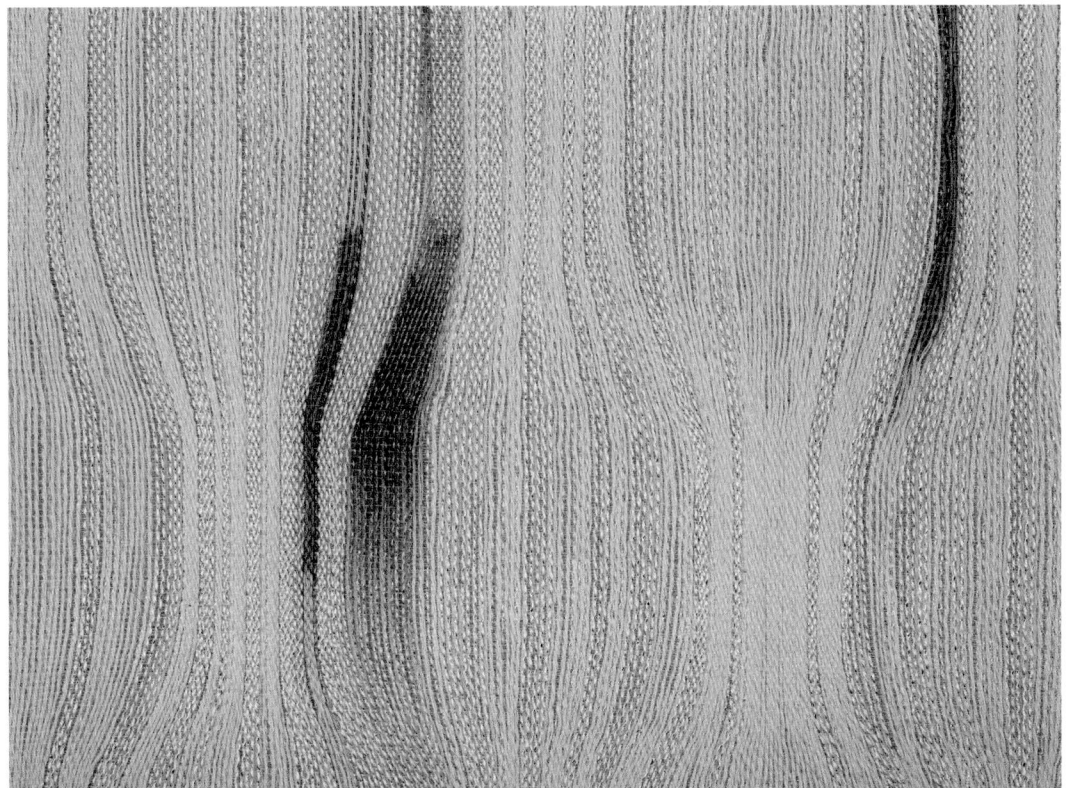

Smudged, detail; photo:
Steve Mann.

Diptych; two silk panels, resist dyed with natural dyes; 58" × 80"; photo: Steve Mann.

Resist dyeing is a technique that combines with warp ondulé beautifully. I have applied shibori and ikat resists to cloth and fabric to achieve color areas that emerge and gently fade in random or intentional patterns. My large wall piece woven in warp ondulé titled Diptych was included in the Contemporary Art of Shibori and Ikat exhibition at the 9th International Shibori Symposium in Hangzhou, China, in 2014. The all white pair of silk panels measures 58" by 80" when installed, and incorporates resist dyeing with natural dyes of madder, black walnut, and osage orange. The exhibition was installed at the China National Silk Museum, and at the close of the show I was contacted by the director of the museum to purchase the piece for the museum's permanent collection. Diptych is now one of the few examples of warp ondulé to be found in any museum collection.

Primaries. 90" × 18"; photo: Steve Mann.

57

Karina Nielsen Rios; photo:
Ole Akhoej.

Japanese yoroke (fan) reed, showing
combination of 70/10 and 30/10 dpi fans;
photo: Ole Akhoej.

Karina Nielsen Rios lives in Copenhagen, Denmark. She studied gauzes at the Bauhaus Archiv in Berlin, in Japan, and at the Museo Amano in Lima, Peru. She is interested in high-tech materials and the cutting edge of textile product development.

I am educated as a textile designer from the School of Design in Copenhagen (1995–2000). Before this I studied to become a teacher in weaving at the VIA University College (1992–94). It was here I first saw the fan reed described in a book, Ideas in Weaving *by Ann Sutton, which the school had bought. At the VIA University College my class went on a study tour to England. Here I had the opportunity to visit Peter Collingwood at his home studio in Essex. Peter Collingwood did not work with the fan reed, but the ways he approached weaving have always been a big fascination for me. His macrogauze wall hanging as well as his shaft switching for weaving rugs was of deep interest. The way he, with very simple tools and methods, was able to create very complex patterns is, for me, a sign of both being a big creator and innovator in a field.*

I did not start weaving with the fan reed at the VIA University College; this was several years later. In 1998, when I did an exchange program at Philadelphia University, I came across some beautiful samples at a nearby little museum which was connected to the University. These were woven with the fan reed in different techniques such as plain weave and a simple leno structure.

When I got my own studio in 2000 I purchased my first fan reed. Today I have three fan reeds with different setts and therefore I am able to use different kinds of thick and/or thin yarns for the warp material. The setts are 70/10 and 30/10. Besides this I have one fan reed which is a combination of one fan in 70/10 together with one fan in 30/10, etc. My first fan reeds came from Sweden and the last one which was customized for my needs I bought through Woolgatherers. They had it made in Germany. (The Japanese name for a fan reed is yoroke.*)*

When working with the fan reed for the first time I used my contramarch loom from Lervad, which has an overhanging beater. On the top part of the beater there are a lot of holes, and by changing the position of the reed with these holes I am able to raise or lower the warp threads in the reed during weaving. Later on I purchased a wooden tool from a Swedish company which I can put on the loom to help me in an easier way to change the position of the warp threads. This is a very simple method and is easy to work with. Today when working with the fan reed I use a simple Texsolv cord string in nylon.

58

Loom with Lervad fan reed attachment; photo: Ole Akhoej.

When travelling to Japan in 2009 to study the mojiri-ori technique, also known as complex gauze, I was lucky to visit a reed maker in the Nishijin area of Kyoto. From here I bought a nami reed which gives the movement in the weft direction. I have used my nami reed on my Patronic ARM loom with twenty-four shafts which is a computerized loom.

Ever since I was a child I have been fascinated by laces. My sweet grandmother taught me to do bobbin lace when I was fourteen years old, and I still remember the feeling of sitting close to her while she helped me to learn this special technique. I also remember my grandmother used to have special curtains in her window in a lace-like pattern. Weaving with the fan reeds, together with the gauze weaving, takes me, in a way, back to these days and the feeling I had inside me. The reason I like to combine these two techniques with each other is that in the gauze weaving you are able to weave an open pattern/ design as the warp threads are twisted around each other and held in place by the weft. This means the threads are not displaced into one another. Woven together with the fan reeds, this gives me an extra way of expressing a design/pattern.

I have always liked the idea of using a simple tool in the weaving process to create a new pattern. Here the yoroke and nami reeds are amazing tools. As I'm fascinated by the gauze weaving myself and have been doing a lot of research of this technique I have been combining these two techniques with each other. Also, today I'm working on another simple way to get a pattern in the loom, with just a little modification on top of the loom. All these small things are what I'm drawn to when weaving.

The textiles I weave in my studio with either the yoroke or the nami reed are mainly used as room dividers or wall hangings.

Japanese nami (weft ondulé) reed; photo: Karina Nielsen Rios.

59

Marea Azul, detail; photo: Ole Akhoej.

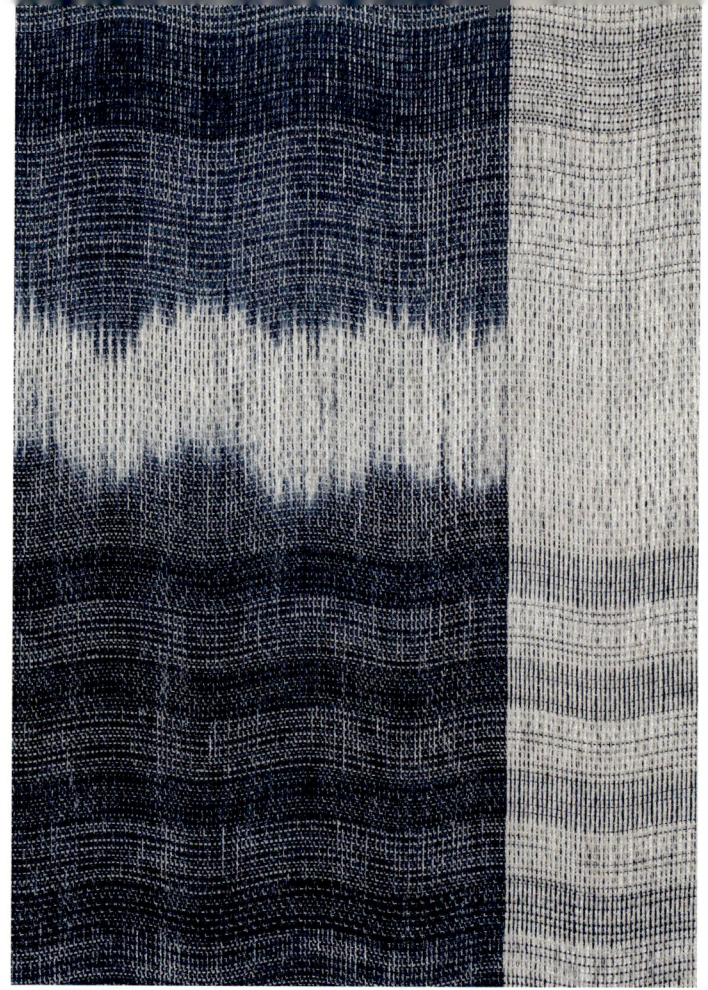

Indigo triptych, series of room dividers, woven with nami (weft ondulé) reed, bamboo and linen, indigo dyed. 2014–2015; photo: Ole Akhoej.

Unnamed, detail; photo: Ole Akhoej.

Room divider, detail; photo: Ole Akhoej.

Room divider, handwoven with fan reed, leno, silk, stainless steel, cashmere. Talente Exhibition, Munich, Germany. 2002; photo: Ole Akhoej.

Thread Five; room divider, polyester, monofilament, coated polyurethane. 2007; photo: Ole Akhoej.

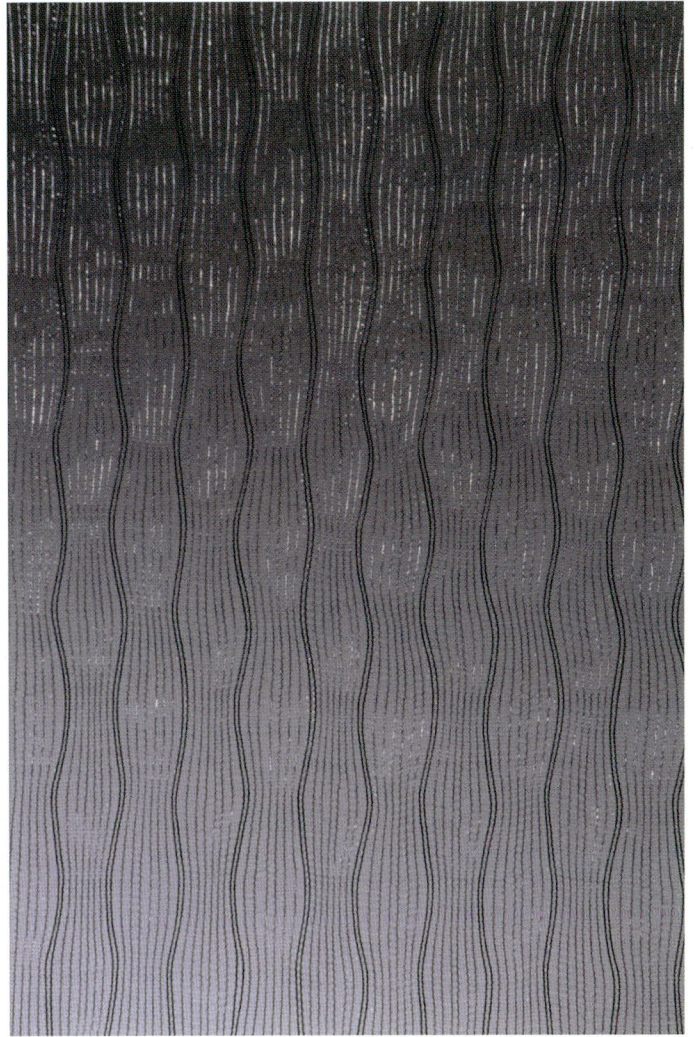

Thread Three; photo: Ole Akhoej.

Anne Selim; photo: Anne Selim.

Anne Selim, born in Germany and now living in Great Britain, produces a range of contemporary handwoven textiles for fashion and interiors. She was the recipient of the 1998 Theo Moorman Trust for Weavers Award. Although they are not ondulé, I have included a photo of her impressive eight-meter-high wall panels in triple weave, with curves and pleats made of nylon thread and copper and steel wire.

I first learned about an ondulé reed in Ann Sutton's book Ideas in Weaving *in 1992, which fascinated me a great deal. Then, in 1993, there was an article published in the German magazine* Textile Forum *about a weaver, Pia Filliger Nolte, who used such a reed and created the most amazing textiles with it. I was very intrigued by this article, and became very keen to get such a reed myself and start working with it. But it took me five more years until I could find and buy such a reed myself along with the lifting device for my Öxabäck loom from Sweden. That worked very well, and I began to explore the possibilities of the ondulé reed with different materials and techniques, such as gaps in the reed, satin stripes on plain weave, alternating blocks of warp and weft faced satin stripes, etc. I was always very fascinated by the distortion of the warp threads creating these soft vertical wave lines and shadow effects in the cloth.*

Later on I got a beater specially made with the same lifting device that I was able to put into my AVL dobby loom. So I could produce more advanced textiles with the reed, e.g., double cloth or triple layered fabrics as you can see in the photos.

Weaving with the ondulé reed was always more fascinating for me than using a normal reed. It became sort of a trademark for my work and is still very important to me. I used mostly very fine silk yarns, weaving scarves and shawls with it, but also screen fabrics made of linen and cotton.

In the future I'd like to explore other materials like synthetic yarns or copper wire or stainless steel. I would also like to get a mixed ondulé reed with straight parts in it as well to get more variety.

I am sure the ondulé reed will always be part of my work as a weaver.

Studio showing loom with lifting device; photo: © Anne Selim.

Scarf in silk double
weave; photo:
© Anne Selim.

Triple weave wall panels in nylon, copper, and steel; installed in the Fortis Building, City of London; photo: © Anne Selim.

Room divider; photo: © Anne Selim.

Three silk scarves in plain weave; photo: © Anne Selim.

Scarf in plain weave with satin stripes;
photo: © Anne Selim.

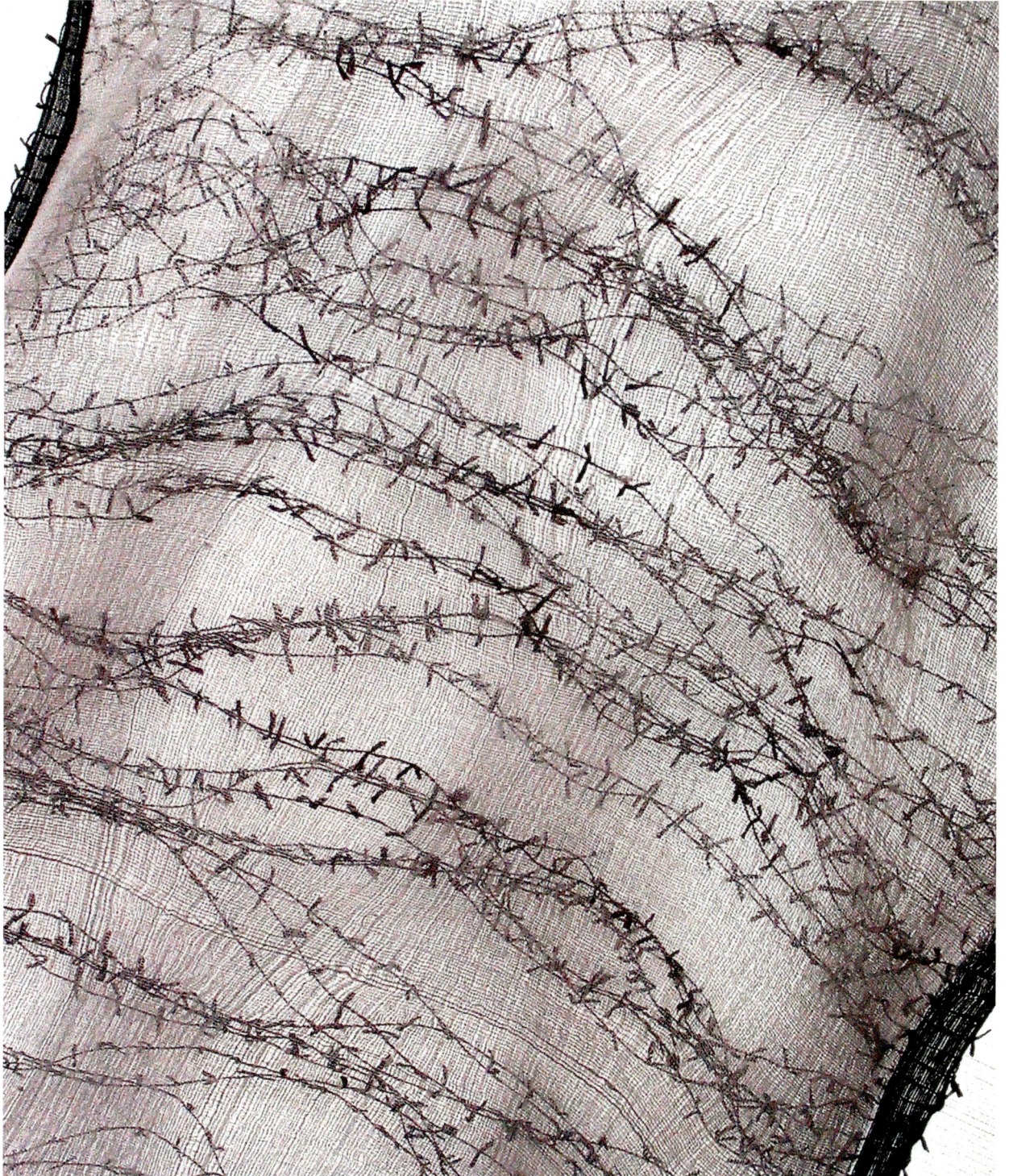

Organza silk scarf in double cloth with paper yarn woven between the layers; photo: © Anne Selim.

8| The Fan Reed

At Convergence 2010 in Albuquerque, on a whim I signed up for a seminar on the fan reed with Sara von Tresckow. I thought my weaving school assistant would be interested in information I could bring back to her. What I did not expect was that I would be the one to become so enamored of undulating warps that weave off the grid. Within thirty minutes of the end of that seminar, I was in the Vendors' Hall where I found a fan reed on display at the Glimåkra booth. It was accompanied by the March/April 2009 article in *Handwoven* by Suzie Liles, "Tired of Straight Stripes?"[1]

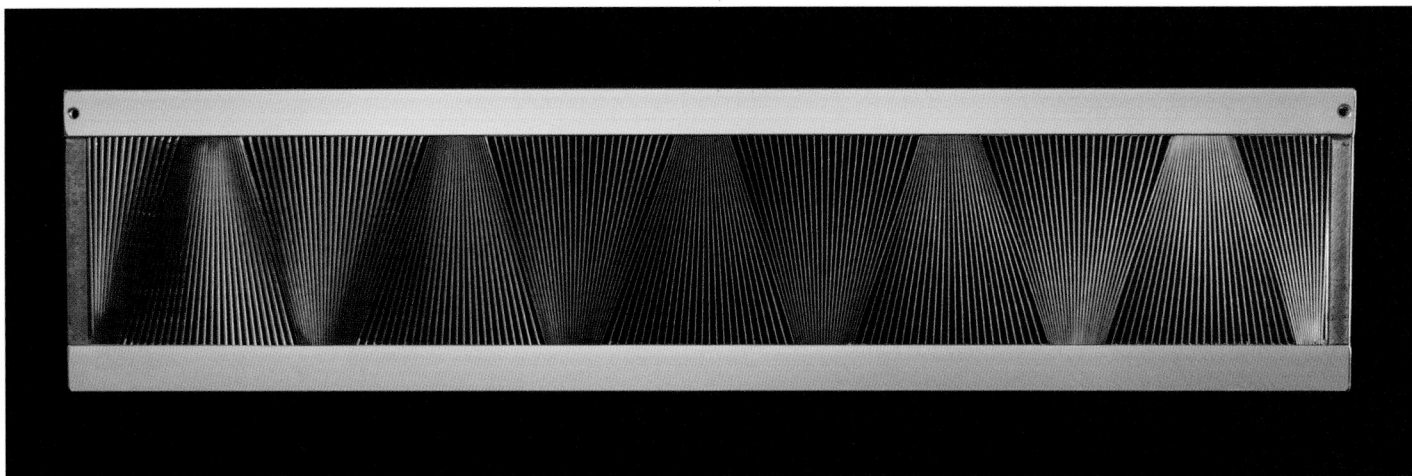

Lars reed. 12.5 dpi at mid-height. 22" long.

The first decisions I had to make when purchasing the fan reed were reed width and dents per inch (dpi). There was a choice between a 12-dent and a 15-dent reed, measured at the vertical center of the fans. These reeds, which are made in Sweden, are metric; the 12-dent reed I chose was actually closer to 12.5 dpi. This would be the most practical for me since I frequently weave with 10/2 cottons and 20/2 linens. Reeds with other dents per inch could be special ordered. The reed I chose had a 20.5-inch weaving width, the length recommended. I was told that longer reeds could be made. The 50/10 reed I ordered means there are 50 dents in 10 centimeters or 5 dents in 1 centimeter, approximately a 12.5-dent reed.

Anatomy of a Fan Reed

The basic building block of a fan reed is the ½ fan

Hybrid fan reeds may include straight wires

The whole fan shown here has 7.5 dents per inch

5 dpi at top
7.5 dpi at middle
15 dpi at bottom

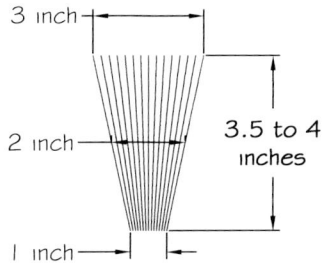

3 inch

2 inch

1 inch

3.5 to 4 inches

Fan shape can vary, but the dimensions shown here are known to be acceptable.

Example of a hybrid fan reed

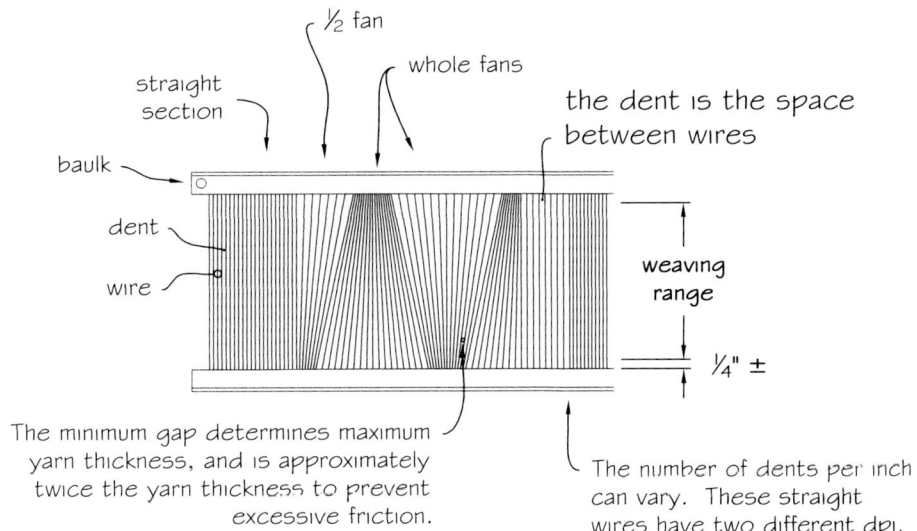

½ fan

whole fans

straight section

the dent is the space between wires

baulk

dent

wire

weaving range

¼" ±

The minimum gap determines maximum yarn thickness, and is approximately twice the yarn thickness to prevent excessive friction.

The number of dents per inch can vary. These straight wires have two different dpi.

Anatomy of a fan reed; figure: Tom Smayda.

I learned that the fan reed Glimåkra previously sold, and the one Suzie Liles used in her *Handwoven* article, was 12.5 dpi in the center, with 10 dpi at the wider and 16 dpi at the narrower base of each fan. Glimåkra had now redesigned their reeds by increasing the maximum angle of the dents, allowing for slightly greater undulation. The width of the broad base had increased and the width of the narrow base had decreased. My 12.5 dpi reed opens to 8.3 dpi at the widest part of the fan, its broad base, and narrows to 25 dpi at the opposite edge. Since I often weave with a sett of 24 epi, sleyed two per dent in a 12-dent reed, that would give me a range of approximately 16 epi to 50 epi within a fan. This seems to be the maximum angle for fans because of the abrasion of warp at the common wires.

After I began to use this reed, I realized that one actually weaves in the center of the shed, not at the absolute top or bottom, decreasing the overall usable weaving height from 3.5 inches to approximately 3 inches. Thus the range of minimum to maximum dpi is somewhat less.

I ordered a standard fan reed. For ease of terminology I will designate adjacent fans as ∧ **(caret) fans** and V **(vee) fans**, based on their orientation, and will describe the broad end of the fan as the **wide base** and the small end as the **narrow base**.

A ∧ fan has its narrow base at the top and wide base at the bottom. The opposite is true for the V fans. **Wires** are the metal strips separating the **dents** or spaces through which the warp threads pass. Each fan shares wires with the adjacent fans. These are designated **common wires**. The top and bottom horizontal bars of the reed are called **baulks**. The shape of a fan is an isosceles trapezoid, and half fan shapes, with one side adjacent to a fan and the opposite side adjacent to a straight wire, are right trapezoids. My 20.5-inch reed has nine whole fans plus a half fan at each edge (see photo on p. 68). The half fans at each edge allow me to weave straight selvedges. Using only whole fans will produce scalloped selvedges. At the vertical center or **median** of the reed the width of a fan is 2 inches; that of a half fan is 1 inch. Fans measure 3 inches at the wide base, and 1 inch at the narrow base. Each fan has 25 dents, and each half fan has 13 dents. Half fans can be inserted within the reed, but must have a fan on one side and straight wires on the other side. (See description of hybrid reeds in chapter 10.)

Distinguishing between ∧ and V fans is mostly of no consequence, since ∧ and V fans must alternate in the reed. Unless I find a reason to change, I will position my reeds with the corner holes on top. These holes are drilled in the upper corners of the reeds so they can be suspended with Texsolv cords if desired. The reeds could as easily be positioned upside down, thereby reversing the direction of the fans. I try to be consistent when possible, such as positioning the reed in the beater, for there are many other variables to consider.

Fan reeds have been adapted for use by handweavers. Sources that refer to reeds used in industry describe fan reeds as about twice as high as normal handweaving reeds. That would make their overall height about 10 inches. The fan reeds available to handweavers are perhaps 1 inch higher than regular reeds. Many of the looms commonly used by handweavers have beaters that open to about 5 inches, so higher reeds would not fit in our looms.

I have since ordered two additional reeds from Hans von Tresckow of The Woolgatherers, and I asked him to explain how a fan reed is designed. His detailed description can be found in Appendix II.

Jean Hosford

I know Jean Hosford from the Weaving History Conferences we have attended for many years. Trained as an engineer, Jean works as a house builder while pursuing her interests in both historical and contemporary weaving. Her experience in loom repair and modification led to an interest in drawlooms and other technical experimentation. What I did not know until recently is that she has an interest in fan reeds, and makes her own! What follows is her interesting and innovative process.

Like many weavers, I find weaving books published in Great Britain to be immensely inspiring. Great photographs without projects leave lots of room for speculation and the incentive to investigate further. Thus was my exposure to ondulé reeds, or fan reeds as I prefer to call them, since I'm shy about my French pronunciations. In Ann Sutton's Ideas in Weaving *are a couple yummy photographs of ondulé fabrics. Immediately after seeing the photos I wanted a fan reed of my own—but found the purchase price too high a hurdle. Being a carpenter and an engineer as well as a weaver, and not easily thwarted, I decided to try to make my own.*

I have a collection of antique reeds—some of which are broken—which I studied for construction details. These reeds are made by inserting the splint material between two split baulks and wrapping with waxed string. I reasoned that in order to create the fanning splints, I would need multiple wraps on the top of the reed and a single wrap on the bottom (and vice versa.) My first attempt using a 2:1 ratio of wraps between the widely and closely spaced sections didn't cause enough warp deflection in the fabric.

A first attempt, this fan reed, made with splints from a broken antique reed, doesn't have a large enough ratio between the wide and narrow spacing (ratio 2:1); photo: Jean Hosford.

71

I start by inserting the decorative reed end between the baulks and lashing it in place with the cord. Then I start inserting splints one at a time, wrapping between each insertion. I compact the splints into place with a couple good whacks of a thin bar of steel. A pair of clothespins helps to hold the wrappings in place when I have to go off and do something else. When finished, I carve the series number on one side and label the dent distribution on the other. The splints usually need to be trimmed; a small angle grinder works great for this.

Materials and tools for constructing a fan reed; photo: Jean Hosford.

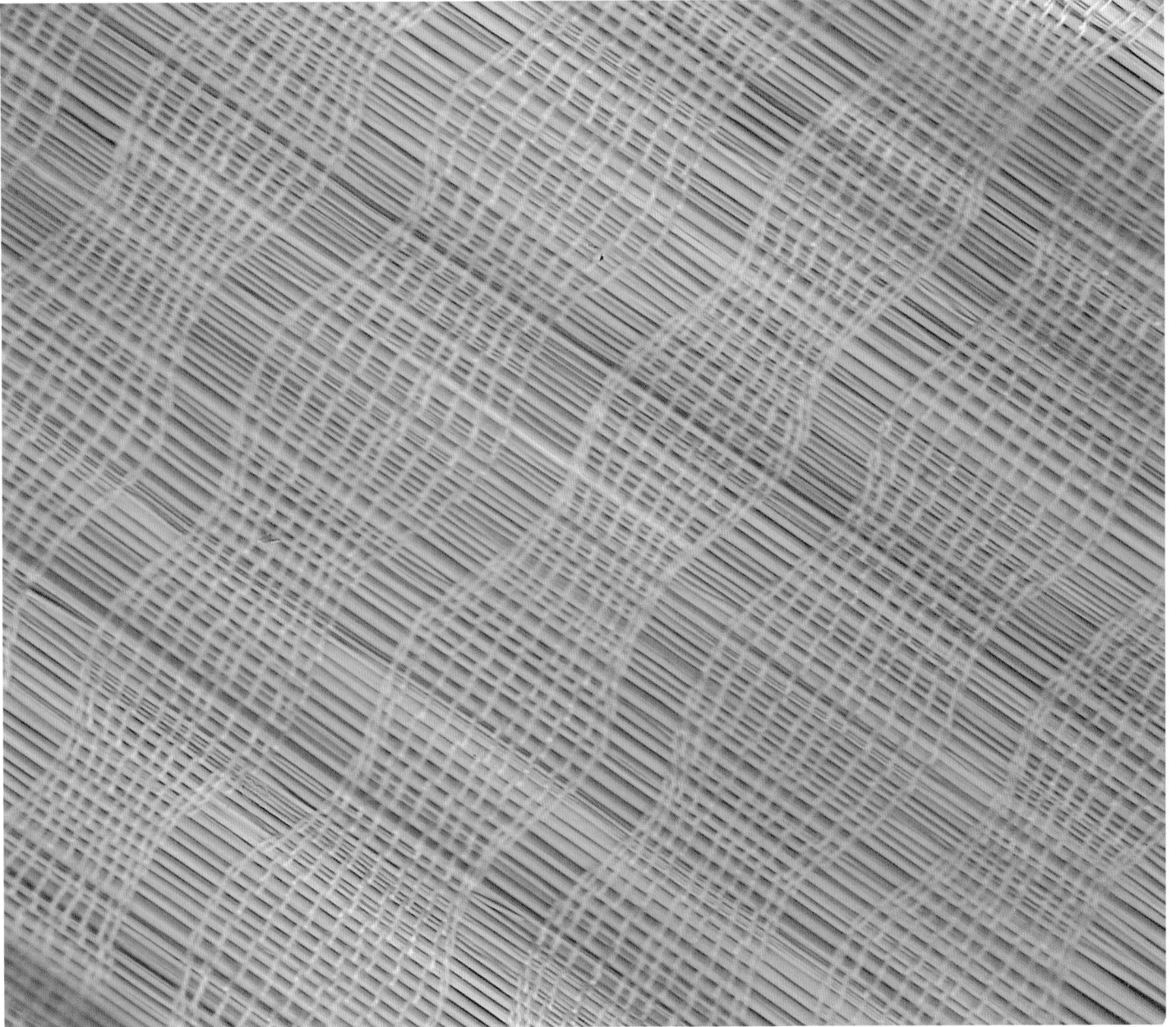

A detail from *Along South River*. Empty dents create a meandering path through a field of dried grasses collected along a stream bed; photo: Jean Hosford.

Loom Adaptations

It has been rewarding to connect with other fan reed weavers who are as passionate about weaving ondulé textiles as I am. Because there is so little written on this subject, we, who use fan reeds, have to be creative and adapt our looms to work the best way for each of us. That is clear in chapter 7, which describes how each of those five weavers approached this problem. One marvels that there are any ondulé weavers at all, until one sees the beautiful fan reeds and the resulting lovely ondulé textiles. Then it is all worth it!

That Amy came up with a way to adapt the breast beam of her loom is a marvel. She raises and lowers the supplementary breast beam rather than raising or lowering the reed, and it works well for her. Pat and Margaret have constructed ways to raise and lower the beater on their table looms. Karina and Anne use an Öxabäck attachment which must certainly be easier than my arrangement. They do not have to get up from the loom bench after every few picks.

Sara von Tresckow also uses this attachment and describes it here: "To facilitate lifting and lowering the beater and reed when using an ondulé reed, Öxabäck makes a device that attaches to the hanging beater of standard counterbalance or countermarch looms. The lifting device is attached to the side bars where beater height is adjusted, replacing the pins or dowels that normally support the beater. There are bars and connections to the lifting portions in the center of the device. Six predetermined positions are available to rest the lever handle. When the handle is lowered, the cords pull the beater higher. When the handle is raised the beater is lowered. By counting picks and using this lifting device, it is fairly easy for the weaver to keep a consistent rise and fall of the reed so that consistent fabric over fairly long yardage is possible."[2]

It is important to note that the distance moved by the lever handle is considerably greater than the vertical distance moved by the beater.

Sara added that she did not use this attachment when she used textured yarns that did not slide through the dents near the narrow portions of the reed. It was necessary for her to hang the reed from elastics. With the reed centered for a good shed, she pulled the weft into position, and finished the beat by bringing the reed up or down manually to the desired height for undulation. This mirrors the process used in some industrial applications, where the shuttle moves through the maximum shed and the reed is then lowered/raised to the appropriate position for beating.

Sara von Tresckow's loom with attachment;
photo: Sara von Tresckow.

Sara von Tresckow's loom, side view;
photo: Sara von Tresckow.

Section Two

Ondulé: A Warp Runs through It

Ornamental pattern work must possess beauty, imagination, and order.

William Morris

9| And So It Begins

In the past I have woven functional items, pieces for exhibition, and samplers for teaching. Now I approach my next projects based on the configuration of the reed. I believe that ondulé textiles are suitable for numerous applications: hangings, hung vertically or horizontally, and for pillows and table runners, maybe lampshades, curtains or room dividers, and certainly for scarves and clothing material. My next weavings will be designed based on the effect I hope to achieve, although with an end product in mind. I have yet to pursue repeated washing of ondulé fabric; I worried that the ondulé effect might decrease or disappear. Therefore I was glad to read of Pat Foster's test of repeated washings (see chapter 7).

The most notable characteristic of ondulé textiles is the undulating, curving warp. But also as interesting is that the intensity of the warp and weft colors change as the weaving shifts from warp emphasis to weft emphasis, alternating across the cloth. This is especially apparent in plain weave and twills. Areas of greater warp emphasis have a smoother feel and appearance, whereas areas of less warp emphasis seem rough and grainy. This has been described as having shadow effects, also referred to as shaded satins by John Murphy.[1]

Plain weave is often suggested as the weave structure of choice for ondulé textiles, largely because other weave structures may detract from the undulating design. This is clearly exemplified in the works shown in chapter 7, and even more in the lovely Japanese textiles in chapter 6. However, exploring weave structures has been a significant part of my development as a weaver, and this continues to be important in my journey with fan reeds.

I have used the following weave structures with the fan reed:

- plain weave, plain weave with spaced denting
- straight twills: 3-shaft, 4-shaft, 5-shaft, 6-shaft
- 8-shaft Ms and Ws twill
- traditional overshot and variations
- summer and winter: 4-shaft, 7-shaft, 8-shaft
- 8-shaft two-block double weave
- 8-shaft two-block twill
- 4-shaft lace and plain weave
- 6-shaft combined weaves—point twills and advancing twill
- 7-shaft combined weaves—lace and tabby, lace and twill
- color-and-weave effect—two blocks on six shafts

A basic draft is included for each project in Appendix III. Each project warp can become one or several finished pieces. Where appropriate, for example with summer and winter, a threading key is given, along with a profile draft, if possible. My projects are organized chronologically, rather than by weave structure or final use, because each one presented questions I wished to pursue with further work.

There were two things I needed to remember when designing these projects. First, warp threads are the focal point; other design elements may detract from the simplicity of ondulé design. Second, the yarns chosen for the warp should be determined by the smallest space between two wires at the narrow base of the fan. Yarn thickness should be approximately the size of that smallest space, or half that space if the piece is double dented. Bouclé yarns, eyelash, or other very textured yarns that could get caught in the narrow part of the fan are not suitable, nor are elastic yarns. Many yarns I have chosen for these projects are those which can be easily sleyed two per dent in a 12.5-dent reed, that is 25 epi.

When I got my fan reed I knew only Sara von Tresckow who wove with one, so almost everything was trial and error for me. What follows is a record of all my experiments, some successful, some less so. It is a record of my growing familiarity with the fan reed. I had already woven undulating pieces, but had not used a specialized tool.

I. My First Attempt: A Sampler

My first attempt using the fan reed was a sampler, becoming familiar with the reed and beginning to discover its possibilities. I wanted separate color areas in the fans, a tonal color change in the center of some fans where no deflection of the warp occurs, and to emphasize a warp color line or stripe at the edge of each fan.

Having ordered the reed from Sweden, I set about designing a warp that was inspired by a weaving I had seen in von Tresckow's seminar. Designing is easiest if the colors and weave structures coincide with the 25-dent fans, and I thought it might be most effective. Using 22/2 cottolin in assorted colors, I warped the loom to have five solid color fans, and two color areas divided at the middle of a fan, where straight warp lines occur. A half fan on either edge allowed for straight selvedges. I separated each fan with one warp end in black on each side of the common wire. Warping back to front as I normally do, I threaded the heddles, then sleyed the reed.

Extra care must be taken when sleying the reed. Each fan's mid-section is not hard to sley, where the wires are sett at 12.5 dpi. At the wide base of the fan it is very easy; it is next to impossible at the narrow base. I found it is easiest to lay the reed flat on a pair of angel sticks, which extend from breast beam to back beam. When sleying, I either worked at the back wide base or in the next fan in the front wide base. To hold the warp threads forward where I could see them, I laid a flat stick across the width of the reed just behind the warp; I could see that they were being sleyed correctly.

During weaving, undulation is caused by raising and lowering the reed incrementally after a determined number of picks. At each incremental change the warps go through a different horizontal space, moving either to the right or to the left, or remaining straight if at the center of the fan. My Glimåkra countermarch loom, a Standard, has a high castle from which the overhead beater is suspended and can easily be removed for this process. Following directions from Sara von Treschow's seminar and those that came with the reed, I suspended the reed from the castle using the Texsolv buttonhole cords, arrow pegs, and S hooks that were supplied with the reed. After sleying the reed using the angel sticks, the warp was tied onto the front rod, and the Texsolv cords were adjusted so that the top baulk of the reed just rested on the warp. I marked every third hole of the cord as a guide and located those holes that would place the warp at the top, center, and bottom of the reed. For me, this was easier than the process Suzie Liles had used. She did not have an overhead castle, so she used paper markers fastened on both ends of the reed to gauge its position. While weaving, she had to hold the reed steady, parallel to the fell as well as at a constant height, always checking the paper markers. (See the measurements marked on reed shown in the photo on p. 42.)

My plan was to combine a study group project of an Ms and Ws twill with my first attempt using the fan reed. The warp was threaded to an 8-shaft 50-end repeat. I had designed the 8-shaft Ms and Ws twill to have exactly fifty ends in a repeat, neatly fitting into each fan. Even if it meant altering a threading design slightly, I wanted to fit my threading repeats into fifty ends (2/dent in twenty-five spaces in each fan).

The advancing twill treadling repeat of twenty-four picks proved to be far too complicated when combined with remembering when to move the reed up or down. I quickly realized I needed to simplify wherever I could, so I went to an 8-pick straight twill treadling and I advanced the reed up or down one position every repeat. (Appendix III, Draft I, Treadlings 1 and 2.) My biggest challenge was to hold the freely swinging reed parallel to the fell, preventing an unwanted weft undulation. At least the Texsolv held it at the correct height, so I was thankful for the high castle.

As I sat at my loom, making slow progress, I glanced at the loom's beater assembly leaning against the wall. The tops of the upright swords of the beater have eight holes one centimeter apart, designed to place the reed at the proper height for weaving. I could use the beater with pegged swords much more easily than the Texsolv cords and hanging reed! So I rehung the beater, put the reed in place, and continued weaving. I then had a reed always parallel to the fell. What a huge difference! Suddenly this slow process became manageable. Because my loom is 54" inches wide I can't reach the holes from my bench. I get up after every eight picks to move the pegs up or down a position. Nonetheless, I much prefer this way of weaving, and I have gradually developed a rhythm.

Advancing the peg to the next position or hole in the sword is equivalent to moving to the next hole in the Texsolv cord. I refer to the top position as #1, which lowers the reed so that the warp touches the top baulk, while #8 is the lowest position on the sword, and this setting raises the reed so that the warp rests on the bottom baulk. Weaving with gray tones of cottolin, perle cotton, and bouclé yarn, I wove the sampler, familiarizing myself with the

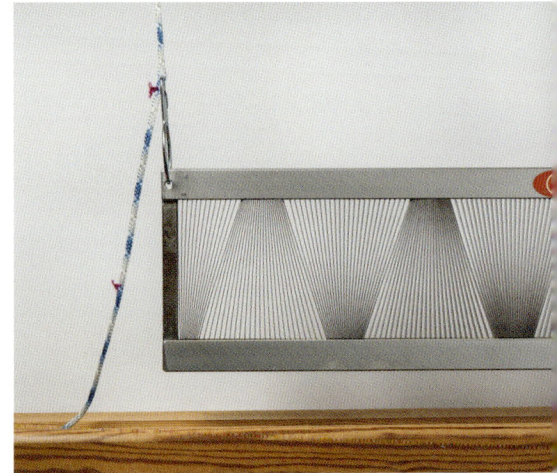

Fan reed suspended with Texsolv cord in a Glimåkra loom.

Peg holes in beater sword, pegged at position eight.

Two interlacements used in A Sampler; figure: Gretchen White.

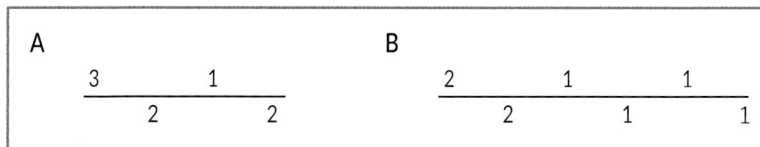

A		B		
3	1	2	1	1
2	2	2	1	1

characteristics of the reed. For some sections I used a temple, something I seldom do. One fan reed weaver said she always uses a temple, another said she never does. I needed to find out which is better for me. I needed to find out whether it made better cloth.

I worried that the undulations I was creating might shift back to straight warps once off the loom and wet finished. Because of this concern, I changed the tie-up halfway through the sampler from that shown in A on the next page's tie-up diagram, to that shown in B, to provide for more warp-weft intersections.

Regular twills are referred to numerically, based on the number of shafts, and on the number of adjacent warp ends up versus those down in one repeat. Thus a 2/1 designation means two warp ends are up and one is down in each repeat of a 3-shaft twill. Adding the numbers together equals the number of shafts needed, as well as equaling the number of ends and picks per repeat. This twill designation can be expanded to more shafts.

I had begun with a 3/2/1/2 twill, and changed to a 2/2/1/1/1/1 twill to allow for more interlacements and less chance for the undulations to shift back to perpendicular lines. Using this second designation, the warps and wefts interlaced six times per repeat, rather than four times using the first one. These are two of the many possible tie-ups for 8-shaft twills. Figure A, above, indicates 3 warps up, 2 down, 1 up, 2 down in the tie-up. Figure B shows 2 warps up, 2 down, 1 up, 1 down, 1 up, 1 down. Here interlacement occurs more frequently and the floats are shorter. Hence there is less chance for the warp to shift.

Using the second tie-up on the facing page, I wove sections in both straight and point twills. A detail of this sampler shows the difference in appearance caused by the two tie-ups. The bottom, with the darker gray weft, was woven with the first tie-up. The top, with lighter gray weft, shows the use of the second tie-up (Appendix III, Draft I,

Treadlings 3 and 4).

After wet finishing the cloth, there were no apparent differences in the curves, no apparent shifting of warp threads between portions of the cloth using these two different tie-ups. The sampler was steam pressed, then machine washed, air dried, and hard pressed while damp. There was no discernible difference in the width of the cloth or undulations nearer the selvedges, whether I used a temple or not. Puckering, movement of warp and weft perpendicular to the plane of the fabric, disappeared after wet finishing, except for the short distance where I advanced the reed height after every four picks. To my great joy, no obvious change in the undulating warp was seen throughout the sampler.

A few things I learned from this sampler: that I can become more experimental without losing the undulations; that a busy threading detracts from the simplicity of the undulating design; that a color change down the center of the fan can offer an interesting contrast to the undulating edges; that the black warp ends chosen to mark the edges of the fans produced too strong an accent in this sampler; and that puckers may be eliminated by wet finishing, or they may be kept to actually enhance the cloth. Subsequent projects will show how I have incorporated these design decisions. To me, the most important and practical thing I learned was to use the pegged positions in the swords to raise and lower the beater, making the weaving process more accurate and more pleasant.

Sara von Tresckow had recommended moving the reed up or down after every two to fourteen picks. More than fourteen would give only slightly curving warp lines, and she suggested that it was perhaps not worth the effort. In sections of the sampler I varied the frequency of moving the pegs, from every fourteen picks to every four picks. As expected, the puckering increased noticeably when the reed height was moved more frequently. In areas of warp

Two tie-ups for 8-shaft twills used in A Sampler; figure: Gretchen White.

A

SHAFTS								
8				8	8		8	8
7	7				7	7		7
6	6	6				6	6	
5			5	5				5	5
4	4		4	4				4
3	3	3		3	3			
2		2	2		2	2		
1			1	1		1	1	

TREADLES

B

SHAFTS								
8	8		8		8	8		
7		7		7	7			7
6	6		6	6			6	
5		5	5			5		5
4	4	4			4		4	
3	3			3		3		3
2			2		2		2	2
1		1		1		1	1	

TREADLES

A Sampler, detail, showing difference in fabric structure due to two different tie-ups.

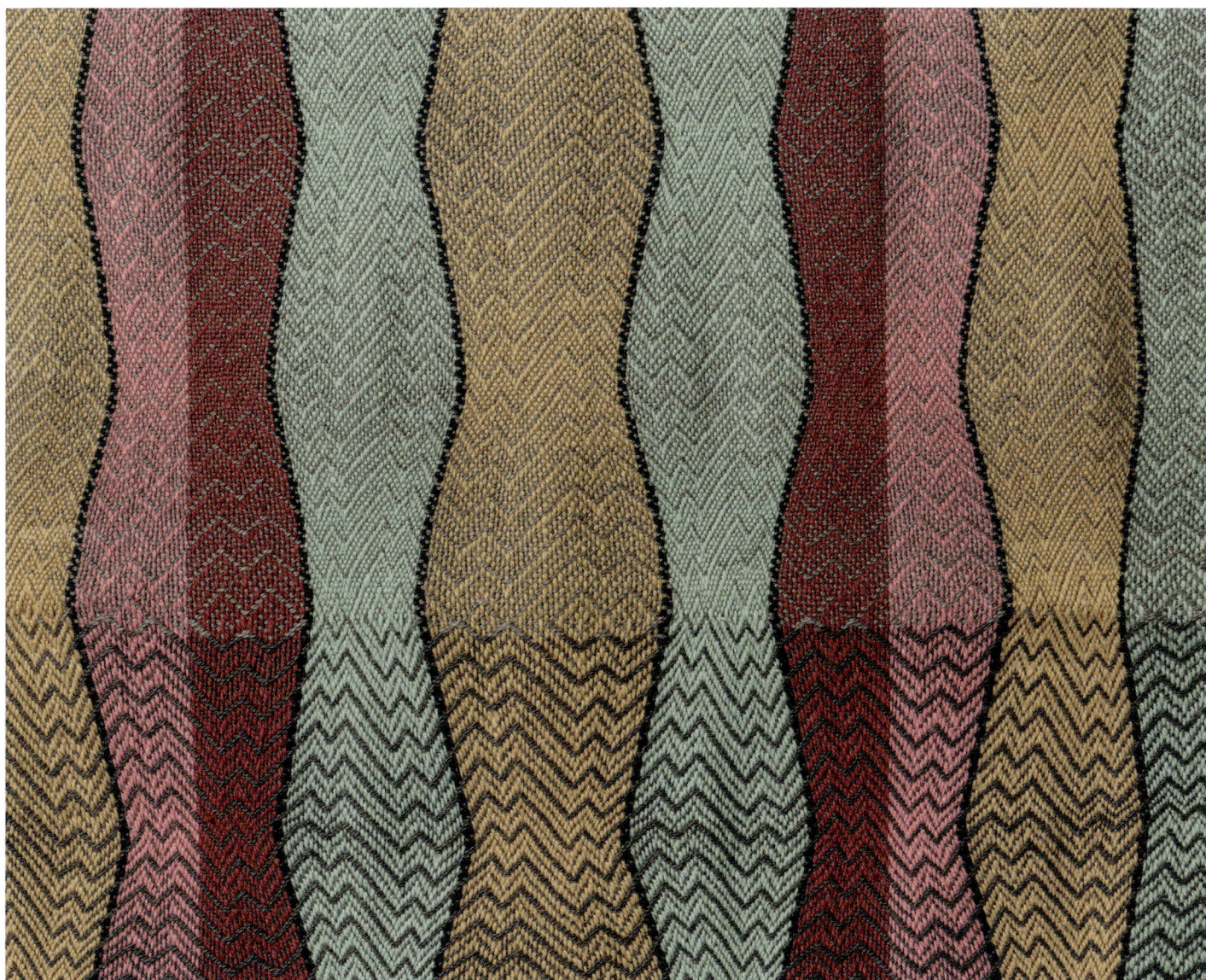

expansion, puckering or dimpling of the fabric occurs, where the widely spaced warps and the weft have room to move. There is no room for puckering in closely spaced, tightly woven areas.

Puckering is caused by differential take-up. The warp threads at the outer contours travel a longer distance than those in the center of the fans. Therefore those in the center compensate by moving up and down out of the cloth's normal plane, causing this puckering. Compressed warp areas in adjacent fans don't allow the weft to shift, so the weft also puckers in less dense warp areas. Photographer Larry Ackmann nicknamed these *Proper Puckers*. If they are not extreme, and are not wanted in the final piece, they can be flattened during wet finishing. On the other hand, for me, there is a charm in this dimensionality, and I often prefer to keep these *Proper Puckers*.

I knew it was wise to advance the reed height at the same time that I finished a treadling sequence in order to keep my place. It is impossible to see exactly where that change in reed position is made during the weaving, but I learned that any slight change in undulation will show in the finished cloth. I chose the number of picks woven in each position to coincide with the treadling sequence.

A high castle countermarch loom has two distinct advantages when using a fan reed. The first I learned when I changed from using Texsolv cords to using a beater that could be raised or lowered as desired, providing eight equally spaced vertical positions. The second is less obvious, but just as important. The pivot point of the overhead beater is a greater distance from the reed than that of an underslung beater. This means the reed is more nearly perpendicular to the fell, hitting it closer to the desired height for the undulation. Being able to move the beater back in its cradle helps as well. The overhead castle also provides a place for positioning the Öxabäck attachment. On whatever loom one weaves with a fan reed, it can not be emphasized enough that the beater should be in a vertical position as it hits the fell. Suspending the reed using Texsolv cords provides better vertical control. The weaver can hold the reed perpendicular to the fabric as the weft is beaten in. However, my large countermarch loom has other advantages that outweigh using Texsolv.

Because the design is primarily in the warp, and I have so many projects in mind, I keep my warps short so I can complete one and get on to the next on my list of ideas. In addition, I was concerned that I would experience poor warp tension, which would only get worse with a longer warp. Because warp ends nearer the common wire travel a greater distance than those in the center of the fan, I expected those ends in the center of each fan to get progressively looser. This has not happened, and instead, the extra warp lengths form into the puckers in the ovals where the cloth becomes three-dimensional.

II. Klee's Line Drawings: *Tamed Waters* Series

Michael Rohde, who wrote about his design influences in a recent *Handwoven*, says, "I honor the grid of the loom in my designs and (do) not aspire to emulate perfect circles or even organic curved lines."[2] In contrast, I have become excited about leaving the grid, even in an organized way, to stretch the curvilinear warp for varying effects.

Rohde is inspired by ethnic textiles, using the inspiration to create something of his own, and calling it a meditation on the ethnic object. I too look for inspiration, and wonder how the essence of a piece of art or a glimpse of nature could be incorporated into an ondulé weaving. My inspirations come from many diverse sources: weavers, of course (Theo Moorman, Peter Collingwood, Weaver Rose, Bertha Gray Hayes, James Koehler), painters (Paul Klee is a favorite), music, architecture, and nature.

Paul Klee, a Swiss artist and teacher, taught in the Weaving Workshop at the Bauhaus from 1920 to 1931. The Bauhaus philosophy was to rediscover harmony among the various areas of art. Most especially there was to be no division between the strictly artistic work and the handicrafts. Klee developed a design course specifically for weavers and taught color theory to the weaving students. He was interested in the subtleties of color that occur by crossing warp with weft, of transparent colors, and of a dynamic rhythm.[3] He told the weavers to "take a line for a walk," and Anni Albers, who studied and later taught at the Bauhaus, did so in many of her hangings.

Klee was an accomplished violinist who drew inspiration for his painting from musical rhythms and structures. Fabric designs produced in the Bauhaus were often based on Klee's ideas of the careful placement and motion of colors, color theories, and abstract designs. In his theoretical class, Klee taught principles of rotation, color swapping, repetition, multiplication, and division to the weaving-workshop students. These principles have a relationship to the woven structure, especially as it relates to the grid, and to color placement. He occasionally painted on burlap, which produced a textured ground with warp and weft showing. Klee was said to be the only master who showed any real interest in the weaving workshop, and he was clearly influenced by his weaving students.[4] In his *Pedagogical Sketchbook*, Klee's line drawings illustrate how he started with a static dot and created linear dynamics. His drawings on perspective

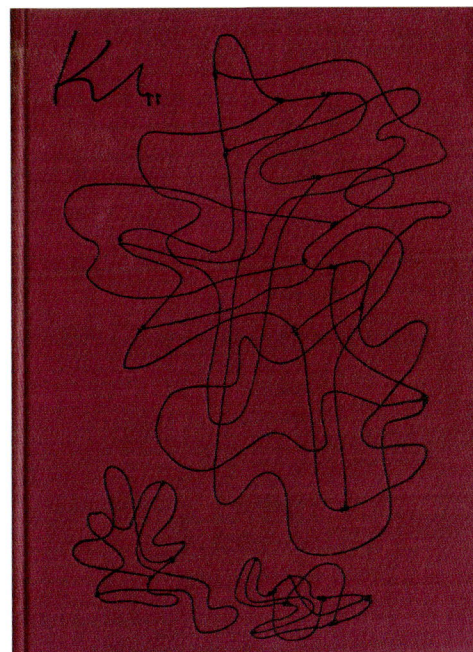

Cover of book, *Klee* by San Lazzaro, showing line drawing and signature.

look like sketches for a fan reed, and suggest ideas for placement of warp stripes within a fan.

Anni Albers, Peter Collingwood, and Theo Moorman, three weavers who have influenced my work, were also inspired by Paul Klee. Albers considered him her "god." "I come always back to Klee as my great hero . . . his art is lasting, and that is what interests me . . . . We were so full of admiration for Klee . . . ."[5] Collingwood said: "I have only to hear a few bars of Bach or to glance at a Paul Klee to have it hammered home that any creativity I have is of a different, infinitely lower, order."[6] And Moorman said: "An evocative mood can penetrate a near-abstract work. In the works I have chosen by Klee, Bissier, and Moore this is clearly seen . . . . The depth and space can be suggested through the subtleties and contrasts of texture. The painting by Klee, in particular, exemplifies this point."[7]

Klee's use of nearly parallel lines creates movement and energy in his drawings. Weaving, by virtue of the horizontal and vertical grid, can appear static. What can be learned from Klee to produce a feeling of motion in wall hangings? I frequently page through my copy of *Klee: A Study of his Life and Work* by Gualtieri di San Lazzaro,[8] and am inspired by his bold use of color, his pen and ink drawings, and even the woven texture of his ground.

In my studio I have a loom that originally belonged to Gertrude Liebman, a weaver at the Bauhaus during the 1930s. Perhaps Anni Albers wove on it, and certainly some of Paul Klee's spirit remains in the loom.

A series of three small hangings, *Tamed Waters*, was inspired by Klee's *Untamed Waters*. This project used a warp of 16/2 linen threaded to a 4-shaft straight twill.

The reed was advanced one position every eight picks for the first two hangings. The first piece was woven in plain weave with a fine neutral weft, and has a rough homespun look and oval areas that appear smudged. Here the linen sheen is obscured, unlike in the second, woven in straight twill. I was concerned that the undulating twill lines in the second weaving would give the appearance of an uneven beat. However, they provided a sinuous visual movement. I was glad to see the effect that the dense and open warp areas had on the straight twill. The ovals evoke images of celestial bodies, or phases of the moon. This one with a yellow linen weft has a smooth sheen, due in part to the linen and in part to the twill treadling. The result looks much more complex than it really is.

The third piece was woven in crepe weave (also called pebble weave), and I advanced every twelve picks or two repeats of the treadling: two picks of plain weave followed by four picks of straight twill. There is a distinct vertical striping of four ends that undulates within the oval area, and it also has a lovely linen sheen. I often use a crepe weave when I want some texture, but not an obvious diagonal twill line. Two plain weave picks and four twill picks combine in whatever combination works best for the project; other variations of these six work as well. This intermingling of plain weave and twill provides a more stable cloth than twill alone, which means the undulations are held more securely. This weave provides a more interesting texture than does plain weave. Combining two simple weave structures can often make a considerable difference in appearance and hand. (See Appendix III, Drafts II and VI, for examples of crepe weave treadlings.)

These three textiles were steam pressed, hand washed, air dried, and hard pressed.

What is fascinating about these weavings is how different they are, yet they share one strong characteristic. I see oval shapes in the open warp areas, and am not as aware of the contour lines as with the sampler.

While half the fans produce a looser weave, the other half is densely spaced and requires a uniform and firm beat. The average density of warp threads in compressed and relaxed areas combined is the same as the density of warp threads in intermediate areas and is constant throughout the piece.

Cover of book, *Pedagogical Sketchbook* by Paul Klee on
Take a Sea Green Line for a Walk.

Tamed Water 1. Plain weave. 22" × 11.5".   *Tamed Water 2*. Twill. 23" × 11.5".   *Tamed Water 3*. Crepe weave. 27" × 11.5".

III. *Scarf in Red and Black*

By now I was sleying the reed when it is in the beater. I can sley Λ fans easily. To sley the V fans I clamp a lease stick lengthwise to the back of the reed and work above it.

Could ondulé textiles be used for scarves and clothing? I wanted to see how the material would drape. I chose a red wool-silk for warp, with two ends of black mohair separating the fans, and sett it approximately 20 epi. The mohair was dented singly. The black ends at the perimeter of the fans were modified by the black weft and were not as jarring as they were in the sampler. Five fans, 10 inches in the reed, provided undulating selvedges. A 5-shaft straight twill with a 3/2 tie-up produced warp emphasis on one face and weft emphasis on the other. The reed was advanced every five picks to coincide with the straight twill treadling sequence.

Two processes here cause a change in warp/weft dominance. One face of the scarf is more red than black; the other face shows more black than red. This warp and weft imbalance is caused in part by the 3/2 twill structure, with 60 percent of the red warp and 40 percent of the black weft showing on one surface and the reverse on the other. In addition, on each surface, there is more red or more black caused by the changing density of the warp threads. This scarf very graphically shows these differences and is equally satisfying on both sides. It has a comfortable drape, with the undulating selvedges adding an interesting feature.

Scarf in Red and Black. 69" × 9".

Towels for Tie-ups Study

In order to explain how the fan reed and weave structure combine for the final color effect seen in this scarf, I looked back at an earlier study in unbalanced weaves in which I used a standard straight wire reed.

A 2/1 twill is unbalanced, meaning that one side shows a warp effect and the other side a weft effect. Warp colors are stronger on the top surface of a 2/1 weave structure. A 2/2 twill produces even amounts of warp on both sides of the cloth. To increase warp emphasis on one side of the cloth, 2/1 (3-shaft), 3/1 (4-shaft), or 3/2 (5-shaft) unbalanced twills can be used. Often, when using a 3/1 weave, there is a tendency for the edges of the cloth to curl, because there is considerably more weft on one side. This is an effect I don't want to conflict with my ondulé designs or the puckering. A 2/1 twill has less tendency to curl, and a 3/2 twill even less. With a 5-shaft twill there is a noticeable color difference between the two sides, and even more so with a 2/1 twill. I would choose a 2/1 twill if I wanted distinctly different sides, or a 3/2 twill if I preferred a more subtle difference (photo of the *Scarf in Red and Black*, p. 91).

Wanting to demonstrate this effect in woven examples, I set up my loom with a striped cottolin warp in a 3-shaft straight twill threading and wove one towel in a 2/1 twill. I cut off and rethreaded the warp to a 4-shaft straight twill, and wove two towels, one in a 2/2 twill, the other in a 3/1 twill. Again the towels were cut off, and rethreaded to a 5-shaft 3/2 straight twill for the fourth towel. This gave four towels, each with a different warp emphasis. The towels are identified by the number of weft stripes woven in at one end, the number of stripes being the number of shafts used. The photo shows the towels arranged in the order in which they were woven.

Four cottolin towels in straight twills, folded to show front and back differences in 2/1, 2/2, 3/1, and 3/2 twills, shown from top to bottom. Each approx. 26" × 16". Note that green weft stripes correspond with number of shafts used.

These four figures illustrate differences in the weave structures used in these towels. Ends per inch and picks per inch are the same in all. In these figures the upper half of the drawdowns represent the fabric as woven on a rising shed loom. The lower half of the drawdowns represent the reverse, and was created here using a tie-up for sinking shed.

I often use odd shaft weaves with their unbalanced tie-ups for the effects I can get, and the impact of this with the fan reed can be seen in several of these projects. With ondulé weaving the desired result is to see the undulating warp. This can be enhanced by something as simple as the tie-up. This is also important when designing warp stripes that are not at the common wire. They will stand out more with a warp emphasis weave than with a 50/50 weave.

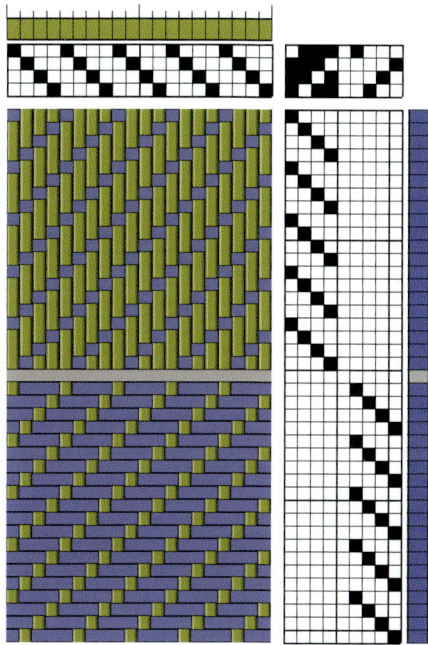

4-shaft 3/1 tie-up: 75 percent of the warp is on the top surface, 25 percent is on the under surface; figure: Gretchen White.

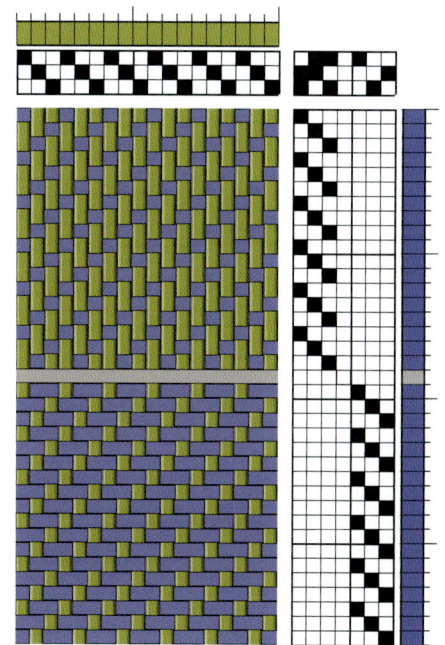

3-shaft 2/1 tie-up: 66 percent of the warp is on the top surface, 33 percent is on the under surface; figure: Gretchen White.

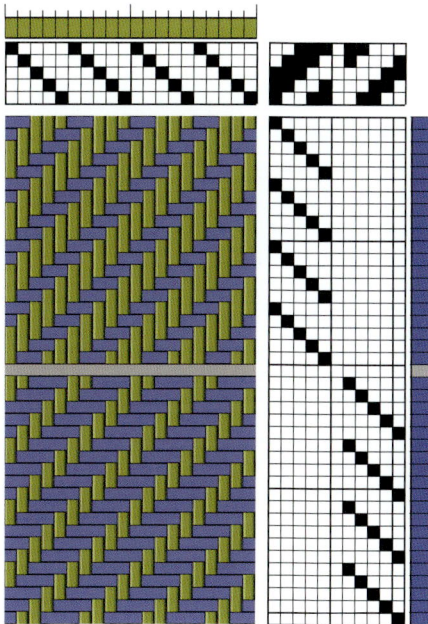

5-shaft 3/2 tie-up; 60 percent of the warp is on the top surface, 40 percent is on the under surface; figure: Gretchen White.

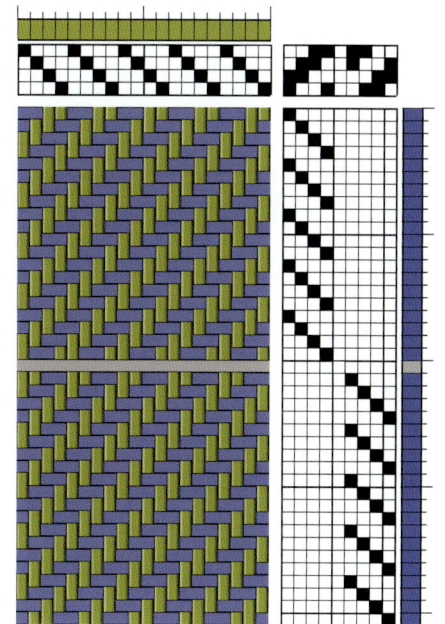

4-shaft 2/2 tie-up; 50 percent of the warp is on each surface; figure: Gretchen White.

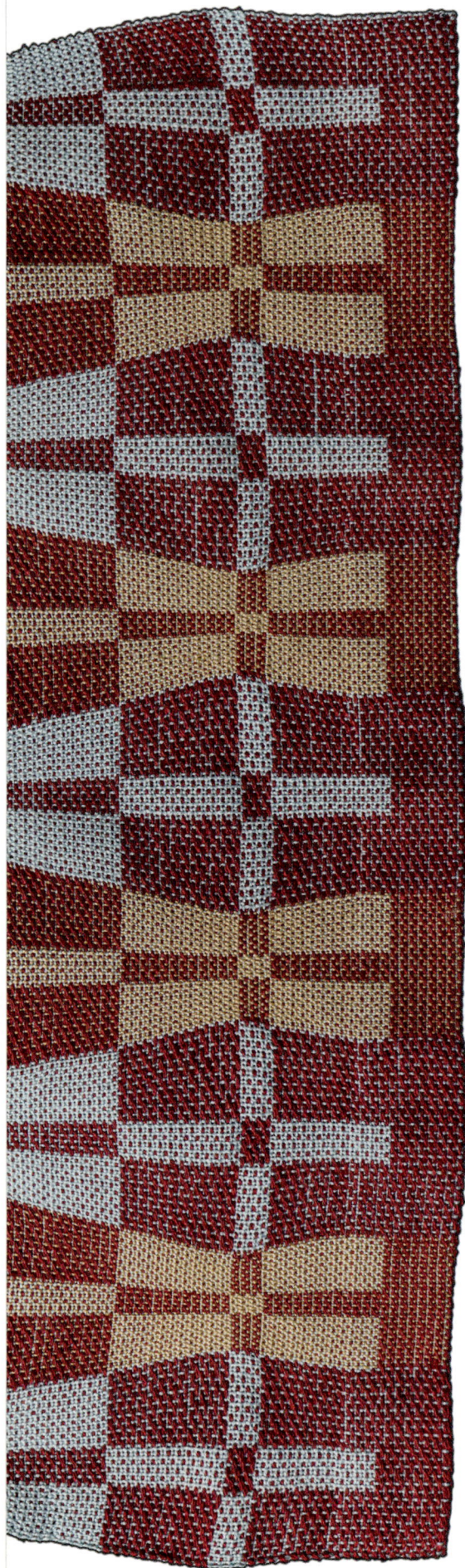

Using 10/2 cotton in light blue in the Λ fans and caramel in the V fans, and having straight selvedges, I first wove it tromp as writ, producing a very busy piece. The undulation is not a focus, and one does not notice the densely and loosely sett areas.

To enhance the effect of vertical curved lines I decided to add scalloped edges. I cut off the first try, and added twenty-four ends, a half fan, to each side. Then I continuously simplified my treadling changes. In the second sample the major color shifts occur at the midpoint in each undulation, with the narrow stripes providing an accent at the peak of the curves. The third sample, woven predominantly with one pattern block, sleek and clean, has dark and light thin center lines showing a slight expansion and contraction. The tabby and pattern wefts obscure the changes in warp density, which were so apparent in the previous two projects, and seen slightly in the top of *Tradition with a Flair 3*. The frequency of changing back and forth between pattern blocks is what gives a busier or calmer effect. The simpler the graphic image, the more noticeable the undulation becomes. This project was a learning process for me. I began with a traditional approach to weaving an ordinary two block pattern, and so obscured the intended design. To highlight the ovals, hourglass shapes, and warp curves I had to keep simplifying the design.

The oval areas lay flat even before they were hard pressed. I wonder if this is because the combination of tabby and pattern uses twice as many weft shots as ends per inch. There are many paths to investigate.

Tradition with a Flair 2. 11" × 17".

Tradition with a Flair 3. 18" × 17".

V. *Estrellita* Series
Estrellita, Italian Fashion, Flame Point, Crystalline

For my fifth warp I chose a small traditional overshot pattern. I looked through *Weaving Designs by Bertha Gray Hayes: Miniature Overshot Patterns*[9] until I found a pattern with fifty ends per repeat, which would fit neatly into the twenty-five dents per fan. *Estrellita*, or "little star," #22, has a star-shaped motif, and I envisioned the star points dramatically extending or shrinking horizontally. As I did with the summer and winter project, I alternated fan colors, this time in pale blue and white. This was treadled tromp as writ, adding a silver metallic thread to the blue pattern yarn as Bertha Gray Hayes might have done. I was surprised to see no visible undulation in the warp stripes, and no apparent horizontal movement of the motif, even though both are there. The undulations of the blue and white stripes are masked by the movement of the points of the stars in the overshot motif. I had to look very closely to see the undulation. Normally changes in color from fan to fan enhance this effect, so it was a surprise to find that the overshot motif negated it. This was definitely counterproductive!

I then experimented with polychrome and lace treadlings. When woven in Italian fashion in teal, gray, and tan, and flame point in greens, the undulations became obvious. Italian fashion uses three weft colors (a,b,c) in rotation within each block, with the transition thread in color a. Flame point uses four weft colors (a,b,c,d) in rotation. Colors for block A are a,b,c,d; for Block B, b,c,d,a; for Block C, c,d,a,b and for Block D, d,a,b,c. Each block is repeated several times and the four-treadle sequence never changes.

In some sampling I changed the color and/or texture of the weft yarn for bands of weaving. This produced distinct weft breaks and disturbed the vertical flow of the design. For a final sample I treadled lace fashion, even though I did not expect to see any undulation. Each block is treadled twice, omitting the last pick when transitioning to the next block. To my surprise, this sample was the most successful attempt. The blue weft strengthened the blue warp stripes, and the lace sections clearly became a denser and then a looser weave. The selvedges undulated the best, and altogether I think this would make lovely curtain material. Treadlings for these three techniques are shown in Appendix III, Draft V, *Estrellita* Variations.

A photo on the facing page shows Miss Hayes's handwritten drawdown from her working notebook, and the card with her handwoven sample.

Estrellita series. *Estrellita*. 27" × 17".

Estrellita series. *Italian Fashion*. 17" × 17".

Estrellita series. *Flame Point*. 25" × 17".

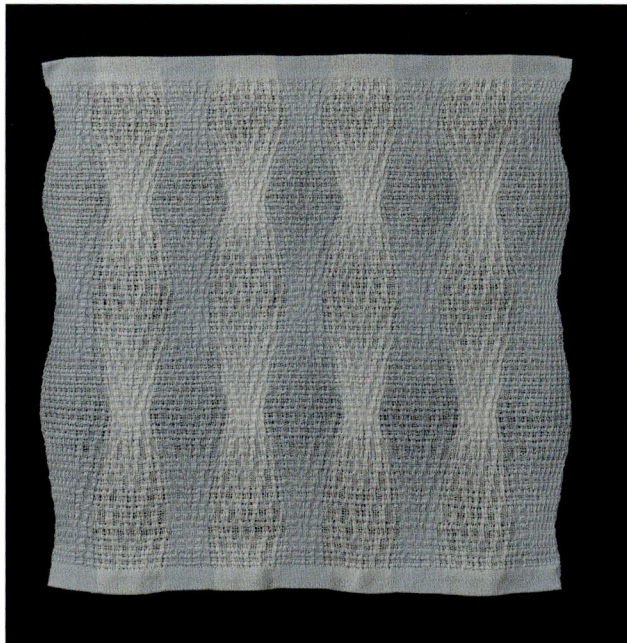

Estrellita series. *Crystalline*. 18" × 17".

Miss Hayes's handwritten draft page and card #22 with woven sample, on *Estrellita*.

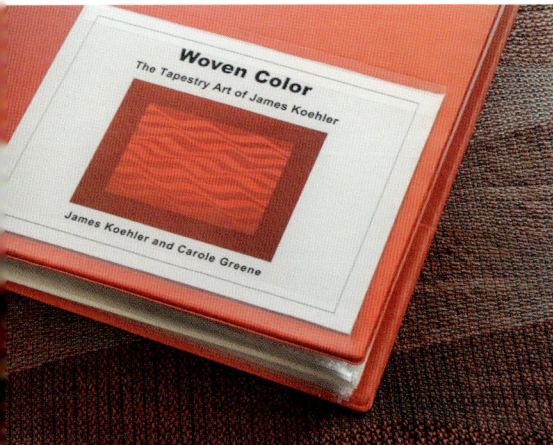

Ondulé projects binder with inspirational photo of Koehler tapestry.

VI. Landscape Series with *Lars*
Coastal Fog, Twilight Moon over the Bay, Cranberry Bog

For my sixth warp I used seven tones of 10/2 gray cotton from Lunatic Fringe, threaded to a 4-shaft twill in a dark to light scale. My inspiration came from several tapestries by James Koehler, depicting Southwest landscapes. A postcard of his weaving decorates my ondulé projects binder. Curves can create a feeling of comfort by mimicking nature's organic forms. I wanted to create rolling hillsides, or sandy ripples on the beach.

Could I hang these pieces horizontally, creating the feel of a distant landscape? For that I would want straight selvedges, so they could be mounted with the selvedges top and bottom. Hence I used half fans at each side. In order to avoid diagonal twill lines, and for a more stable cloth, all three were woven with some version of crepe weave. I liked the effect and named these three *Coastal Fog, Twilight Moon over the Bay*, and *Cranberry Bog*. The first two I see as horizontal landscapes. *Cranberry Bog* is more pleasing hung vertically. Is there more movement with the vertical undulations? Is it the color? I will try this landscape idea again, adding a more subtle play of colors as Koehler did, and varying the length of the undulations for interest.

The intensity of the warp and weft colors changes as the weave shifts from the hourglass warp-emphasis shape to the oval weft-emphasis shape. This feature seems especially noticeable in these three pieces, due in large part to the gray scale warp.

I sampled the remaining warp with a monofilament weft, wondering if the undulation would hold its place or move back to vertical on this slippery thread. Even weaving with twelve picks twill, two tabby, there was no shifting of the undulating warp ends. This could make a very striking room divider or unusual curtain material. I had never woven with monofilament before, but now it is something I will continue to try with some of these fan reed warps.

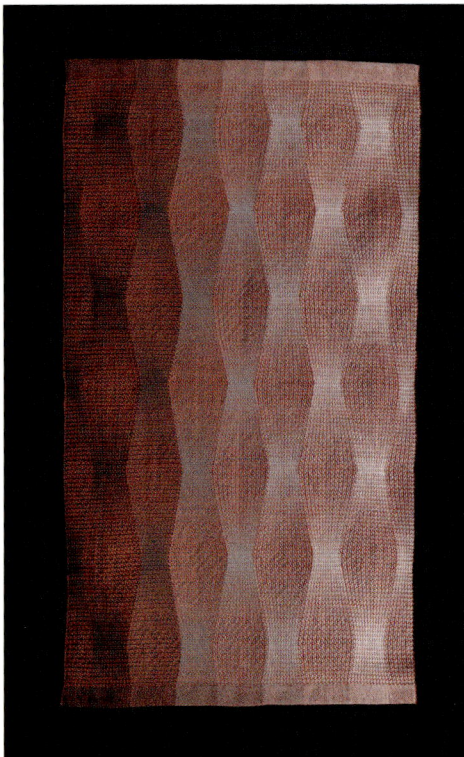

Landscape series with *Lars. Cranberry Bog.* 30" × 16".

Landscape series with *Lars. Twilight Moon over the Bay*. 16" × 24".

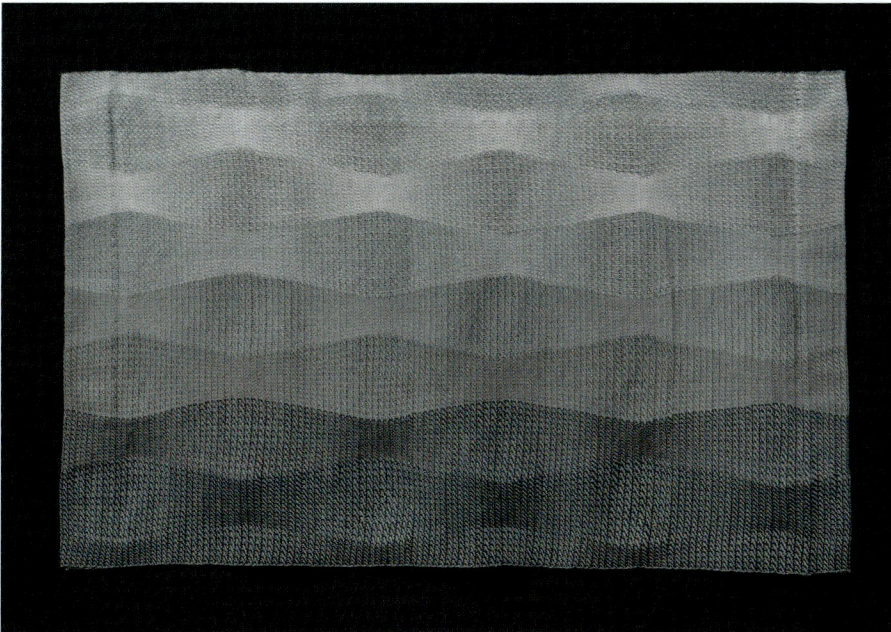

Landscape series with *Lars. Coastal Fog.* 16" × 24".

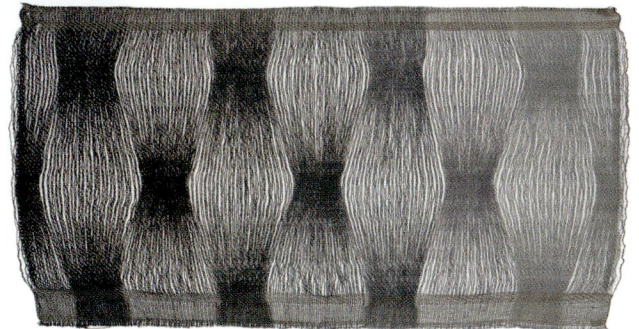

Landscape warp woven with monofilament. 9" × 16".

Lagoon City on loom; photo: Larry Ackmann.

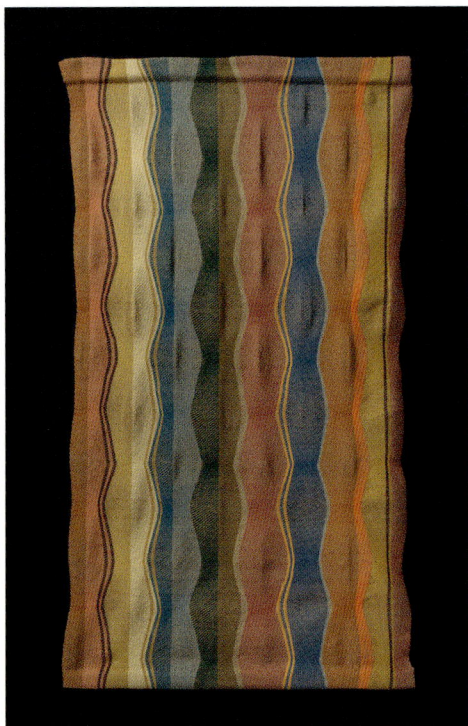

The Colors of Klee series. *Lagoon City*. 27" × 15".

VII. The Colors of Klee Series
Lagoon City, Monument in Fertile Valley, With Green Stockings

Inspired by Klee's vibrant use of color, I chose many cones of yarn in order to achieve the fluid effect of his water-colors. An advantage of having a large stash of yarn, even in small amounts, is being able to play with warp stripes. I eventually decided on this multi-color sequence, designing the stripes around placement within the fans.

I like the effect of narrow stripes, which show more movement, ribbons of undulating color, so these stripes were placed at or near the edges of the fans. A 3-shaft straight twill was chosen for warp emphasis that would not cause additional puckering. The straight vertical lines, where a color change occurs near the center of a fan, offer a strong contrast.

I wanted to use eight complete fans for undulating selvedges, which meant weaving 2 inches off center in the reed. This produces selvedges which undulate simultaneously to the left or to the right. *Lagoon City*, my 3-shaft twill of many colors, was exhibited in the Complex Weavers exhibition, Complexity 2014.

I was not satisfied with the bright orange stripe, so after weaving the first piece I replaced those twelve ends with six ends gray and six ends light yellow, unifying the palette. I advanced pegs after three treadling repeats (nine picks) for two pieces, then for the third piece I advanced after every six picks for a more puckered effect. In *Monument in Fertile Valley* and *With Green Stockings*, to break up the strong vertical elements, I wove in weft emphasis stripes at peg positions 1 and 8 where the greatest compression and expansion of warps occur. The weft twill lines in *Monument in Fertile Valley* are less pronounced, moving in the same direction. *With Green Stockings* was woven with a clear golden weft and with a more rapid advancement of the pegs. This emphasized a rounded oval and caused puckering because the warp was more frequently deflected. Where the column is expanding the point twill line is most noticeable. It may look embroidered at the horizontal stripes, but is a surface weave effect. There is a subtle but noticeable right hand, then left hand, weft twill in the ovals.

To soften the impact of the strong verticals I added weft emphasis stripes. However, I found the resulting effect more disruptive than successful. The sweep of the warp ondulé is diminished by the addition of these stripes. In a later project I will search for ways to incorporate weft design elements that will not lessen the vertical movement. Using the simple twill treadling of these pieces, and reversing the treadling at the maximum width of the ovals, might add interest without detracting from the primary design.

The Colors of Klee series. *With Green Stockings*. 22" × 15".

The Colors of Klee series. *Monument in Fertile Valley*. 30" × 15".

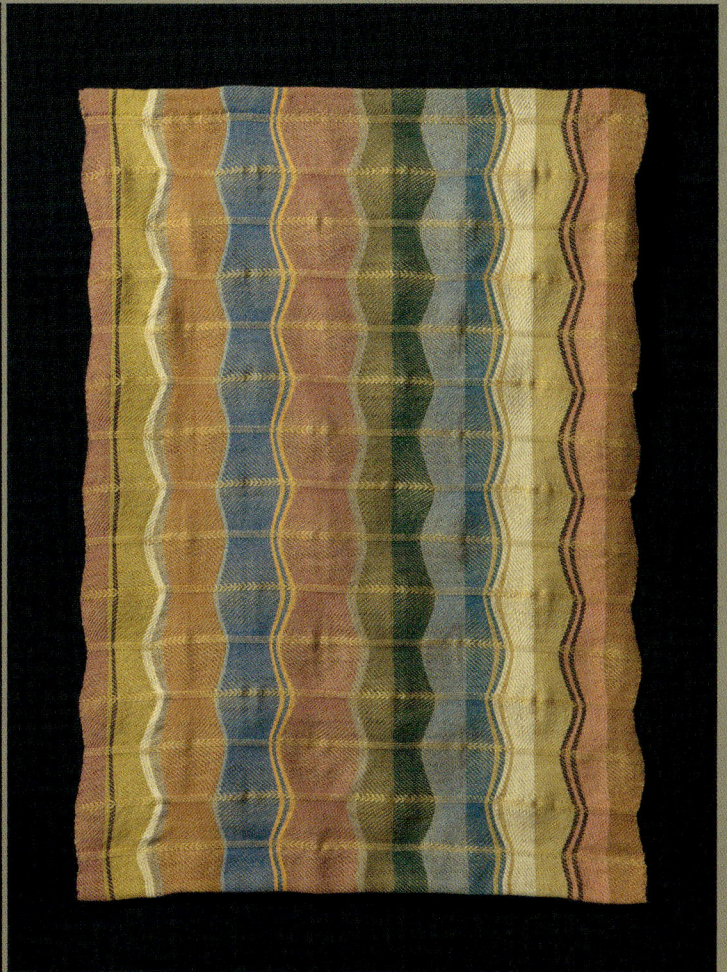

Double Weave series. *Circus Day*. 24" × 19".

Double Weave series. *Double Canals*. 34" × 19".

VIII. Double Weave Series
Circus Day, Double Canals, Landis

The next project started with inspiration from a two-block double weave hanging by Richard Landis seen at HGA Convergence many years ago. It had a fascinating strong circular movement caused by differences in color values. While his use of double weave was my jumping-off point, my ideas soon took a totally different tack. I became interested in how two layers of colors could play against one another, and as I spread out many cones of 10/2 cotton for possible warps, the color choices seemed endless. I arranged cones of yarn that worked together in pairs for double weave blocks and for blocks that are adjacent to one another. I realized that with double weave there would be twice as much weaving to get the same amount of undulation, but I needed to try it. The edge half fans with one pattern block at each straight selvedge are blue on both layers. This project is sleyed full width in the reed.

The right half of each fan is Block A, and the left half is Block B. Colors change from fan to fan. The center of each fan has an obvious vertical line, the division between two blocks. These are either woven with the same color weft for solid blocks or with a different weft for color blending. In previous projects the center of each fan was never a focal point, whereas here it contributes to the patchwork-like effect.

In each of the three pieces woven on this warp, I advanced to the next position after twelve picks (six picks per layer) and each block was woven with half of a complete undulation. That is, moving from position 4 up to position 1 and back to position 4. The next block was woven from position 5 down to position 8 and back to position 5. There was no difficulty with the shed or with warps sticking, even in the closest sett at the narrow base of the fans, where the warp is most dense. It was about 50 epi at the center of the reed and nearly 100 epi at the narrow base!

First I wove *Circus Day*, with a bright color weft sequence matching that of the warp, producing a very busy and cheerful piece. It definitely has the effect of a patchwork quilt. The second, *Double Canals*, has two salmon-colored vertical stripes that pop unexpectedly and surround a darker center section. The darker sides frame and contain the piece. I alternated aqua and rust for one weft block, reversing to rust and aqua for the next block. The weight of the heavy wooden mounting for *Double Canals* contributes to vertical ridges. As in looking at an Escher painting . . . what is ground and what is pattern? When you look at the bright salmon convex shapes, your eye is drawn upward into the entire column. Or, from an adjacent blue concave block, your focus shifts to that line. For the third, *Landis*, I simplified even more, using only beige for the weft on both layers. The curves and color added a liveliness and rhythm to these pieces.

I had enough warp left to again sample weaving with monofilament, alternating that with rust cotton weft. The monofilament piece showed the most puckering, with the two layers separating. The monofilament, an unforgiving weft, did not weave well. In the ovals, the block with monofilament weft appeared to split, whereas the block woven with cotton did not. Most of this sample was woven alternating picks of monofilament and cotton. The top block was woven only in monofilament, and clear spaces between the blocks show even more distinctly in this section. Holding this piece to the light produces the most amazing color changes, enriching the colors.

Double Weave series. *Landis.* 26" × 19".

Double weave warp woven with monofilament. 18" × 20".

IX. *Lilacs and Dandelions*

To honor the history of the fan reed in Japan, I chose silk, a fiber traditionally used in Japanese ondulé textiles for kimono and obi. Would the feel of vertical movement shift if the placement of the vertical lines shifted? I answered this question by incorporating both straight and undulating warp stripes.

I used a brightly colored silk warp, a 6-shaft straight twill threading, and a 2/2/1/1 tie-up chosen to minimize shifting of the silk warp at the fans' edges. I advanced every six picks. The placement of stripes of contrasting color is as important as the color itself in creating a subtle or a striking design. Subtle color changes reveal areas of warp and weft emphasis within a fan, based on the changing sett. Warp colors changing near but not at the edge of a fan, mask the exact place where the change in undulation occurs. These changes make following the curving twill lines more interesting. A gold stripe defines one edge, in contrast to the straight gold line near the other edge. Black mirrors the gold stripe on that same edge, and marks the center of the wide gold stripe. They complement each other. Within a partial fan, the wide rose stripe has one deeply undulating edge and the other with gentler curves. After washing and hard pressing, the undulations did not shift, and the puckers were removed. The scalloped selvedges accentuate the undulating design. Subtle weft stripes accent each end. The straight twill threading appears as an undulating twill. Looking at this scarf makes me smile.

Lilacs and Dandelions. 72" × 11".

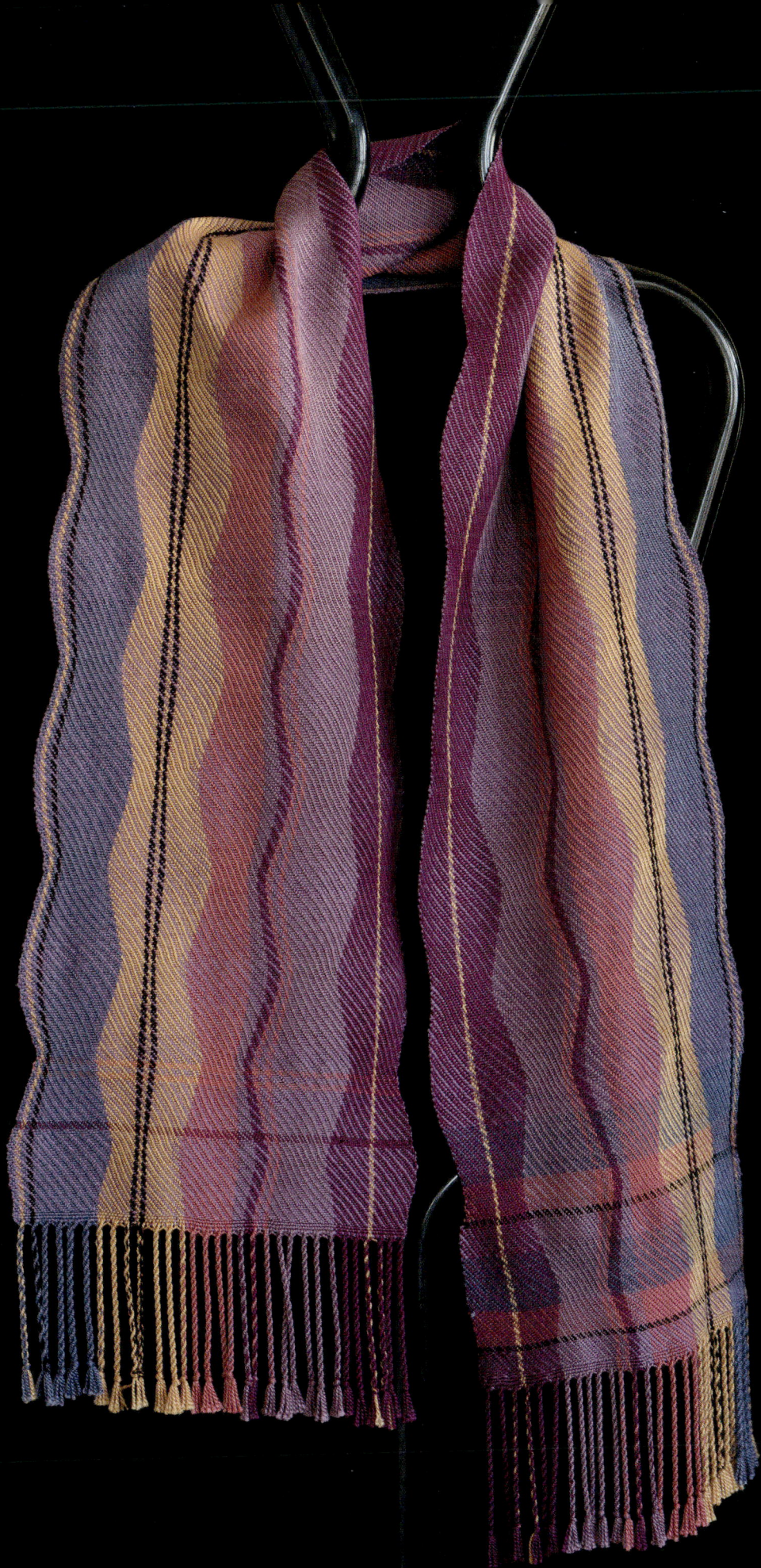

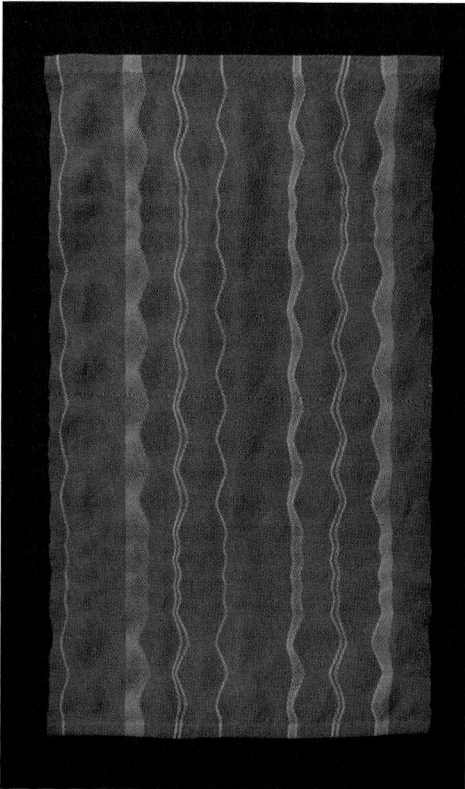

Counterpoint series. *Take a Marine Blue Line for a Walk*. 33" × 19".

X. Counterpoint Series
Take a Marine Blue Line for a Walk,
Take a Sea Green Line for a Walk, Anne-Sophie's Vest

Just as a composer puts hundreds, thousands of notes together to create a symphony, or a pointillist places a myriad dots on his canvas to create a painting, so does a weaver arrange hundreds of warp threads to interlace with thousands of weft threads to create woven works of art. Listening to classical music often provides a pleasant background while weaving. Attending a live concert is very different. There I am involved with the music in a more visceral way, and often find myself thinking of how I might interpret a musical section in weaving. These two hangings and the vest were inspired by watching violinist Anne-Sophie Mutter, standing tall and slender in her teal gown, playing Dvorak's Violin Concerto with the Boston Symphony Orchestra. The staccato rhythm, the shape of her gown, and the physicality of her performance were on my mind as I designed this warp.

The teal warp was similar to the color of her gown, with narrow stripes of silver, gold, and pale turquoise. This warp was designed to have straight selvedges, and a single straight line in pale turquoise. Then I played with curves and with the stripes in varying places within the fans. Sometimes two or three narrow stripes undulated at the edges of the fans. Other stripes occurred with less movement. I find that narrow stripes placed near a common wire reinforce the impact of those stripes at the common wire. The wide blue stripes spread across parts of adjacent fans. In both the *Marine Blue* and *Sea Green* hangings a shimmering iridescence is most apparent where the warp density is shifting. The *Sea Green* piece with a teal weft has a more subtle warp and weft interaction in those oval areas.

The two hangings, which I call *Take a Line for a Walk* (the reference is to Klee's instruction to Albers, to let the thread do all it could[10]) were woven on three shafts. With both I varied the rate at which I advanced the pegs, adding a subtle interest.

Something I had not previously tried was raising the reed less than a full oscillation; moving from position 5 to 8, then back to 5 and repeat, or 4 to 1 and back to 4 and repeat. This half oscillation would occur at one extreme of the curve or the other. These are shallower in breadth and shorter in height than full oscillations. I chose not to move the reed from position 3 to 6 and back to 3, which would be the same amount of vertical movement of the beater. This would, however, produce a barely discernible shallow sideways shift. The frequent and uneven oscillations of *Marine Blue*, especially, remind me of sea foam on cresting waves. These two hangings were woven in a double-faced 3-shaft twill for a firm textile.

I wove the third piece on this warp with a blue wool weft and a point twill treadling for more drape, and a more interesting cloth structure. This portion also was treadled for warp dominance to emphasize the undulating curves, which showed especially in the light stripes. I wanted this to become the front of a vest. Curves have an inherently graceful appeal, suitable for a garment. I was planning a vest using three warps. This was the first, and the only panel to have undulating warp stripes.

The other two warps used a standard reed. Both are 3-shaft double-faced twills, one in blue wool to complement the ondulé section, and one in cotton, in variations of cream and gray for the back.

Weaver and master seamstress Judy Schaefer designed this vest. She used a piece of the undulating cloth for a surprise effect, inserting it within a center back pleat. She also used some of the vest back material to line the vest front, which shows when the front lapel is folded back. Thanks to Schaefer's design and sewing skills, this vest received a Judges' Choice Award at the New England Weavers Seminar in 2015.

I wove off the last inches of the ondulé warp using monofilament as weft. This would make a wonderfully dramatic lampshade or curtain material. The monofilament holds its place in the open areas, forming two-end columns. This is most likely due to its being sleyed two per dent. However, the unusual treadling may also contribute to this effect. The gray and cream stripes are visible, even against the light. Some puckering occurs, but if this were stretched as a lampshade, for instance, the puckers would be stretched out. Ironing monofilament is not an option. One more avenue for exploration.

Counterpoint series. *Take a Sea Green Line for a Walk*. 29" × 19".

Counterpoint series. *Anne-Sophie's Vest*, front.
Approx 28" × 20"; photo: Judy Schaefer.

Anne-Sophie's Vest, back; photo: Judy Schaefer.

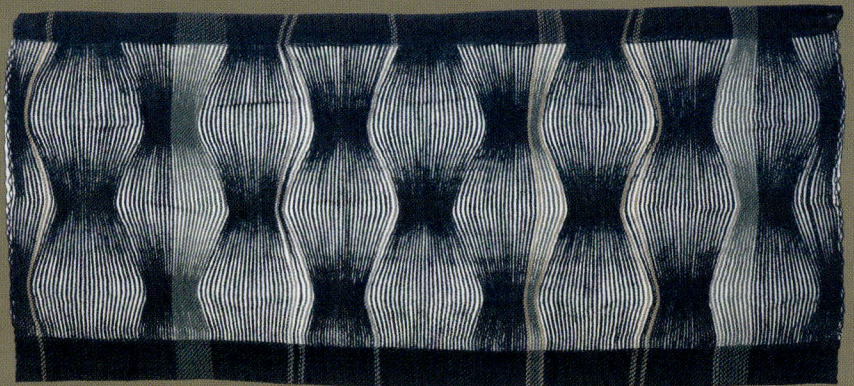

Counterpoint warp woven with
monofilament. 9" × 20".

XI. *Prokofiev's Linen Runners*

My assistant author, Gretchen, suggested I combine tabby or twill with lace to see how this would be affected by the undulating warp. I wanted to include narrow stripes in these linen table runners, evoking the memory of another Boston Symphony Orchestra concert. The cheerful, fast-paced, and melodic rhythm of Prokofiev's *Classical Symphony No. 1* inspired the design of stripes. The blue stripes were woven in twill for one runner and in plain weave for the other. The contrasting stripes of natural linen were woven as lace.

I was concerned that weaving lace would potentially cause tension problems. I experienced none, even with the unforgiving linen warp. It seems that the warp dense areas hold warp and weft in place. Any unevenness forms puckers in the widely spaced warp areas, only to be constrained again in the next warp dense area. There was little puckering on the loom, and none after wet finishing. A few weeks later slight puckering appeared, as the yarns had a chance to relax and move. Ideally, table runners should lie flat. Moving pegs from one position to the next less frequently, perhaps after eighteen rather than twelve picks (meshing with treadling repeats) might eliminate puckering. I like the length of oscillations in these lace runners, chosen to fit the scale of the table they were designed for. Another good choice for table linens would be a weave that lies flat when using the fan reed, such as overshot or summer and winter.

The blue stripes in plain weave seem darker, more striking, and are rough in appearance. The twill stripes are softened and seem more uniform. Although the pegs were advanced after twelve picks in both runners, the twill weave beat in more densely and undulations are shorter than those for the tabby woven runner.

Prokofiev's Linen Runner 1. Lace with twill. 50" × 15".

Prokofiev's Linen Runner 2. Lace with plain weave. 44" × 15".

111

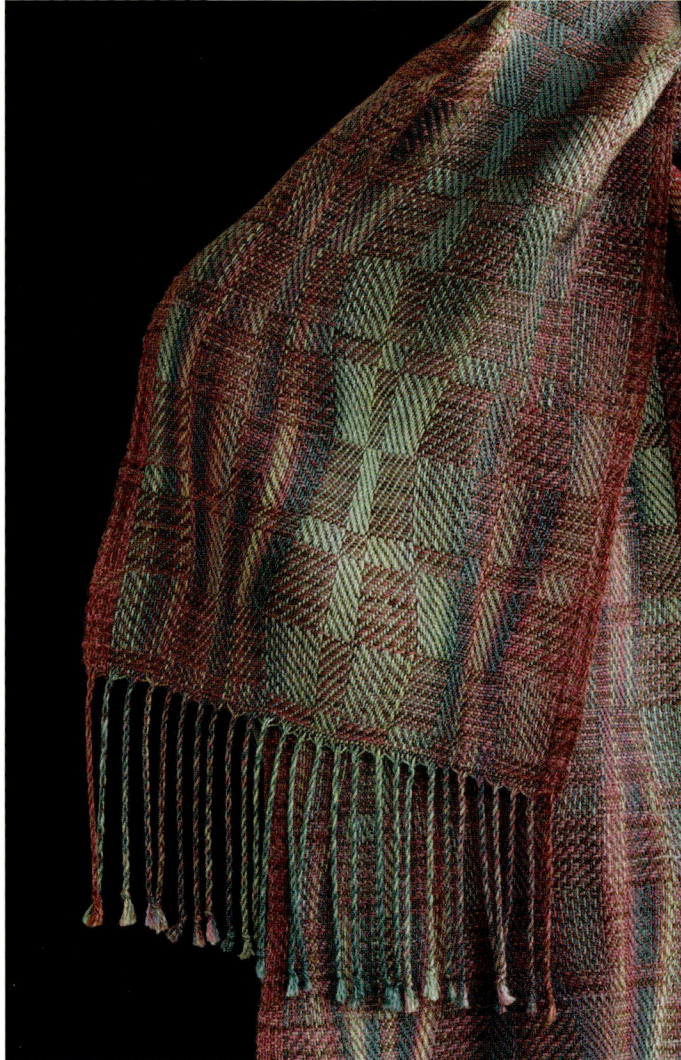

Detail of twill blocks in green *Scarf of Joy*.

XII. *Scarves of Joy*

The yarn for these scarves is hand-painted 10/2 Tencel, from Just Our Yarns, woven in a two-block twill. The first scarf was an exploration of shifting twill blocks on an undulating warp. This warp was woven in the same block sequence as it was drawn in, with a different but related palette for the weft. Treadling alternate twill blocks somewhat masks the vertical warp undulations, and a cross motif shows down the center of the fans. The effect is more of shifting muted colors and less of undulation. The photo at left shows a detail of the two-block twill weave.

The second scarf with a hand-painted cherry weft was treadled with a single pattern block and provides a more striking graphic design. The constant contrast of alternating warp-faced and weft-faced twills emphasizes the straight versus the undulating lines. The straight lines occur because the twill blocks change within the fans as well as at the edges of the fans. These scarves have a lush iridescence in the warp-faced blocks.

Two *Scarves of Joy*. Each 70" × 8".

XIII. *Alpaca with Proper Puckers*

I combined space-dyed merino wool, JaggerSpun wool-silk yarn, and alpaca in the warp, not knowing how each would respond to undulation. The warp wound on easily and evenly, with no tension problems. The alpaca developed Proper Puckers due to qualities of the alpaca yarn, in addition to its central location. Alpaca has more drape and more stretch but less elasticity than wool. When tension was released and the scarf taken off the loom, the wool and wool-silk yarns bounced back to their original length. The alpaca remained stretched. The yarn had to move somewhere, so it puckered dramatically in the center of the less dense warp areas. This was enhanced by wet finishing. More surprises and more room for exploration.

It is worth speculating what might happen if this alpaca yarn were used in selvedge stripes, especially if whole fans were used for scalloped edges. The space-dyed warp with pleasing asymmetric placement held its undulations after wet finishing, adding to the complexity of the design. The color changes accentuate different portions of the curves. Altogether this was an exciting and, I think, a very successful project.

Alpaca with Proper Puckers. 70" × 7".

114

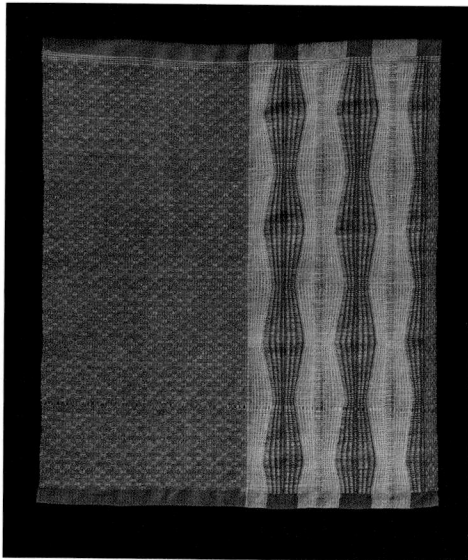

Garden Tulip series. *Lyric*. 24" × 21".

Lyric

Next, the treadling was simplified by using one pattern block in the fan areas, creating an unbroken, uninterrupted flow. A muted palette of variegated pastels was used. The narrow central dark blue line within the variegated column is echoed by a broader pastel stripe within the light blue column. On the right edge of the two dark columns is a fine dark blue outline, like a shadow, caused by the dark blue tie-down thread. It should be noted that the darker variegated columns are weft-faced, while the light blue, finer grained columns are warp-faced. The light blue columns physically advance from the cloth. The predominant pattern areas on the surface of *Lyric* occur in the 7.5 dpi fans. The repetition of a single pattern block causes a smooth surface. The light and dark columns share the visual impact. This will be seen to contrast with the next piece where the pattern block occurs in the finer 15 dpi fans, and yet it recedes visually.

Columbine

This piece retains the simple one-block treadling, the alternate pattern block from that used in *Lyric*, and has a copper colored pattern weft for a dramatic contrast. In all three pieces the straight wire sections were woven in the same diamond motif, which I consider as background. The central vertical copper lines within the dark blue columns can be seen to expand and contract. The visual emphasis is on the dark blue warp-faced stripes. Because the weft-faced pattern block is woven within the finer fans, where there are twice as many narrow units, the weft line is broken more often by the warp tie-downs. The copper pattern areas appear as ground beneath the dark blue stripes. In the previous piece the pattern block creates the figure. In this piece the pattern block creates the ground.

I shared my thoughts about this project with a friend who was studying William Morris's ability to show motion through his large motifs. When she saw these pieces she liked the results and suggested that this fabric would make a smart jacket. She envisioned the bold areas accenting the sleeves and perhaps a front panel, with the body of the jacket made from the small diamond background. Again, each development sparks new ideas.

Curved shapes engage the viewer, but it is important to strive for balance. Sometimes having too many curves may defeat the purpose of the piece. Better that a curve acts more like an exclamation point! I think this happens in the *Garden Tulip* series.

126

Landscape series with *Sara*. *Janet's Wood*. 29" × 50".

Landscape series with *Sara*. *Woods 2*. 29" × 21".

Janet's Wood

This weaving was conceived of as a landscape. Hence, the color shifts from the rich earth to the meadowlands, to the horizon and cloudy sky above. The width gives the sense of a broad panorama, suggesting a story. It allows for less regular oscillations with varying depths, and the longer wave-like lines provide a calm scene. The muddy, dark brown yarn bubbles up from the earth; the middle, dark olive green, provides the large meadow area with rolling hillsides, organic in feeling. The pale blue sky occupies two fans. The open areas, appearing cloudlike, are darker because of the gray weft. The juxtaposition of the dense and open warp areas is noteworthy. Some color changes were pushed beyond the fan edges to create softer undulating lines.

Woods 2 and Woods 3

In the next two pieces we look as if through a window to a restricted view. The first piece, woven straight twill, shows more dimpling in the oval areas, perhaps because of frequent oscillations. This textile appears opaque and substantial. The lavender weft provides a slightly warmer palette. In the second piece the oscillations are less regular, and thus more interesting. The broken twill treadling opens layers in the clouds, is translucent and laminar.

Landscape series with *Sara*. *Woods 3*. 29" × 21".

Deve series. *Deve boynu* on loom.

XIX. *Deve* Series
Deve boynu, Deve boynuzu, Deve tabani

This series of hangings, again woven with the *Sara* reed, uses colors reminiscent of Turkish carpets, and is named for symbols commonly seen in kilims and soumak rugs. A variety of linen yarns was used. Using summer and winter motifs designed to fit within the 9 dpi and 14 dpi fans, pattern blocks can be woven to give profiles facing right or left, or narrow vertical stripes. The profile drafts vary from fan to fan. The black and green borders reference the static center stripes, which contrast boldly with the muted curvilinear forms. All three were woven dukagång fashion.

In the first one, the yellow weft warms and lightens the warp colors. *Deve boynu* ("camel's nose") is a hanging in which I wove two and three block profiles. This warp, as with the Landscape with *Sara* series, was a challenge to design, to thread, and, especially, to sley. I find the results exciting, and worth the challenge.

The profiles are clearly visible, with the three-block motifs facing right and the two block motifs facing left. The gold of the pattern weft is similar to that used in the straight wire sections. Single pattern blocks were treadled within the straight wire stripes, softening them. There are two dark red stripes. The one on the right is tightly dented and is a pure dark red. The one on the left is widely spaced and is much altered by the yellow-green weft.

Again I simplified as I wove. The second, *Deve boynuzu* ("baby camel's nose"), was especially interesting because of the warp colors and shadows that occurred where the ovals expanded and contracted. In addition, the green weft is present in different proportions as the density shifts. It mutes and blends with the colors of the warp. The motifs within the less dense areas move forward physically; those within the more dense areas remain flat. Only one pattern block was used in each fan and the blocks, which are discontinuous, overlap each other from fan to fan.

The woven profile differs in each piece. The third, *Deve tabani* ("camel's foot"), is woven with one pattern block in each fan and it is treadled continuously. The warp colors are intensified by the black weft. The straight wire stripes are less emphatic by comparison because of the strength of the black motifs. Oscillations remained constant within each but varied from weaving to weaving. They are minimal in the last one. These works are richly textured because of the use of heavy tow linens in the warp.

Deve series. *Deve boynu*. 23" × 28".

Garden Tulip series. *Columbine*. 36" × 21".

XVII. *Morning Mist Shawl*

This rustic shawl reminds me of a foggy day, the lighter shiny ondulé being reminiscent of the sun breaking through the mist. I had a small amount of hand-spun, indigo-dyed cotton yarn, a gift from Rowland Ricketts, that I had been saving for a special project. I wanted to try that yarn here, with just three narrow stripes to provide a color contrast. I was concerned this hand-spun yarn would shred, or pull apart, especially between the tightly spaced wires. I used it sparingly in the 7.5 dpi fans, where the sett would vary from approximately 5 to 15 epi and have less abrasion than in the closer dpi fans. In the 7.5 fans I also used a slub cotton of approximately the size of a 5/2 cotton, and it worked well sett at two per dent. My instinctive choices were successful here.

The weave structure of this shawl alternates plain weave and lace spots in the straight wire section, with plain weave in the fans. This contrasts with *In and Out of Sync*, which has bold fan areas and less dramatic straight wire areas. *Morning Mist Shawl* is monochromatic with the exception of those thin indigo stripes which add interest near the edge of the undulation. It was hard to get a smooth flowing contour line when I advanced to the next position after eighteen picks. The slubs of the textured yarn influenced these lines, decreasing the ondulé effect. The contours appear more irregular. In the ovals the fluid versus rough grainy texture is dramatically apparent, differing between 15 dpi silver and 7.5 dpi light gray fans. The color variations are soft edged and cloudy. Tracking around the lace units as well as in the fans adds texture, as do reed marks which are not strictly vertical. I wear the shawl with the lacy portion draped around my shoulders, and the ondulé section across my back where it is more visible.

In the future, I will try another shawl with this reed, using heavy and fine silks. For a narrower shawl I might place the straight wires for a straight selvedge on one side and a whole fan with a scalloped selvedge on the other. Perhaps I will weave the fine fans and straight wires in one weave structure and color, and the coarser fans in another.

Morning Mist Shawl using *Hans* reed. 78" × 22".

Deve series. *Deve boynuzu.* 45" × 28".

Deve series. Detail of *Deve boynuzu.*

Deve series. *Deve tabani.* 26" × 28".

XX. *Scarf in Green and Violet*

Using the *Sara* reed, I wove a scarf with straight wires to left of center, some fans on each side, and parallel scalloped edges. This meant positioning the warp a few inches to the left of the center of the reed for a 12-inch wide scarf. The yarn I chose was North Light Fibers Forever Lace in an 80 percent alpaca/20 percent bamboo blend. The fans were threaded to 6-shaft point twills, which contrasted with the 4-inch straight wire section threaded in an advancing twill. When woven, the diamonds retreated and expanded, while the width of the advancing twill remained constant. In working out the point twill threadings, since the number of ends varied from fan to fan depending on the dpi, I wrote out the threadings symmetrically, starting from the center of each fan. For much of my work involving fan reeds I have not used my Fiberworks PCW program, because their drawdowns cannot properly represent undulating cloth. However, for this project, I worked out the draft on the computer in order to look at different tie-ups as well as different treadlings, to be sure the twill structures would weave well together. I like the interplay of twill movement. The advancing twill in the straight wire section moves to the right and then the left as I reverse the treadling. Simultaneously, the twill diamonds expand and contract within the undulations.

Had I designed this on ten shafts, and given the advancing twill its own shafts, I could have had a more dramatic central design, but I am satisfied with the results of this scarf. Because the dark weft is similar in value to the edge stripe color, there is subtle movement here, contrasted with the waves in the lighter green stripes. The black weft has overtones of garnet, which show as red tones in the edge stripes of forest green. The half fan light green stripes expand and contract symmetrically around the straight violet section.

While it may be difficult to keep good records and accurate draft sheets when using the hybrid reeds, I believe it is very important to keep good notes, tracking the thought process and the successes and problems that occur.

Scarf in Green and Violet. 80" × 11".

XXI. The Next Warp: Work in Progress

Project XXI is on the loom now. I am using the same yarn and essentially the same fans and straight wire configuration as in the last project. However, the weave structure is very different. The green scarf was woven in combined twills, while this one in light browns and tan is woven in a straight 2/2 twill. Will working with lighter yarn produce a different, more grainy look in the oval areas versus more shiny in the hourglass areas? I won't know until it is wet finished. I do know that these last two scarves are easy, pleasant projects to work on, and that it is good to have the variety of challenging projects and easier ones as a balance in my weaving life.

Work in Progress.

136

Conclusion

There is magic in a warp thread that curves off the grid in a controlled manner.

The Warp Continues

Having tried angle fell, macrogauze, and the shaped shuttle for variations on undulating warps or wefts, I know that I am happiest working with my fan reeds. It is not how easy—or difficult—the process is, for angle fell is quite easy and relatively fast to weave. With the rigid heddle sections, macrogauze as Collingwood conceived it is not too difficult to weave. Using fan reeds has limitations, but they are amazingly beautiful tools that produce fascinating curving warps, and I expect that ondulé weaving will keep me busy for a lifetime.

I am fascinated with curving warp effects on lace weaves, and even more with the striking designs that summer and winter motifs offer. Using an off-center section of a hybrid reed sparks new ideas. It is a challenge to design with the *Hans* reed, with its bold asymmetry, and obtain balance in the woven piece. I am working on a design for pillows using the *Sara* reed, and also have chosen a warp to weave ribbons. Will I go back to the *Lars* reed with its regular fans? Definitely. This reed is the one I will use for ribbons. Single fan reeds were developed in the early 1800s to weave ribbons with scalloped edges. I will weave variations of this idea. This expands the concepts used in creating *Triptych*. Based on warp placement in the fans, multiple forms will develop.

I noted that Karina Nielsen Rios uses leno to contain threads at the edges of fans. I have yet to try that, but will in a future project. I also want to weave a monochromatic plain weave piece, which will be in total contrast to much of what I have woven thus far, e.g., the *Deve* series. Another challenge will be to weave softly shaped rectangles, as seen in John Marshall's textile, Fukuro-obi, on page 40. I am intrigued with the effect this reed has on different weave structures, and there are many more to investigate.

Looking at the variety of lovely textiles woven with fan reeds has made me realize how much more there is to pursue. Contemporary weavers have taken the fan reed in different directions, and used a variety of materials, techniques, and design sensibilities. From the lovely silks of Japan to the crisp linens of Scandinavia to man-made fibers with their newly discovered potentials, from opaque to transparent cloth, from monochromatics to brightly colored textiles, we have revisited the source of our craft, stretching the boundaries toward the future of undulating textiles. I want to share with you this information I have gleaned, and now look forward to seeing what others will do with these reeds.

My ondulé work will be exhibited in a two-person show with fiber artist Jan Doyle at Hera Galley in Wakefield, Rhode Island, in September 2017. In addition, a select number of my pieces will be part of a three-person exhibit at the 2017 New England Weavers Seminar held at Smith College, honoring Antonia Kormos, Jan Doyle, and myself.

Exploring ondulé with fan reeds has been an important part of my development as a weaver. In writing about my work with ondulé, I have looked back over fifty years. I am intrigued by my journey. I see how each firm step has followed the previous ones, not in a straight line but always leading on to more adventures, along further paths to learning. I know where I am headed—more ondulé weaving.

Norma in front of Saunderstown Weaving School. The silo houses her Glimåkra loom.

Appendix I

Hints and Helps

I have developed a list of "hints and helps" to make the process easier for me, and to help maintain a rhythm in my weaving. Even though I have worked with fragile yarns, slub yarns, and singles wools, I've had no serious problems with broken warp ends. And this, although at two per dent, my usual denting, means 30 to 60 epi at the narrow bases of the fans.

These hints are meant to help you get started with the fan reed; you will undoubtedly discover additional techniques that work best for you.

- I had been concerned about differences in warp tension. Warp ends near the common wires travel considerably greater distances than those in the center of the fans. The more frequently I advance from one position to the next, the greater the warp curvature, and, I concluded, the greater chance tension problems would arise. And yet, I've had none. The puckers absorb the unevenness of the warp. The warp and weft are tightly woven together in the warp emphasis areas. That leaves extra warp and weft length to float above or below the flat plane of the widely spaced warp areas, forming puckers.

- Plain weave minimizes puckering, as does alternating tabby and pattern wefts, and more gradual movement on the pegs.

- A five yard warp will allow enough length for three wall hangings, two scarves, or one garment. I know that my first treadling idea often produces busy designs. By simplifying the pattern, my second or third piece is often more successful.

- Sleying the reed must be done with care. Margaret Arafat, dressing her loom front to back, does that off the loom where she has best light and control. I prefer to wind on first. Originally, I laid the reed flat, resting on angel sticks. That way I could look straight down through the reed. I sleyed the reed going through the widest dents, at one edge of the reed for one fan, then the other edge for the next fan. By clamping a lease stick lengthwise across the reed at mid-section, the warps can be held closer to the widest part of the dents. Once it was sleyed, I positioned it in the beater. Now, I position the reed in the beater to sley, again clamping a lease stick to hold warps up or down in the widest part of the fans. I recheck the denting frequently, at least once for each fan.

- For even tension I tie on with the reed set at position 4, where the sett across the reed is most constant.

- I begin weaving most projects at position 4, with the warp close to the middle of the reed and at the median sett. This is best for hems, especially with a striped warp, to insure that the stripes line up at the hem line. If you choose to begin your weaving at a different position, then weave the entire amount for the hem pegged to the same position, again so the warp stripes line up.

- Using an unbalanced tie-up, with more warp on the upper surface, heightens the visual effect of the sinuous warp curves.

- I *always* move the beater to the next position just *before* weaving. I always weave one or more complete treadling repeats before moving to the next position. Only then will I take a break. This helps me to know where I am in the process of raising and lowering the reed. Whatever your process, be consistent.

- I have several ways to note whether I am moving the reed up or down. Sometimes I choose a warp stripe and note whether the undulation has moved out or moved in at position 1. I can also count the pattern repeats in an overshot or summer and winter weave. I lace a smooth thread into the weaving to keep track of where I am when I advance from one position to the next. If necessary, I keep paper and pencil beside me to note whether I am moving up or down the length of pegged holes.

- The "sweet spot" for ondulé (mechanically the ideal distance from beater to fell for optimum performance) is not the same as for ordinary weaving. Always keep the beater as vertical as possible. This means weaving close to the beater, normally considered poor technique, and advancing the cloth frequently. I also adjust the beater position in the cradle as needed. This insures that the weft will be beaten in as close to the correct reed height as possible. An overhead beater is preferable to an underslung one, because the pivot point is farther from the fell. Having the reed suspended with Texsolv cords is better still for maintaining the vertical beat, but less desirable for its inconvenience.

Weft extender, made of clamps and weights, and extended over side of loom.

- I always change the shed when the beater is at the fell to hold the last pick in place. I generally beat firmly to get a consistent weave. Although half of the warp is widely spaced, the other half is densely spaced. Because the oval and hourglass areas alternate, it is not possible to over beat the looser areas.

- I use narrow shuttles for ease in weaving.

- Advancing the reed height does not need to be done regularly. Undulations can vary by irregular increments as in the *Take a Line for a Walk* series.

- I have tried weaving both with and without a weft extender, which I prefer to a temple because of its ease in use. I now regularly use a weft extender, and I believe it is especially necessary to help maintain scalloped selvedges. Half-pound weights are added at each selvedge. Using a temple and having to readjust its width continuously would be nearly impossible when weaving scalloped edges.

- Undulating selvedges are more noticeable than straight ones; in fact, they have a charm and should be noticed. If I use floating selvedges, I make them of the weft yarn. It produces a tidier edge.

- Make sure the warp yarns will fit through the narrow part of the fans. Bouclés, eyelash yarns, and elastic yarns are not suitable. Also, the warp yarns should be strong. A singles that might be acceptable in a regular reed is challenged in this reed, where it can fray as it rubs against the narrowed dents.

- Use straight selvedges when turning the weaving sideways to a landscape position, in order to hang it. Twill tape can be sewn onto top (and bottom) selvedges for a hanging device.

- Many weavers use only plain weave with the ondulé reed. After much experimentation, I have found that using busy patterns often defeats the purpose. It can conflict visually with the undulating movement of the warp, and can obscure the lovely subtle color changes seen in the hourglass and oval areas. However, different weave structures offer different effects, and should not be ignored.

- To accentuate the ondulé, other design elements should be kept to a minimum within each fan. Designing for a fan reed is not as straight forward as designing for a standard reed. Uneven denting may detract from otherwise interesting pattern areas. Consistent denting often can be more effective. Plain weave was the structure used historically, and twills are also very satisfactory. Should you use another structure, the units should fit within the fan, or the correct threading must continue into the next fan.

- Before purchasing a fan reed you must decide what sett is most useful. 12.5 and 15 dpi were setts offered when I bought my first reed. You can order one to your specifications. What yarns do you use most often? What sort of projects are you most likely to make? How will you make the reed work with your loom? These factors should be considered before ordering your reed.

- Fan reeds are more versatile, but hybrid reeds can yield remarkable and almost magical effects. They definitely present more of a challenge when designing. Using a standard fan reed for several projects will prepare you to design with hybrid reeds. Consider the dpi, the number of fans, half fans, and straight wires when designing. Ends per inch change with the weaving. Picks per inch do not.

Appendix II

Fan Reed Design

The fan reed is a weaving reed where the reed wires are not vertically attached to the upper and lower binding profile, but on an angle. A number of reed wires create a fan-like pattern, hence the name.

Fan reeds can be composed of alternating fan sections mounted into the binding profiles, or can be combined with normal straight sections in between or just on the ends. To get a continuous reed with straight sections, you have to use half fans before the straight section begins.

Since the reed has to be raised or lowered during the weaving process to get the ondulé effect of the warp, the reed should be higher than a standard reed, a minimum of 5 inches (127 mm) to about 8 inches (203mm).

For a reed consisting only of fans the weaving width should be a multiple of the fan width at the center of the reed. Since the number of dents per inch (dpi) or dents per 10 cm changes over the height of the reed, the nomenclature is defined as the dents per length unit at the centerline of the reed. Fans, half fans, or straight sections with different dents can be combined in one reed.

Another design factor is the enclosed angle of one fan section. The greater the angle of the fan the greater the possible undulations in the fabric. A maximum angle should not be more than 60 degrees, since the higher the angle is, the higher will be the forces and friction on the individual warp thread when it is moved sideways by the fan reed.

This angle can be changed by the height of the reed and/or by the ratio of the fan width at the coarse side, divided by the width at the fine side.

A good ratio is 3:1 (3-inch coarse; 2-inch middle; 1-inch fine = 75 × 50 × 25mm). The upper limit would be 6.5:1.

The minimum fan width at the fine side should not be less than 0.78 inches (20 mm) to avoid too much crowding at this end of the fan section.

The definition of a good working reed of any kind is: At least one half (50 percent) of a reed is the open space between wires.

The most restricted area of a fan is the fine end. Theoretically you can achieve that 50 percent air space at the fine end by reducing the reed wire thickness. The reed wire is produced down to a minimum thickness of 0.004 inches (0.10 mm) and up to 0.079 inches (2.0 mm) for carpet reeds. Unfortunately the thinner the wire gets, its resistance to bending forces is reduced by the factor of 4, when you reduce the wire thickness by half. If possible keep the wire thickness not lower than 0.012 inches (0.3 mm).

If a fan reed includes straight portions or ends, it is advisable to use an even number of dents per fan section, because you get in the center of the section one vertical straight wire, which can be used as the first wire of a straight section. Otherwise an uneven number of dents can be used as well in any fan reed design.

I have designed, and the reed maker has made, fan reeds from 7.5 dpi (10/30) to 25 dpi (10/98) so far. The maximal length of a fan reed is only limited by the length of the special reed makers bench, which is, at the moment, 20 feet (6.0 m).

Hans von Tresckow
The Woolgatherers Ltd
Fond du Lac, Wisconsin

Appendix III

Weaving Drafts I–XXI

The following twenty-one drafts represent the weaving projects described in chapters 9 and 10. Tie-ups are for rising shed. Project information is minimal. It is merely a guide to my thought process. You will go on from there, weaving your ideas into your creations.

Weaving drafts by Gretchen White.

I. My First Attempt: A Sampler

Weave: Ms and Ws 8-shaft twill
Warp: cottolin   Weft: cotton
                                    cottolin
Reed: Lars   Sett: 25 epi

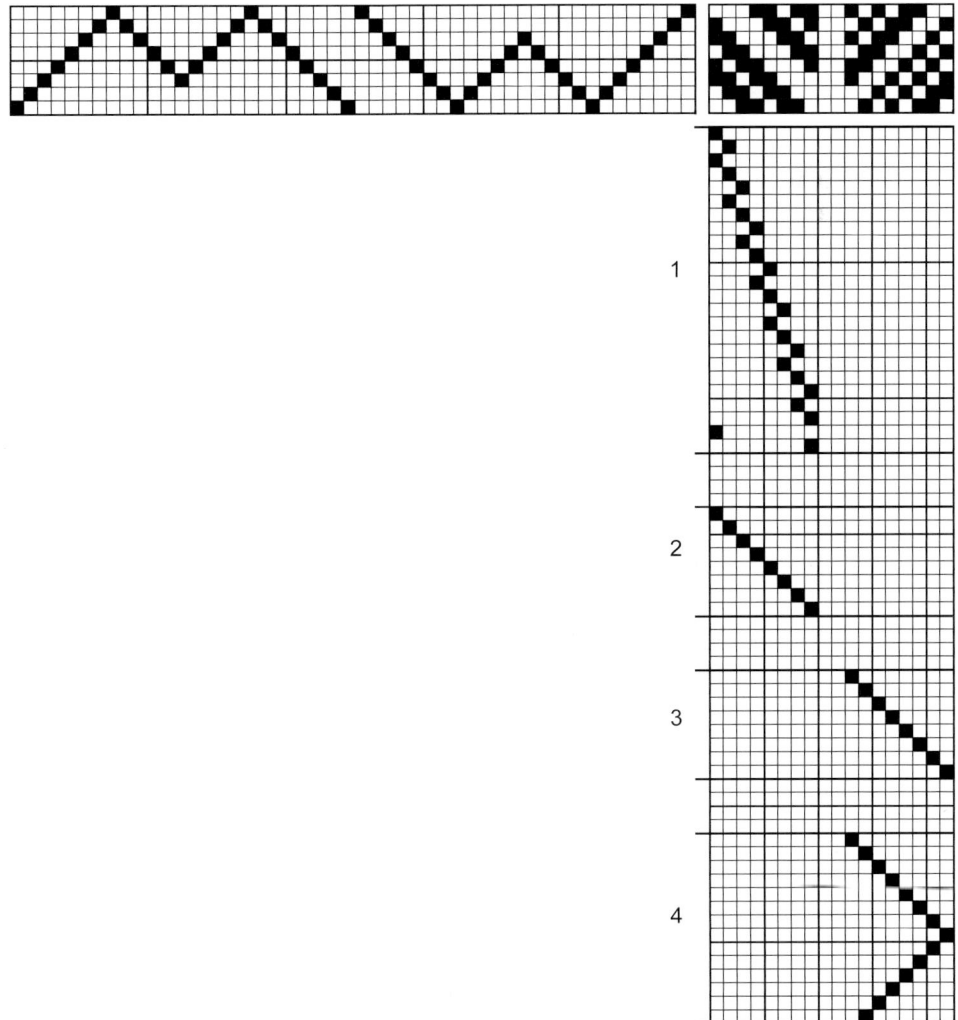

II. Klee's Line Drawings: *Tamed Waters*

Weave: 4-shaft twill
Warp: 16/2 linen   Weft: 16/2 linen
Reed: Lars   Sett: 25 epi

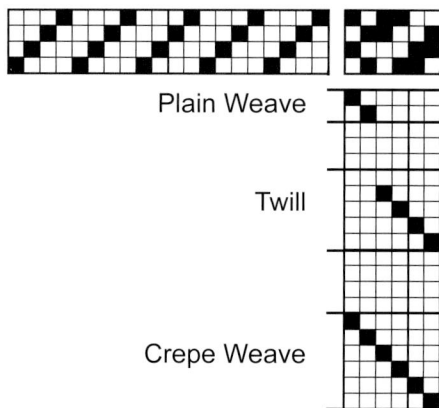

Plain Weave

Twill

Crepe Weave

III. *Scarf in Red and Black*

Weave: 5-shaft straight twill
Warp: wool/silk   Weft: wool
            mohair
Reed: Lars   Sett: 20 epi

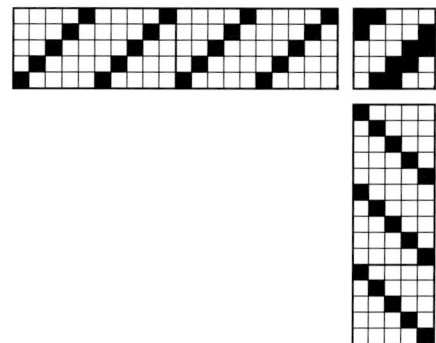

IV. *Tradition with a Flair* Series

Weave: 2-block summer and winter
Warp: 10/2 cotton   Weft: tabby – 10/2 cotton
                              pattern – 5/2 cotton
Reed: Lars   Sett: 25 epi

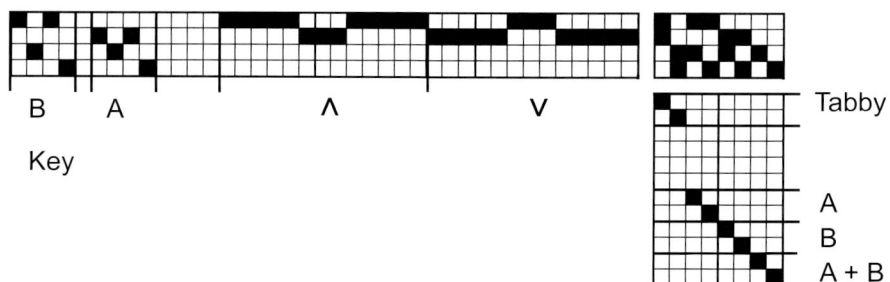

B   A   ∧   ∨   Tabby

Key   A
                                         B
                                         A + B

V. *Estrellita* Series

Weave: overshot
Warp: 10/2 cotton   Weft: tabby – 10/2 cotton
pattern – 5/2 cotton
metallic
Reed: Lars   Sett: 25 epi

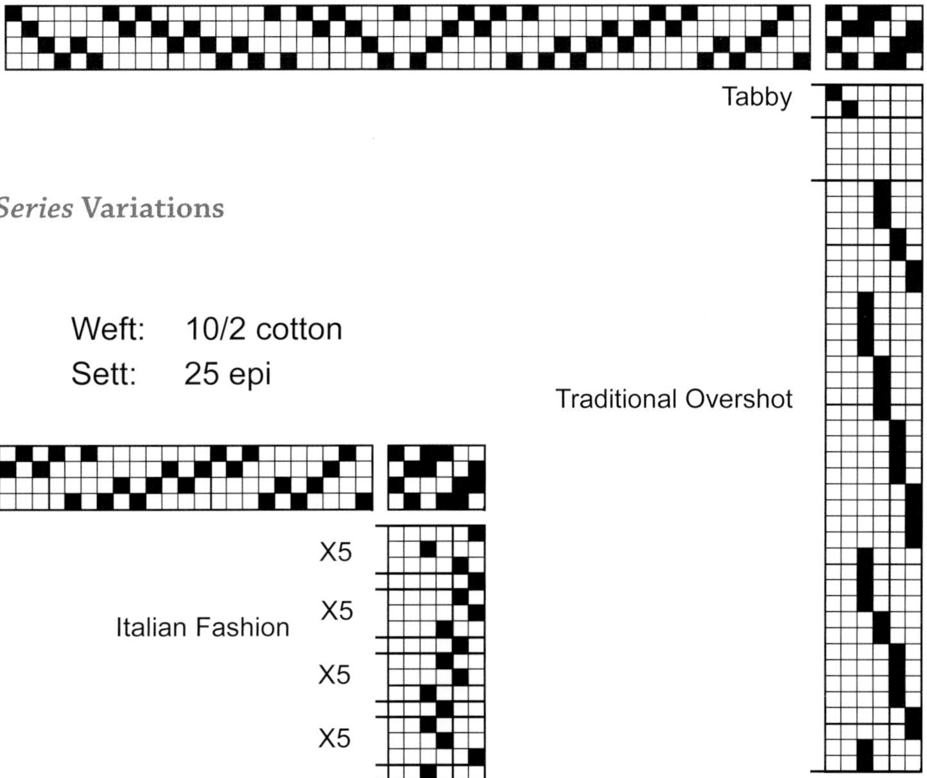

Tabby

Traditional Overshot

Estrellita Series Variations

Weave: overshot
Warp: 10/2 cotton   Weft: 10/2 cotton
Reed: Lars   Sett: 25 epi

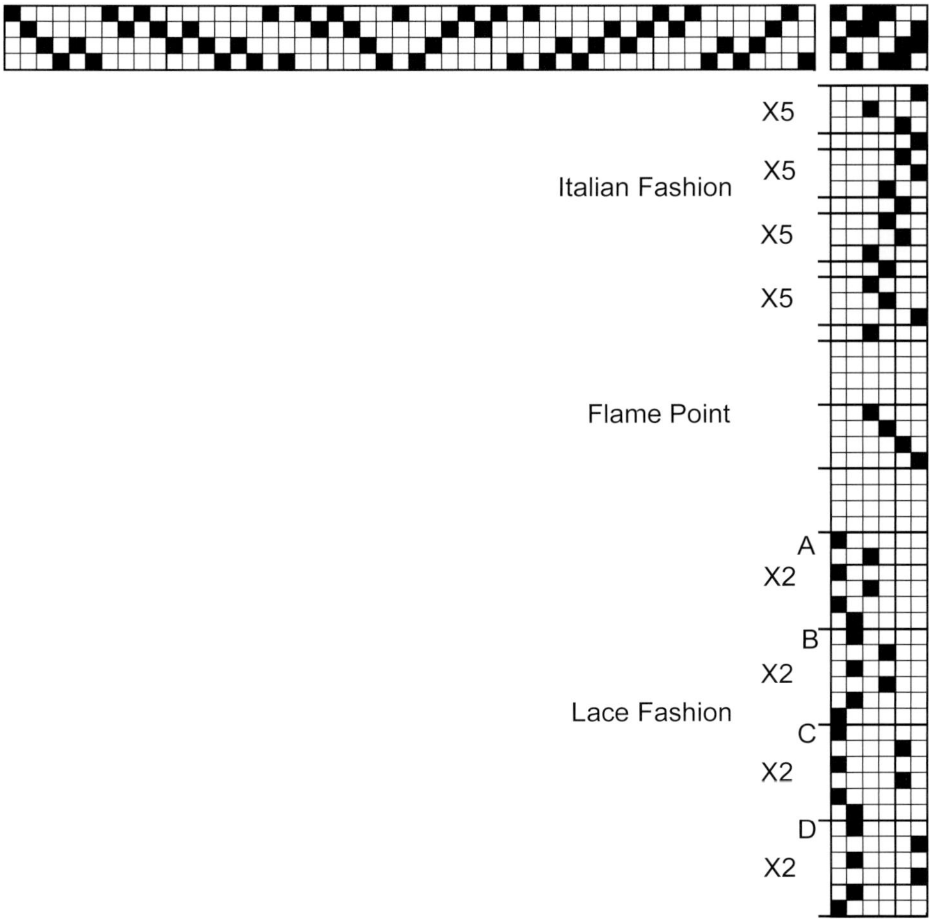

Italian Fashion

X5
X5
X5
X5

Flame Point

A
X2
B
X2

Lace Fashion

C
X2
D
X2

143

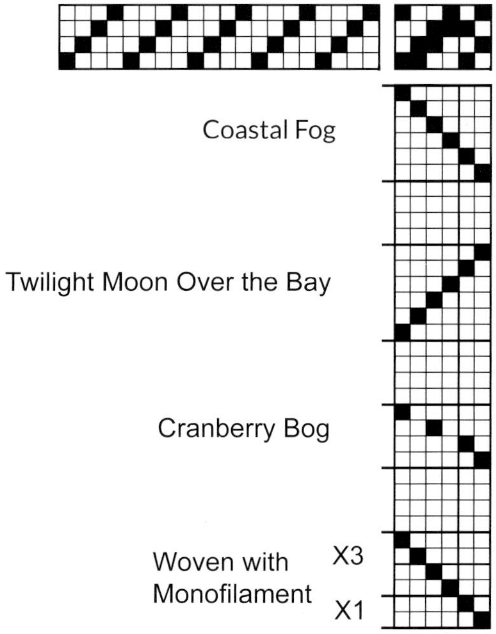

VII. The Colors of Klee Series

Weave: 3-shaft twill
Warp: 10/2 cotton   Weft: 10/2 cotton
Reed: Lars   Sett: 25 epi

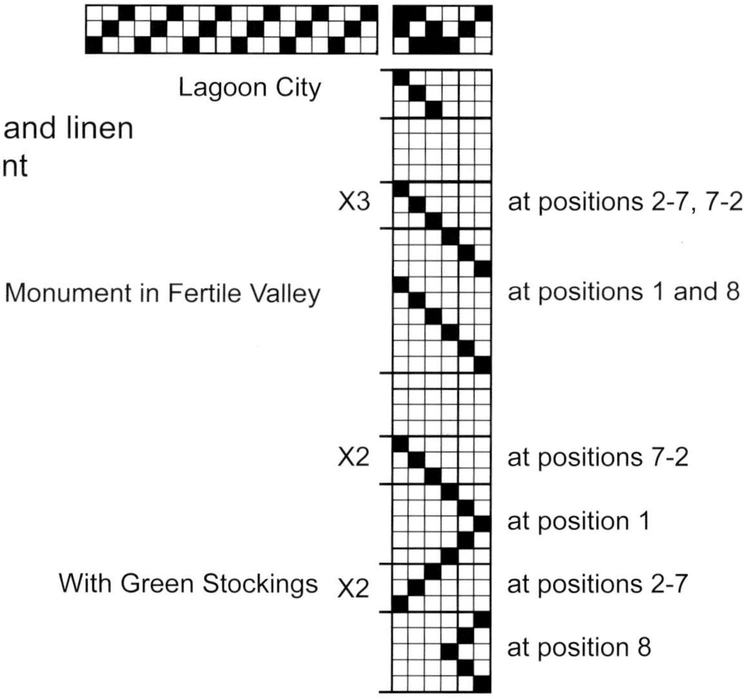

Lagoon City

X3   at positions 2-7, 7-2

Monument in Fertile Valley   at positions 1 and 8

X2   at positions 7-2

at position 1

With Green Stockings   X2   at positions 2-7

at position 8

VI. Landscape Series with *Lars*

Weave: 4-shaft twill
Warp: 10/2 cotton   Weft: 10/2 cotton
                                    24/2 cotton and linen monofilament
Reed: Lars   Sett: 25 epi

Coastal Fog

Twilight Moon Over the Bay

Cranberry Bog

Woven with Monofilament   X3   X1

VIII. Double Weave Series

Weave: two-block double weave
Warp: 10/2 cotton   Weft: 10/2 cotton
Reed: Lars   Sett: 50 epi

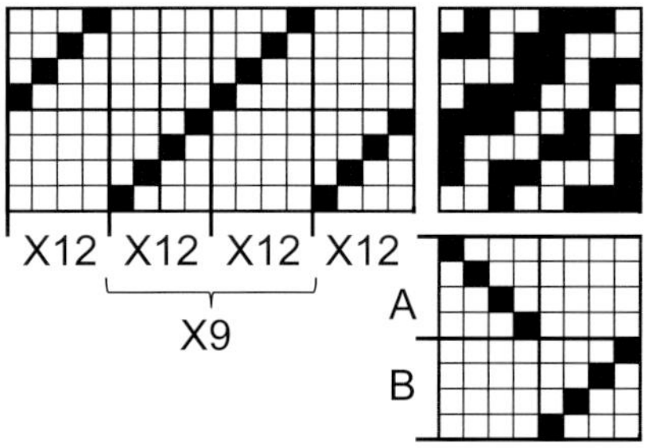

X12   X12   X12   X12

X9

A

B

IX. *Lilacs and Dandelions*

Weave: 6-shaft straight twill
Warp: 12/2 silk   Weft: 12/2 silk
Reed: Lars   Sett: 25 epi

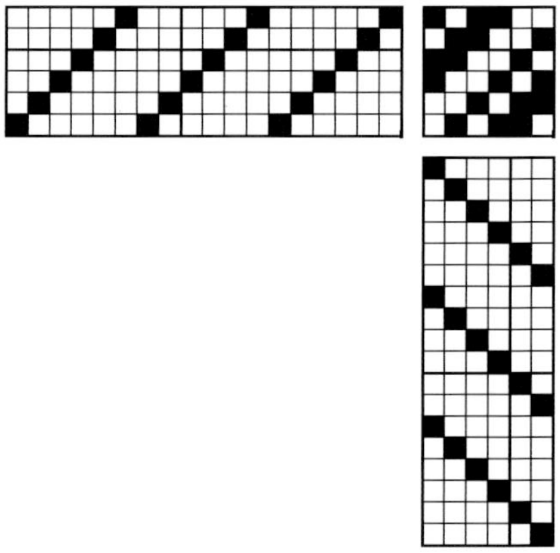

X. Counterpoint Series
Take a Marine Blue Line for a Walk, Take a Sea Green Line for a Walk, Anne-Sophie's Vest

Weave: 3-shaft twill

Warp: 10/2 cotton   Weft: 10/2 cotton (hangings, vest back)
                                     2/18 wool (vest fronts)
                                     monofilament

Reed: Lars   Sett: 25 epi

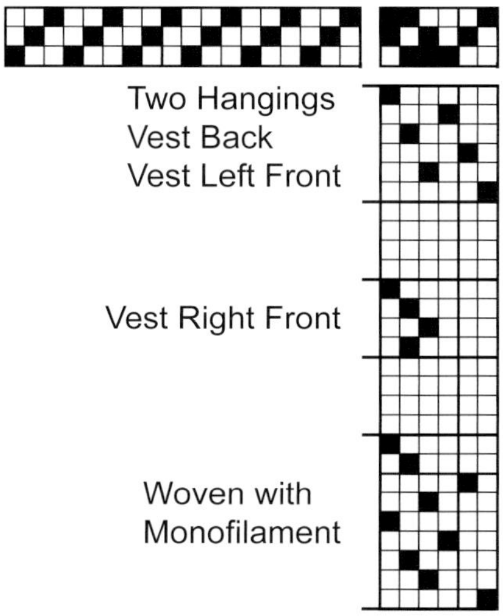

Two Hangings
Vest Back
Vest Left Front

Vest Right Front

Woven with
Monofilament

XI. *Prokofiev's Linen Runners*

Weave: combined weave
          (3-shaft lace and 4-shaft twill)

Warp: 30/3 linen   Weft: 30/3 linen
          2 ply linen

Reed: Lars   Sett: 25 epi

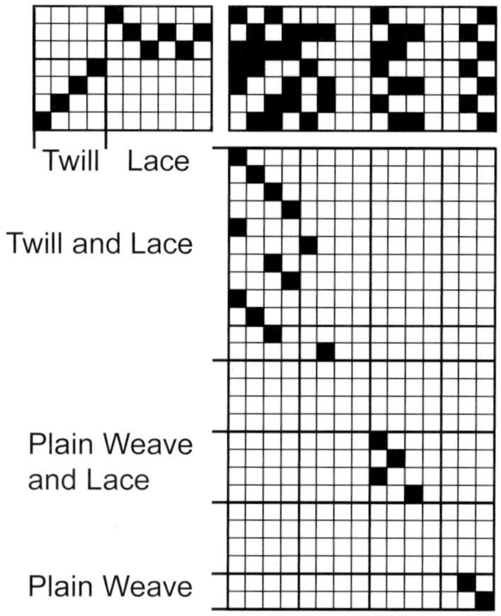

Twill   Lace

Twill and Lace

Plain Weave
and Lace

Plain Weave

XII. *Scarves of Joy*

Weave: two-block 8-shaft twill

Warp: 10/2 painted   Weft: 10/2 painted
          Tencel   Tencel

Reed: Lars   Sett: 25 epi

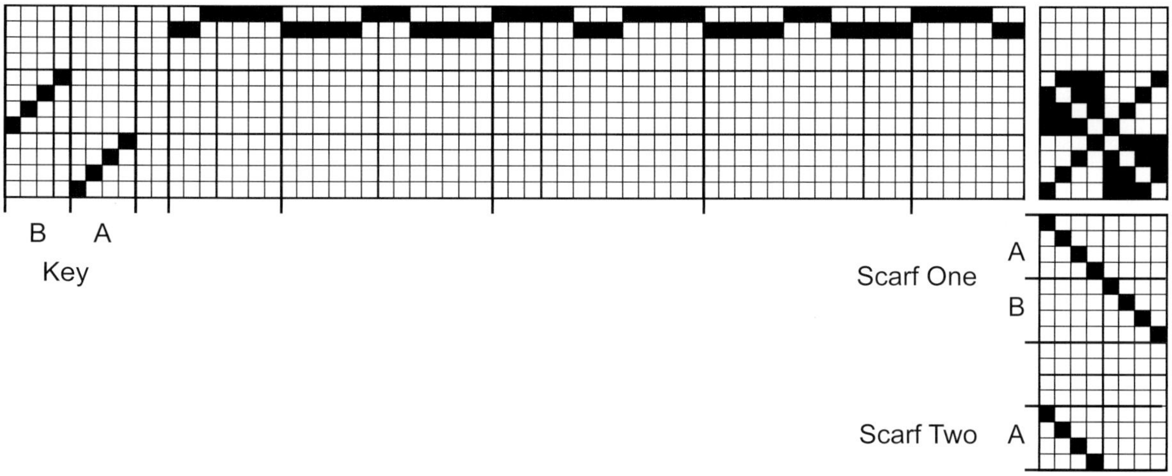

B   A
Key

Scarf One   A
             B

Scarf Two   A

XIII. *Alpaca with Proper Puckers*

Weave: 5-shaft straight twill
Warp: wool/silk   Weft: rayon
         alpaca
         merino wool
Reed: Lars   Sett: 20 epi

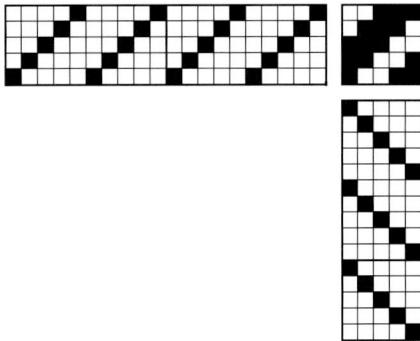

XIV. *Triptych*

Weave: plain weave with spaced denting
Warp: 16/2 linen   Weft: ramie
Reed: Lars   Sett: 25 epi

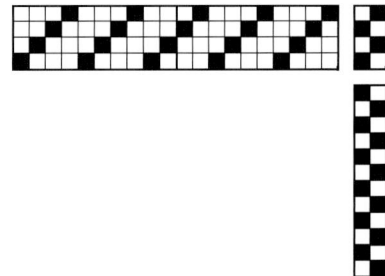

XV. *Kente Series*

Weave: two-block 6-shaft color-and-weave
Warp: 10/2 cotton   Weft: 10/2 cotton
Reed: Lars   Sett: 25 epi

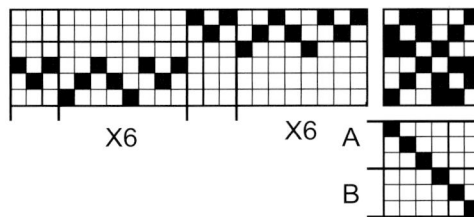

Warp color sequence

Red	1		1					1		1
Black		1			1		1		1	
Light Gray				1						
Dark Gray						1		1		

X6

Weft color sequence: dark gray, black, red

146

XVI. *Garden Tulip Series*

Weave: 7-shaft summer and winter
Warp: 20/2 cotton   Weft: tabby - 35/2 linen
       5/2 cotton   20/2 cotton
                                   pattern - 5/2 cotton
Reed: Hans   Sett: 30 and 15 epi

E   D   C   B   A   Tabby
          Key

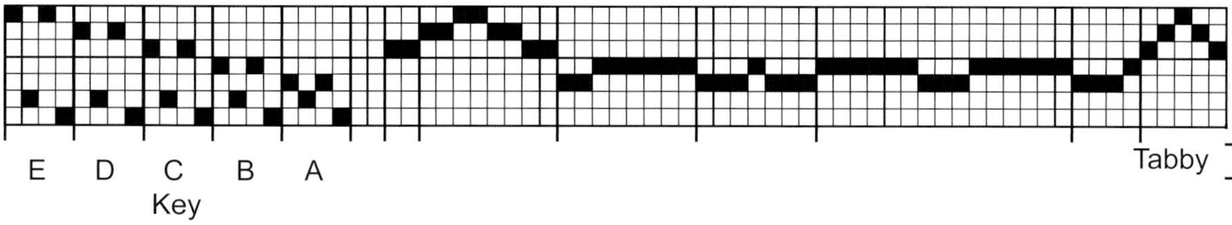

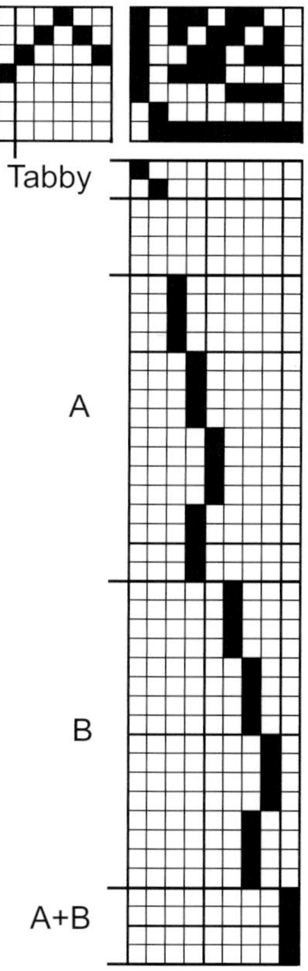

XVII. *Morning Mist Shawl*

Weave: combined weave
        (two-block lace and plain weave)
Warp: 20/2 cotton   Weft: wool/silk
       5/2 slub cotton
       hand-spun/hand-dyed cotton
Reed: Hans   Sett: 30 and 15 epi

B   A   Tabby

A

B

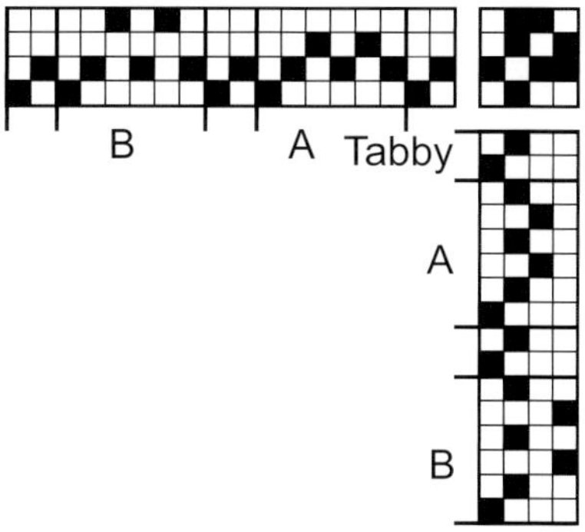

XVIII. Landscape Series with *Sara*

Weave: 5-shaft twill
Warp: linen, various sizes   Weft: fine linen
Reed: Sara   Sett: varied

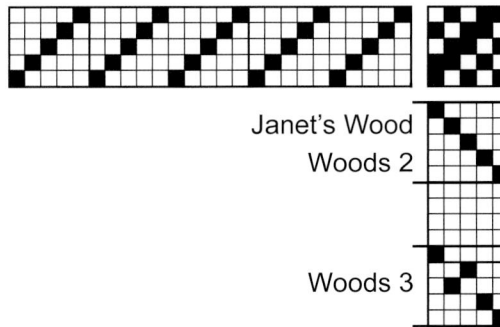

Janet's Wood
Woods 2

Woods 3

XIX. *Deve Series*

Weave: 8-shaft summer and winter
Warp: linen, various sizes   Weft: fine linen
Reed: Sara   Sett: varied

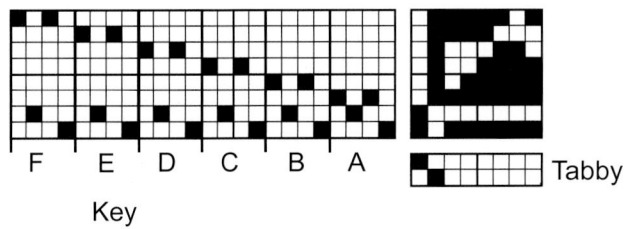

F   E   D   C   B   A   Tabby

Key

148

XX. *Scarf in Green and Violet*

Weave: combined weave
(6-shaft point twills and advancing twill)
Warp: alpaca/bamboo   Weft: alpaca/bamboo
Reed: Sara   Sett: 18 and 21 epi

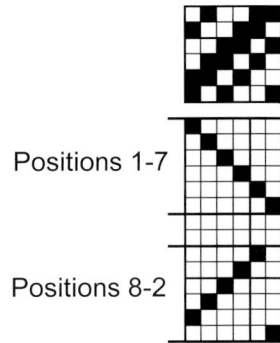

Positions 1-7

Positions 8-2

XXI. The Next Warp: Work in Progress

Weave: 4-shaft straight twill
Warp: alpaca/bamboo   Weft: alpaca/bamboo
Reed: Sara   Sett: 18 and 21 epi

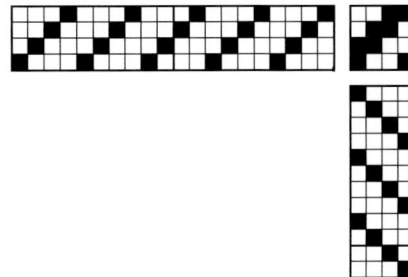

Appendix IV

Fan Reeds with Various DPI

Figure by Tom Smayda.

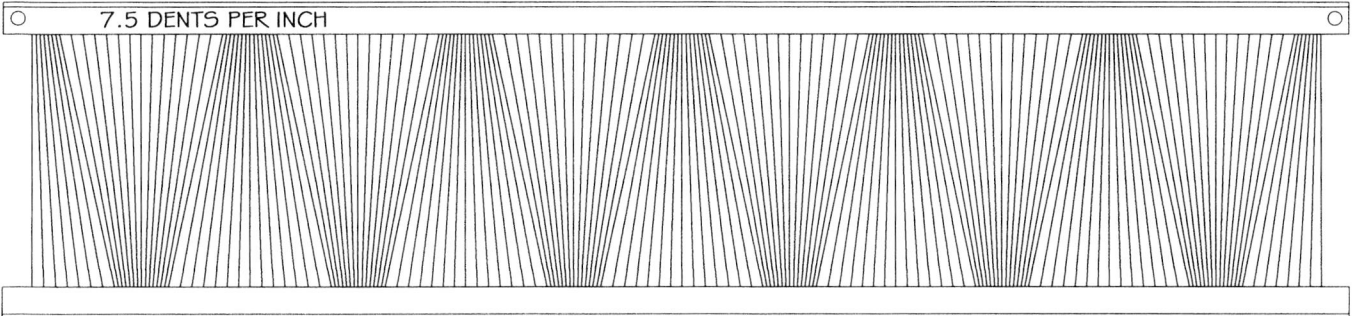

7.5 DENTS PER INCH

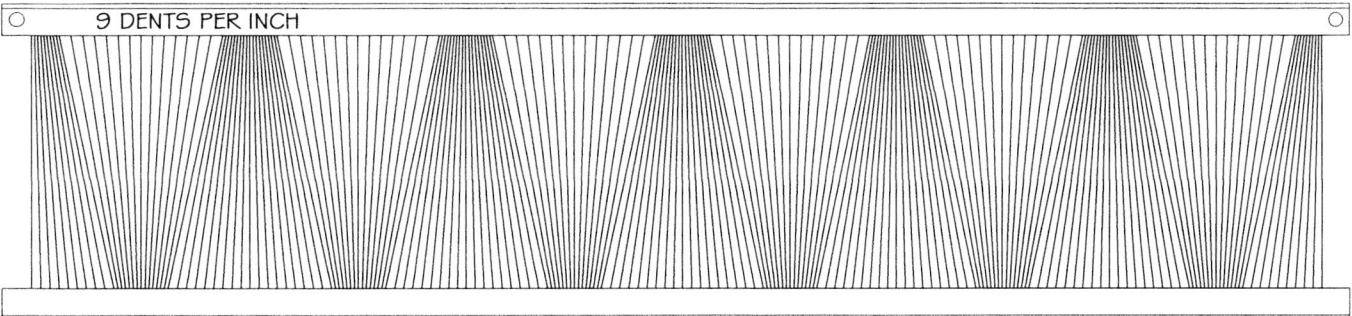

9 DENTS PER INCH

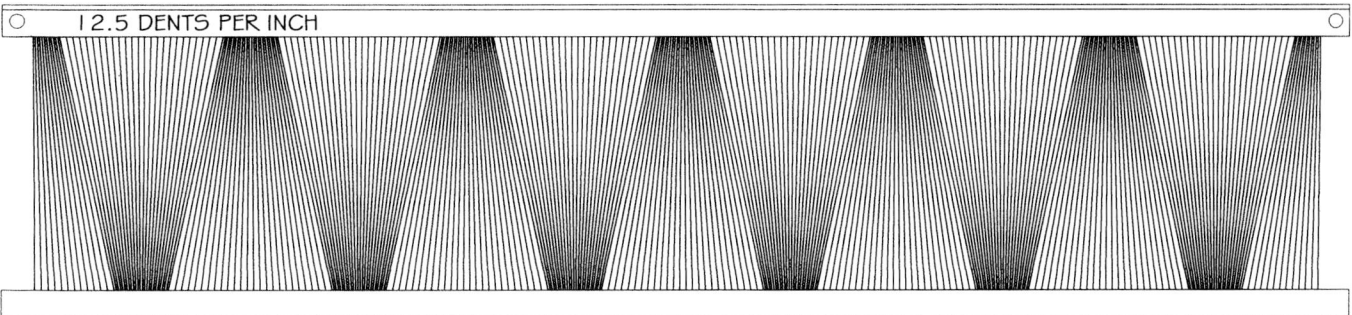

12.5 DENTS PER INCH

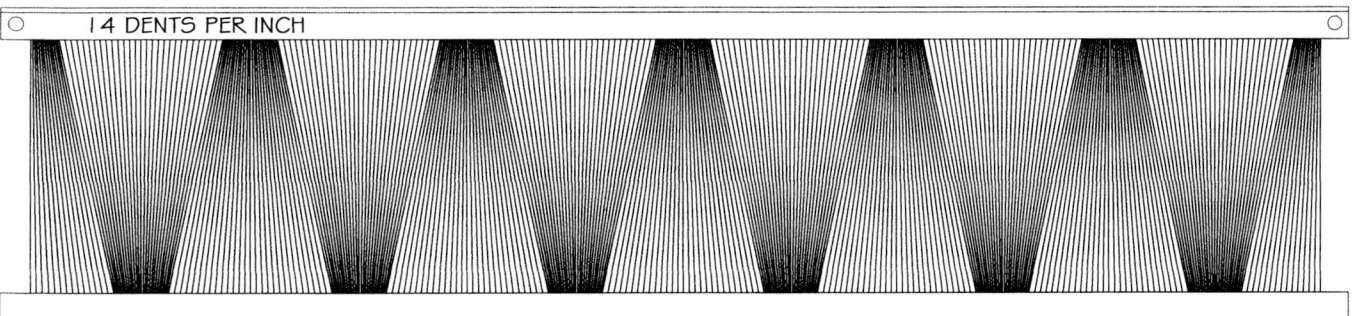

14 DENTS PER INCH

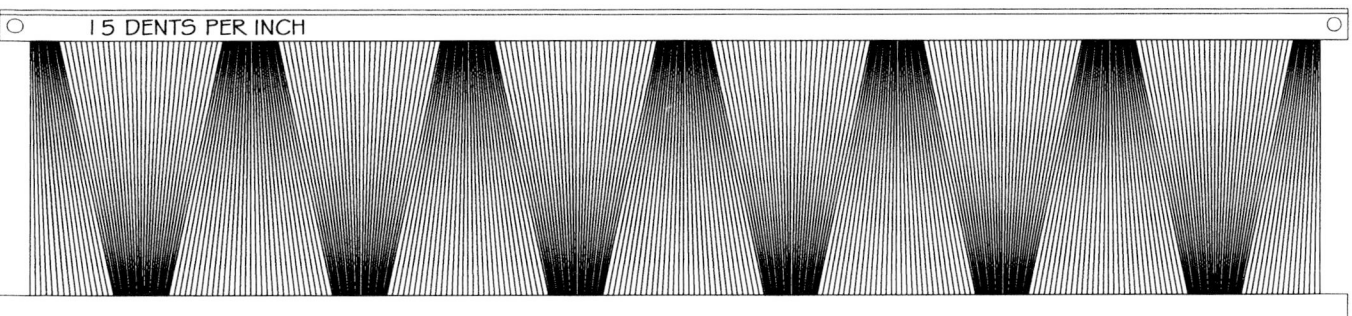

15 DENTS PER INCH

Glossary

Angel sticks: A pair of sticks that lie from the back beam to the breast beam, on which the reed may rest to ease the sleying process. End stops on the sticks help prevent them from slipping off the beams.

Angle fell: The angle at which the reed hits the fell of the cloth.

As Drawn In: The weaving is treadled in the same sequence as it was threaded. Also called *Tromp As Writ*.

Band: The top and bottom parts of the reed, holding the wires. A term used by reed manufacturers. Also called *baulk*.

Base: One of the parallel sides of a trapezoid.

Baulk: The top and bottom parts of the reed, between which the wires sit. Also called *band*.

Common wire: The metal strip shared by adjacent fans. Contours in the warp are most prominent close to these wires.

Cradle: V shapes mounted on the overhead framework of a loom from which the beater pivots. Cradles often have three or more positions, allowing the weaver to move the beater and weave further before advancing the cloth.

Crepe: Crepe weaves are often on a straight twill threading. They have an irregular or pebbly surface and have short floats alternating with longer floats in warp and weft. The amount of interlacement for all warp ends is the same or similar, preventing uneven warp tension.

Dents: Spaces between the wires of a reed.

Differential take-up: The difference in the length of warp at the contour compared to that in the center of the fan. In ondulé weaving it is what causes puckers, warp-wise or weft-wise.

dpi: Dents per inch. In this book, refers to dents per inch at the vertical center of the reed, unless otherwise noted.

Dukagång: A treadling technique sometimes used with summer and winter threadings. Only one shaft is used to lift the ends that tie down the inlaid pattern weft, forming vertical columns reminiscent of the Scandinavian inlay technique.

epi: Ends per inch.

Fan reed: A reed composed of wires grouped in fan-shaped sections.

Fell: The edge of the fabric where the last weft pick has been pressed into place by the beater.

Hybrid reed: A reed having fans with differing dpi, or a reed that has both straight wires and fans. The dpi in these fans may differ.

Kente cloth: Narrow strip cloth woven in Ghanaian West Africa, usually 3.5 inches to 4 inches wide.

Legs: The two non-parallel sides of a trapezoid.

Leno: A woven structure formed when the weft is passed between warp ends that have crossed over each other. This interlacement produces an open, stable cloth. It is often used when weaving ondulé to hold the warp ends in place. The term is commonly used for some types of gauze.

Logarithm: The power to which a fixed number (called the base) must be raised in order to produce a given number. The log of 8 to the base 2 is 3, also written as $2^3 = 8$. Logarithmic graph paper is composed of cycles of nine rectangles of decreasing size vertically and horizontally, which is repeated for the width and length of the pager. Designs can be created that are reminiscent of the op-art designs of the 1960s.

Macrogauze: A term Peter Collingwood used to refer to his large woven hangings in which groups of parallel warp ends were moved sideways, creating large triangular forms.

Median: The line joining the midpoints of the two legs (non-parallel sides) of a trapezoid.

Nami or Namiosa: Japanese weft ondulé or wave reed.

Ondulé: A French word meaning "to undulate or corrugate." This term refers to waved or shaded effects in the cloth. This effect is brought about by causing specific warp ends, in a series of groups, to be forced alternately to the right and then to the left.

Ondulé textile: Cloth designed to show undulation of texture, color, and/or weave structures in the warp or weft. Fan reeds are used to produce warp ondulé.

Paquet: French word for *fan*.

Puckers: Dimpling of the woven cloth in open sett areas.

Sett: Spacing of warp threads in the reed, expressed as ends per inch or epi.

Sley: To draw the warp threads through the dents in a reed.

Sprang: A finger-controlled method of making fabric by manipulating parallel warp threads that are fixed at both ends.

Summer and winter: A weft-patterned weave with a tabby ground and a supplementary pattern weft that moves over or under the ground in three-thread floats.

Swords: Vertical sides of a beater, which hang from an overhead cradle.

Trapezium: Term used in the United Kingdom for *trapezoid*.

Trapezoid: Fan shaped. A four-sided figure, with one set of parallel sides, called bases, and one set of non-parallel sides, called legs. A half fan adjacent to straight wires is a right trapezoid.

Triaxial weaving: A type of weaving formed by three interlacing yarns that meet at 60-degree angles. Essentially two warps and one weft, forming exceedingly strong textiles.

Tromp As Writ: The weaving is treadled in the same sequence as it was threaded. Also called *As Drawn In*.

Wires: Metal strips spaced exactly in a reed to give the required number of dents per inch.

Yoroke: Japanese warp ondulé or fan reed.

Bibliography

American Fabrics Magazine, ed. *AF Encyclopedia of Textiles.* Englewoods Cliffs, NJ: Prentice-Hall, Inc., 1960.

Andreasson, Gullvi. "Japanskt och Svenskt I Skon Kombination." *VävMagasinet.* (2) 1994.

Arafat, Margaret. "On a Slippery Slope: Using an Ondulé Reed." *Complex Weavers Journal.* (103) 2013.

Broudy, Eric. *The Book of Looms.* New York: Van Nostrand Reinhold Co., 1979.

Collingwood, Peter. *Rug Weaving Techniques: Beyond the Basics.* Loveland, CO: Interweave Press, 1990.

Collingwood, Peter. *The Maker's Hand.* Loveland, CO: Interweave Press, 1987.

Diaper, Hilary, ed. *Theo Moorman 1907-1990: Her Life and Work as an Artist.* Leeds, UK: The University Gallery Leeds, 1992.

Dumke, Judy. "An Angle Fell." *Complex Weavers Journal.* (96) 2011.

Emery, Irene. *The Primary Structures of Fabrics: An Illustrated Classification.* Washington, DC: The Textile Museum, 1966.

Falcot, P. *Traite Encyclopedique et Methodique de la Fabrication des Tissus.* Mulhouse, 1852.

Fox, T.W. *The Mechanism of Weaving.* New Jersey: Textile Book Service, 1894.

Global Textile Partner. "Burcklé Fan or Trapezium Reeds." http://www.globaltextilepartner.com/GTP/en/burkle/warpprep/fan/.

Grosicki, Z.J. *Watson's Advanced Textile Design: Compound Woven Structures.* London: Newnes-Butterworths, 1977.

Holmes, James. *Manuscript Notes on Weaving.* Nashville: Tunstede, 1945.

Klee, Paul. *Pedagogical Sketchbook.* London: Faber and Faber Limited, 1953.

Labriffe, Charles. *Manuel de Tissage: matières textiles, tissues simples.* Paris: Baillière, 1928.

Liles, Suzie. "Tired of Straight Stripes? Meet the Ondulé Reed!" *Handwoven.* (144) 2009.

McCann, J., and D. Bryson, eds. *Smart Clothes and Wearable Technology.* Oxford: Woodhead Publishing Limited, 2009.

Moorman, Theo. *Weaving as an Art Form: A Personal Statement.* New York: Van Nostrand Reinhold Company, 1975.

Naylor, Gillian, ed. *William Morris by Himself: Designs and Writings.* Edison, NJ: Chartwell Books, Inc., 1988.

Nisbet, H. *Grammar of Textile Design.* New York: D. Van Nostrand Company Inc., 1906.

Pärson, Åsa. "Weaving with a Fan Reed." *Vävmagasinet.* (4) 2013.

Posselt, E.A. *Textile Machinery: Part 3.* Philadelphia: Textile Publishing Company, 1898.

Poulson, Christine. *William Morris.* Secaucus, NJ: Chartwell Books, Inc., 1989.

Rohde, Michael F. "Keeping My Eyes Open." *Handwoven.* (174) 2015.

Rongde Ge. *Method for Weaving Curved Warp Yarns and a Woven Fabric.* http://patents.justia.com/inventor/rongde-ge/.

San Lazzaro, G. Di. *Klee: A Study of His Life and Work.* London: Thames and Hudson, 1957.

Smayda, Norma. *An Investigation into Means of Translating Colonial Overshot Patterns into Geometric Compositions.* MFA Thesis. Southeastern Massachusetts University, North Dartmouth, MA, 1977.

Smayda, Norma, Gretchen White, Jody Brown, and Katharine Schelleng. *Weaving Designs by Bertha Gray Hayes: Miniature Overshot Patterns.* Atglen, PA: Schiffer Publishing, Ltd., 2009.

Straub, Marianne. *Hand Weaving and Cloth Design.* New York: Viking Press, 1977.

Strong, John H. *Fabric Structure.* Brooklyn: Chemical Publishing Company, 1947.

Sutton, Ann, ed. *Falcot's Weave Compendium.* London: Deidre McDonald Book/Bellew Publishing, 1990.

Sutton, Ann, and Diane Sheehan. *Ideas in Weaving.* Loveland, CO: Interweave Press, 1989.

Sutton, Ann, Peter Collingwood, and Geraldine St. Aubyn Hubbard. *The Craft of the Weaver.* London: British Broadcasting Corporation, 1982.

Tarrant, W. E. "A Study of Warp and Filling Ondulé." *The Bobbin and Beaker.* (16) 1957.

Textile Colored Comprehensive Dictionary. Tanko-sha Publishers, 1977.

Tidball, Harriet. "Undulating Weft Effects." *Shuttle Craft Monograph Nine.* Freeland, WA: HTH Publishers, 1963.

Weber, Nicholas Fox, and Pandora Tabatabai Asbaghi. *Anni Albers.* New York: Guggenheim Museum Publications, 1999.

Weltge, Sigrid Wortmann. *Women's Work: Textile Art from the Bauhaus.* San Francisco: Chronicle Books, 1993.

Yoshida, Kozo. *Teori-no-Jitsugi-Kobo: (Technique of Handweaving).* Senshoku to Seikatsu-sha Publishers, 2002.

Zlatanovski, Diana. *Echoes in Fiber: The Textile Art of Monika Correa.* Pucker Gallery Catalogue, Boston, 2014.

Interesting Online Sources

Amy Putansu. www.putansutextiles.com

Anne Selim. www.anneselim.com

Gowdey Reed Company. www.gowdeyreed.com

Japanese Production Weavers. www.oriza.jp

John Marshall. www.johnmarshall.to/

Just Our Yarn. www.justouryarn.com

Kadi Pajupuu. www.kadipuu.berta.me

Karina Nielsen Rios. www.karinanielsenrios.com byrios.blogspot.com

Kerstin Froberg. www.oddweavings.blogspot.com

Louet Looms. www.louet.nl

Lunatic Fringe Yarns. www.lunaticfringeyarns.com

Nat Rea. www.natrea.com

North Light Fibers. www.northlightfibers.com

Pat Foster. www.purpledonsu.blogspot.com

Sara and Hans von Tresckow. www.woolgatherers.com

Saunderstown Weaving School. www.saunderstownweavingschool.com

Index